For Enerisa and Val

Good Luck for a
Happy Marriage
4-EVER!
To the sweetest couple
from the Library gang.

Best of Everything
Gillian

Thanks for all
your hard work.
Good Luck!
Jenn

All my best!
—Mary

Good Luck
Alan

All the LOVE and HAPPINESS
in the World

I'm sorry that
this book does
not contain any
instant noodle
recipes. Best wishes,
—Jenny

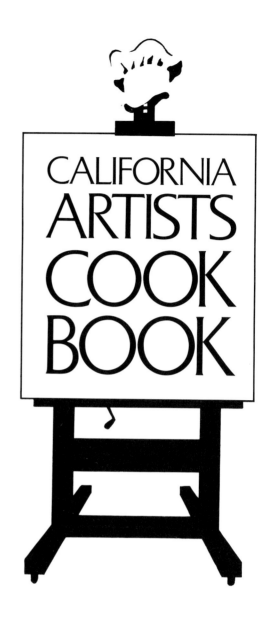

CALIFORNIA
ARTISTS
COOK
BOOK

A Modern Art Council project
Produced by
Chotsie Blank and Ann Seymour
for
The San Francisco Museum of Modern Art
Photographs by Chotsie Blank
Foreword by Henry T. Hopkins
Edited by Jack Van Bibber and Michael Sonino

CALIFORNIA ARTISTS
COOK BOOK

Introduction by JAMES BEARD

ABBEVILLE PRESS · PUBLISHERS · NEW YORK

Jacket and book design: Roy Winkler

On the jacket:
Wayne Thiebaud. *Buffet.* 1975
Collection of the artist

On the title page:
Paul Wonner
Dutch Still-life with Lemon Tart and Engagement Calendar. 1979. Diptych. Collection The San Francisco Museum of Modern Art. Charles H. Land Foundation Fund Purchase

Note: Unless otherwise indicated all works are oil on canvas

Wayne Thiebaud. *Three Shelf Pies.* 1963–64. Courtesy Allan Stone Gallery, New York

Marianne Boers. *Spice Islands.* 1976. Watercolor. Courtesy John Berggruen Gallery, San Francisco

Library of Congress catalog card number: 82–6789
ISBN 0-89659-246-4

CONTENTS

Wayne Thiebaud. *Candy Ball Machine.*
1977. Gouache and pastel on paper.
Collection the artist

JAMES BEARD

INTRODUCTION

I have always pictured the Muse of Gastronomy as a beautiful, sensuous, voluptuous woman who delights in life and all its pleasures. Along with the muses of dance, theater, and painting, she is welcome into the realm of each particular art (especially that of painting) and has her own importance and function, which is startlingly prominent.

It is amazing to look on the number of paintings, by the greatest artists, that depict food and express the appreciation of food through the beauty of still life. This combination of foods and other objects can be exquisite to the eye and sometimes very entertaining. The composition of a still life may have been inspired by the desire to juxtapose something unusual against something extremely beautiful and something that is satiric, amusing, or just downright funny. Such still lifes were created to appeal to more than one emotion, because a laughter-producing beauty is just as important as a serious, melancholy, or even tragic one.

Two paintings that come to mind are Rembrandt's regal and magnificent carcass of beef hanging after slaughter, with the red flesh and the creamy fat interspersed, and the fairly little-known Picasso painting of bread, to my mind one of the most mouth-watering experiences for a bread lover. Picasso, as most of you will remember, also did a painting and designed some ceramics featuring the skeleton of a just-eaten fish, and he expressed in those works a gastronomic wonderment that has caused amusement as well as appreciation of design.

Artists, singers, actors, and dancers all seem to have a

great esteem not only for the beauty but also for the taste of food. Both these values are extremely important in an aesthetic appreciation of what one sees and eats, or what one simply takes in while wandering through a field of fruits and vegetables or a great marketplace. Nothing can make such an exquisite composition as a great market pyramided with brightly colored fruits, furred and feathered game, glistening fresh and colorful fish and meats, and crisp, brilliant vegetables. How exciting to think of the Christmastime market in Caen, where game hangs in enormous quantities, the traditional holiday dishes ooze out into the windows of every bakeshop, and the flowers and fruits of the season shine in splendor!

Wayne Thiebaud. *Three Strawberry Shakes*. 1964. Courtesy Charles Campbell Gallery, San Francisco

Also exciting is the fact that through years of gastronomic growth in the United States, cultural and social organizations have produced some memorable cookbooks. Our gastronomic Americana collections (starting in the nineteenth century), compiled by museums, schools, churches, or women in social work of some kind, have been one of our greatest sources for recipes and culinary methods and ideas and for generally maintaining the kitchen arts in the communities. In our own time, I think you would find the cookbook assembled by the Walters Art Gallery in Baltimore a tome of beauty and memorable good food, and there was an exquisite book brought out by the Portland (Oregon) Art Museum a number of years ago. The Metropolitan Museum of Art has published several finely designed and nicely done books devoted to medieval and Renaissance cookery. Over the years we have been able to capture the

Priscilla Birge. *And the Children Love the Supermarket, Too.* 1975. Montage. Collection the artist

ideas of people of different eras and to notice the changes in cooking habits and processes and in food appreciation. It is a startling record.

So it happens that the San Francisco Museum of Modern Art has created a new book that echoes the present age of this city. *The California Artists Cookbook* is a living record of several dozen of the top artists living and working in the state and of their feelings about food. It will join with a great number of other books in attracting the cook as well as the rapidly growing faction of readers of good cookbooks. And the readers are certainly as important as the cooks, because although they may never cook a recipe from a book, they treasure what they learn and keep it as a record of their gastronomic gratification. A most delightful pleasure!

I have enjoyed the recipes from *The California Artists Cookbook* and I find myself trying out some of them as soon as I read them, and enjoying the artists' remarks and the drawings and paintings that decorate the book. *The California Artists Cookbook* should stand as a record for many years, and I hope it will spread its message far beyond the confines of the Bay Area.

A very amusing and revealing cookbook brought out in Portland, Oregon, in 1883 is now a collector's item and brings quite a lordly price. This is an unusual case, but there are in our collections great books that have come from such worthy producing units as the San Francisco Museum of Modern Art. Let us predict a long life for *The California Artists Cookbook*!

James Beard

Henry T. Hopkins

FOREWORD

It is quite consistent for a museum that sponsored the First Artists Soap Box Derby and brought together a wide community of participants in displays of skill, color, humor, and speed to involve that same art community in another love-of-life venture, *The California Artists Cookbook*. Certainly food for the senses, whether visual or edible, should be of consuming interest to us all.

Lifestyle is part of life, and it sometimes seems desirable for the artists of our community to step a little bit outside their serious role of informing, criticizing, and aesthetically sustaining us and to remind us that no one better exemplifies quality of life than the artist him- or herself. The diversity, the look, taste, and texture, and the implications of a hundred heritages are as representative of the art community as the works they produce.

I want to thank Chotsie Blank and Ann Seymour for their tireless efforts in producing this book under the auspices of the Museum's Modern Art Council. They were ably assisted by Katie Schlafly of the Museum staff, who devoted many hours to organizing the raw material into manageable form.

On behalf of all involved in the production and publication of *The California Artists Cookbook*, it is once again my true pleasure to thank the participating artists for their versatility and for their continuing support of the San Francisco Museum of Modern Art.

Henry T. Hopkins
*Director, San Francisco
Museum of Modern Art*

APPETIZERS

Sandy Shannonhouse. *Luncheon Tray.* 1974. Ceramic. Collection the artist

Salted Asparagus Tips ❧ K. Lee Manuel

Bastille ❧ Frederick Eversley

Chicken Balls ❧ Victor Bergeron ("Trader Vic")

Chicken Livers with Grapes ❧ Hans Burkhardt

Chile con Queso ❧ Betty and Clayton Bailey

Fish Balls ❧ Victor Bergeron ("Trader Vic")

Melanzane alla Gianna Felice (Italian Pickled Eggplant) ❧ Jack Zajac

Flaming Mushrooms ❧ Sylvia Lark

Nutted Mushroom Balls ❧ Sylvia Lark

Salt-Cured Olives ❧ Donna Mossholder

Smoked-Salmon Pâté ❧ Robert Freimark

Snails on the Skid ❧ Jo Hanson

Tofu-Chicken Liver Pâté ❧ Victor Bergeron ("Trader Vic")

Italian Pickled Zucchini ❧ Roland Petersen

SALTED ASPARAGUS TIPS
Contributed by K. Lee Manuel

2 pounds asparagus
⅓ cup coarse sea salt
Freshly ground black pepper
2 teaspoons dried oregano
½ cup dried mushroom chips
   (available in health-food
   stores), crumbled

Cut off and discard the tough white bottom portion of the asparagus stalks and peel the outer skin of each stalk, using a very sharp knife or a rotary vegetable peeler. Wash thoroughly and chill in the refrigerator one hour or more.

Using a salt mill, grind the sea salt into a bowl. Add freshly ground pepper to taste, the oregano, and the mushroom chips. Mix thoroughly.

Just before serving, moisten the asparagus under running cold water and sprinkle each stalk generously with the seasoned salt, or, if you prefer, serve the asparagus and salt separately and allow guests to dip their own. *Serves 6 to 8.*

BASTILLE
Contributed by Frederick Eversley

6 tablespoons sugar
2 teaspoons cinnamon
½ teaspoon ground ginger
½ teaspoon ground nutmeg
2½ cups cooked chicken,
   shredded
Salt
Freshly ground black pepper
1½ cups butter
1½ cups thinly sliced
   blanched almonds
½ medium onion, minced
9 eggs
3 cloves garlic, minced and
   crushed
3 tablespoons minced parsley
16 sheets phyllo pastry
   (available fresh in Greek
   specialty shops, or frozen in
   large supermarkets)

Mix the sugar, cinnamon, ginger, and nutmeg and set aside. Season the chicken to taste with salt and pepper and set aside.

Melt 3 tablespoons of the butter in a large, heavy skillet, add the sliced almonds, and sauté over medium heat until golden brown. Scrape into a dish and reserve. Melt 3 more tablespoons of the butter in the same skillet, add the minced onion, and sauté over medium heat until soft but not brown. Beat the eggs lightly in a bowl with the garlic, parsley, and salt and pepper to taste. Pour into the skillet with the onion and stir gently over low heat. Before the eggs are fully cooked, remove from the heat and continue stirring until barely set but still creamy and moist. Set aside.

Melt the remaining butter in a small saucepan. Brush the bottom and sides of an 11-by-16-inch jelly-roll pan generously with melted butter and fit a sheet of the phyllo pastry in the pan, trimming off any excess. Brush the top of the phyllo sheet with butter, fit another sheet on top, and continue in this manner, using eight sheets of the phyllo. Spread the chicken in an even layer over the phyllo and spread the egg mixture evenly over the chicken. Sprinkle the almonds over the eggs and then about half the sugar mixture. Lay another phyllo sheet on top, brush with butter, and continue until the remaining sheets are used. Do not trim off the top sheets but tuck them around and under the sides of the other sheets. Using a razor-sharp knife, cut into triangular or rectangular serving shapes, but cut only through the top layers of phyllo down to the almonds.

Bake in a preheated 350° oven 25 to 30 minutes. Sprinkle with the remaining sugar mixture and cut all the way through the pastry into the serving pieces previously marked. Serve hot or warm.

Serves 8 to 10.

Note: this recipe is a version of the North African pastela, which uses pigeon or squab. Dark meat of chicken may be substituted in the above recipe as an approximation of pigeon. Bastille may be served as a main course by halving the ingredients with the following exceptions: use 5 eggs and the full amount of phyllo dough called for in the recipe. Line an 11-inch pie pan with aluminum foil, folding the excess outside the rim of the pan. Line the foil with phyllo, following the directions in the above recipe. When the filling has been added, cut off the four corners of the phyllo layers (they will be roughly triangular) and place them neatly on the filling. Cover with remaining phyllo and butter. Fold the excess neatly over on itself, as for a pie pastry. Carefully unfold the excess foil under the rim of the pie plate and, grasping it firmly, gently lift the foil onto a cookie sheet. Sprinkle with the sugar mixture, and proceed as described in the recipe. Cut in wedges, however, when serving.

Serves 6.

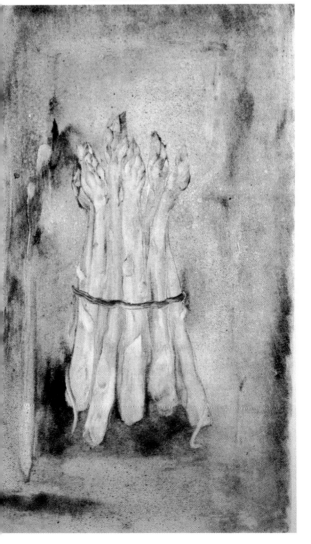

Joseph Goldyne. *Asparagus.* 1977. Monotype. Collection the artist

CHICKEN BALLS
Contributed by Victor Bergeron ("Trader Vic")

1 pound uncooked chicken
  meat
1½ pounds tofu
2 eggs
½ medium onion, quartered
¼ teaspoon white pepper
½ teaspoon salt
¼ cup dry sherry
3 cups fresh bread crumbs
Oil for deep frying

Cut the chicken and tofu in medium chunks. Put them in a food processor fitted with the standard steel blade, add all the remaining ingredients except 2 cups of the bread crumbs and the oil, and process into a paste. Alternatively, force through a meat grinder twice, using the fine blade. Roll the mixture, a spoonful at a time, into ¾-inch balls. Roll the balls in the remaining bread crumbs, coating them thoroughly, and chill in the refrigerator 1 hour. Fry the balls, a dozen at a time, in 375° deep fat 2 minutes, or until golden brown. *Serves 6 to 8.*

CHICKEN LIVERS WITH GRAPES
Contributed by Hans Burkhardt

2 pounds chicken livers
4 tablespoons butter
2 pounds white seedless
  grapes
½ cup port
Salt
Freshly ground pepper

Trim the chicken livers, cutting away any discolored spots. Heat the butter in a large skillet over medium heat until golden but not brown, add the livers, and sauté until lightly browned; 5 minutes. The livers should not be crowded in the pan or they will not brown properly.

Cut a third of the grapes in half, add to livers, and cook until heated through, 2 or 3 minutes. Add the port, season to taste with salt and pepper, and cook only 1 minute longer. Garnish on a heated platter with the remaining grapes, divided into small bunches. *Serves 6 to 8.*

CHILE CON QUESO
Contributed by Betty and Clayton Bailey

2 tablespoons butter
1 large onion, finely chopped
1 clove garlic, minced
1 28-ounce can whole
  tomatoes, drained
2 7-ounce cans Ortega-brand
  diced green chilies
1 teaspoon salt, or more to taste
½ pound sharp cheddar
  cheese, coarsely grated
Corn Fritos

Melt the butter in a large, heavy pot, add the onion and garlic, and stir over medium heat until the onion is soft and translucent but not brown. Add the tomatoes, chilies, and salt. Cook about 20 minutes, stirring frequently, until the tomatoes have formed a thick, fairly smooth sauce. Add the grated cheese and stir just until the cheese is melted. Serve as a dip with corn Fritos or spoon the sauce over corn Fritos on individual plates. *Serves 6 to 8.*

FISH BALLS

Contributed by Victor Bergeron ("Trader Vic")

Butter filling:
  2 tablespoons minced chives
  2 tablespoons minced
    parsley
  1 tablespoon Worcestershire
    sauce
  1½ tablespoons lemon juice
  2 cups grated Parmesan
    cheese
  4 drops Tabasco
  2 tablespoons dry bread
    crumbs
  1 tablespoon garlic powder
  1½ cups butter, slightly
    softened

Fish coating:
  2 pounds raw boneless fish,
    such as cod, halibut,
    or sole
  1 pound tofu, cut in chunks
  ½ cup fresh bread crumbs
  1 egg
  1 teaspoon salt
  ½ teaspoon white pepper

Dry bread crumbs
Oil for deep frying
2 cups soy or teriyaki sauce

Put the butter-filling ingredients into the container of a food processor and, using the standard steel blade, process just until the ingredients are well blended. Alternatively, simply mix in a bowl until well blended. If using the processor, scrape the mixture into a bowl. Chill in the refrigerator 2 hours. Remove from the refrigerator. Using the palms of your hands, roll a scant teaspoon of the mixture at a time into ¼-inch, pea-size balls and place on a chilled platter lined with wax paper as they are formed. Try to work quickly so that the butter does not soften. Chill the balls in the refrigerator at least 1 hour.

During the first chilling of the butter filling, put all the fish-coating ingredients in the container of a food processor and, using the standard steel blade, blend well. Alternatively, force the fish and tofu through a meat grinder twice, using the finest blade; put them in a bowl and beat in the remaining ingredients by hand. Chill the mixture in the refrigerator until the balls of butter filling are ready.

When the butter balls and fish mixture are well chilled, cover each butter ball with the fish mixture. Use about 1 tablespoon of the fish mixture for each butter ball and, again rolling them between the palms, form a ball about 1 inch in diameter. As each ball is formed, roll it in bread crumbs. Chill the balls again in the refrigerator 1 hour.

Just before serving, fry the balls, about 15 or 20 at a time, in deep 375° fat just until golden brown. Put them on a serving dish lined with a napkin and serve small bowls of the soy or teriyaki sauce for dipping.
Serves 10 to 20.

MELANZANE ALLA GIANNA FELICE
(ITALIAN PICKLED EGGPLANT)
Contributed by Jack Zajac

2 medium eggplants
Salt
3 cups red-wine vinegar
1½ cups canned sweet red
   peppers, packed in oil
6 cloves garlic
1 teaspoon dried oregano
Olive oil

Peel the eggplants and cut in ¼-inch slices. Sprinkle both sides of each slice generously with salt and put the slices in a colander (not aluminum) placed over a bowl. Put a flat plate over the slices and weight it to press the liquid out of the eggplant. Drain 24 hours, pouring off the liquid in the bowl occasionally so that it does not touch the slices. Pat the slices dry with paper towels. Marinate the slices in the vinegar 12 hours. Drain.

Put a little olive oil in a wide-mouthed glass jar or terra-cotta crock with a tight cover. Put a slice of eggplant in the bottom and then alternate layers of red pepper and eggplant, sprinkling with pinches of oregano and interspersing the cloves of garlic. Fill the jar or crock with olive oil, cover, and store in the refrigerator 1 week.
Serves 6 to 8.

FLAMING MUSHROOMS
Contributed by Sylvia Lark

½ pound mushrooms
3 tablespoons butter
½ cup sherry
¼ cup brandy
¼ cup heavy cream
Salt
Freshly ground pepper

Trim off only the very bottoms of the mushroom stems. If necessary, wipe the mushrooms clean with a damp paper towel. Melt the butter in a very large skillet over medium heat, add the mushrooms, and shake the skillet until they are lightly browned, about 5 minutes. Raise heat to high, add the sherry, and, still shaking the pan, allow it to reduce until syrupy.

Transfer the mushrooms and any remaining liquid to the top pan of a chafing dish over boiling water. Heat the brandy briefly, pour it over the mushrooms, and ignite. When the flames subside, add the heavy cream and season to taste with salt and pepper. Heat just until the cream is very hot. Do not boil or it may separate.
Serves 4.

Sketch by the artist

18

NUTTED MUSHROOM BALLS
Contributed by Sylvia Lark

½ pound cheddar cheese,
  crumbled, at room
  temperature
2 tablespoons brandy
¼ pound raw mushroom
  caps, cleaned and minced
½ pound salted peanuts

Put the cheese and brandy in the bowl of an electric mixer and whip until fluffy. Stir the mushrooms in thoroughly. Roll the peanuts on a board with a rolling pin until they are finely crumbled. Spread out the peanuts on a sheet of wax paper. Drop a small spoonful of the cheese paste onto the peanuts and roll it around in the nuts until thoroughly coated. Shape it into a firm ball by rolling between the palms of your hands. Continue until all the paste is used. Chill the balls in the refrigerator for 3 hours before serving. *Serves 4 to 6.*

Wayne Thiebaud. *Plate of Hors d'oeuvres.* 1963. Courtesy Charles Campbell Gallery, San Francisco

SALT-CURED OLIVES
Contributed by Donna Mossholder

In California, olives get ripe around Christmastime. If possible, locate an olive grove when the fruit is fully ripe. Pick them when they have turned black; they may have a little red or brown on them, but no green. This recipe is for 10 quarts of olives.

You will need a wooden, slat-sided box to fit the quantity of olives. Staple cheesecloth or clean, undyed burlap to the bottom and sides of the inside of the box, leaving an overlap at the top to serve as a lid.

Wash and pick over the olives, discarding any that have bad spots or are bruised. Lay them out on newspapers or a screen to dry.

You will need about 10 pounds of pickling salt, or you may substitute kosher salt. Sprinkle a generous amount of salt in the bottom of the box and then alternate layers of olives and salt, ending with a layer of salt.

Allow the box to sit in a cool, dry place, indoors or out, for 1 week. Then turn and mix the olives twice a week for 5 weeks. After 6 weeks the olives should have shriveled and lost all their bitter taste.

Rinse the olives thoroughly to remove all the salt and allow them to dry. They may now be coated with either plain olive oil or a dressing made of olive oil, vinegar, garlic, and herbs. You will need about 2 quarts of oil. After coating the olives thoroughly, pack in cooled, sterilized jars.
Makes about 7 quarts.

Sketch by the artist

20

SMOKED-SALMON PÂTÉ
Contributed by Robert Freimark

6 to 8 pounds salmon, gutted,
  heads and tails intact
Pickling (or kosher) salt
Sugar
½ cup mayonnaise, or more if
  necessary
Juice of 1 lemon
1 egg, lightly beaten
¼ cup chopped fresh dill
⅛ teaspoon cayenne pepper
Freshly ground pepper
Unsalted crackers or
  homemade Melba toast

Any fish may be smoked, but fat fish, such as salmon, is preferable. Hickory is the best wood for smoking. Do not use charcoal or ordinary wood, such as pine. In the West I use fruitwoods, such as prune, apple, or pear. Use oak for a real hardwood taste.

Commercial smokers are too small and are inadequate for the real devotee. Find an old refrigerator, remove the motor, and pound holes through the bottom with a cold chisel, so that the smoke can penetrate the airtight compartment. Never use a refrigerator with plastic parts. They can melt out, and the fish will fall to the bottom.

The fish should be gutted but unscaled. Wash thoroughly, dry, and sprinkle generously with a mixture of 3 parts pickling (or kosher) salt to 1 part sugar in any conveniently sized container. Marinate 3 days in a cool place, turning once a day. Remove from marinade and pat dry. Before smoking, large fish should be cut crosswise in 2- to 3-inch slices. Small fish may be left whole.

Start a fire under the refrigerator with paper under the wood to get it blazing. When the wood is well ignited, douse it with water, extinguishing the flame. Smoking is done "cold." Do not use flame or heat. Lay the fish on the shelves and close the door. Smoke about 5 hours.

The fish may then be stored in the kitchen refrigerator, but only for 1 week. Freeze the fish if it is to be stored longer. Once the fish is smoked and stored, make pâté whenever you want it, using just a little at a time.

Remove the skin and bones from ½ pound of the smoked salmon. Cut the fish in chunks, put them in the container of a food processor, and, using the standard steel blade, purée. Alternatively, pound the fish to a pulp in a stone mortar with a pestle and then force through a fine wire sieve. Put the purée in a bowl with mayonnaise amounting to about ⅓ the volume of the fish. Add the lemon juice, egg, dill, cayenne, and pepper to taste. Mix thoroughly and chill in the refrigerator 2 hours. Serve with unsalted crackers or homemade Melba toast.
Serves 6.

SNAILS ON THE SKID

Contributed by Jo Hanson

Locate a favorable spot in your garden to establish a snail farm. Build a wire-mesh enclosure that can be set 4 inches into the ground. The mesh must be fine enough to prevent the snails from escaping.

Snails are very migratory. You cannot assume they were born in your garden just because you find them there. Thus their diet (including poisons) is an unknown factor, unless you find a way to keep them home on the farm.

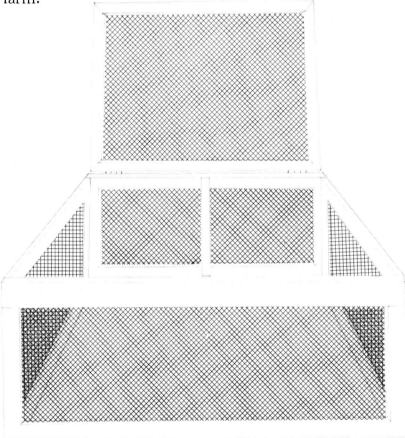

Inside the mesh enclosure—and outside too, for reserve supplies—plant your favorite selection of herbs, including chives and Italian parsley, not the very curly kind but the kind with this leaf:

The adventurous among you may include a very *few* seeds that produce a plant with a leaf that looks like this:

In canary food this seed inspires the birds to sing way over their heads. I have less knowledge of it as snail food, but observation suggests that it causes these little creatures to organize snail derbies in which every contestant is a winner.

When a lush growth has established itself within the corral, begin dropping your snails into it as you encounter them in the garden. In spite of the Edenlike character of this herb enclosure, you will need a hinged cover of the same wire mesh to allow you to put the snails in, keep them in, and, later, take them out.

In this happy environment, the snails are what they eat. They are rich in food nutrients and marvelously flavored.

When you have enough snails of mature size to prepare for eating, remove the desired number (one dozen per person, more or less) to an adequately sized covered container and do not feed them for two days, to allow their digestive tracts to clear.

You may then use your favorite recipe, or my recipe for steaming in a wine sauce.

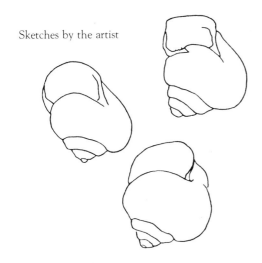

Sketches by the artist

A Jo Hanson assemblage in her studio

STEAMED SNAILS

As you approach the preparation of steamed snails, or escargots, think of the creative variations on steamed mussels served in France and Belgium. There are no rigid rules. The basic elements are (1) snails, (2) other ingredients, and (3) a matrix to carry the ingredients and produce steam. The matrix may become a tasty broth to serve following the escargots. Both (2) and (3) invite variation.

INGREDIENTS: Minced, sliced, or quartered onions; minced or crushed garlic; and sliced celery (optional, but good). Try other vegetables according to your inspiration, but

Jo Hanson

perhaps you might keep it simple the first time. A prepared *bouquet garni* or *fines herbes* provide a reliable selection of herbs and should be used generously. Or you may prefer to make your own selection.

THE LIQUID MATRIX: This can be water, but I prefer white wine or beer, or a little dry sherry added to white wine. Vegetable or chicken bouillon is a good addition, or leftover vegetable or meat juices. Add salt and freshly ground pepper to taste, but keep in mind the salt in bouillon if you use it.

PROCEDURE: Use a large pot with a tight cover. Avoid aluminum; it can interact with some of the ingredients. (Preferably the pot should be wide enough to accommodate the snails in no more than 2 or 3 layers. Pile the snails deeper if you must, but make sure the liquid is steaming vigorously when you do it.) If you use a steamer, the level of the liquid should rise into the bottom of the steamer insert.

Put the liquid, seasonings, onions, garlic, herbs, and a sampling of the vegetables into the pot. Bring to a near boil and then simmer with the lid on for 15 minutes. Taste and make any adjustments. (Personally I disagree with tasting directly from the pot. Try pouring your sample into a tasting spoon, which never goes into the pot.)

Then, timing it to fit your other arrangements, bring the pot to a vigorous steaming point and drop in the well-washed snails, retracted into their shells. Scare them into retraction if necessary, but be gentle; the shells are fragile. After 3 minutes of steaming with the lid on, add the rest of the vegetables and steam, covered, for another 10 minutes. You might wish to do preliminary explorations with one or two snails to establish the ideal cooking time. You want good, firm texture and easy removal from the shells without disintegration.

SERVING: You can serve steamed escargots before the main course or as a main dish. Serve in wide soup bowls with some of the cooking liquid and vegetables. Cocktail forks are my choice of tool, and provide soup spoons.

24

TOFU-CHICKEN LIVER PÂTÉ
Contributed by Victor Bergeron ("Trader Vic")

1 tablespoon gelatin
1½ pounds chicken livers
5 ounces compressed tofu
1 6-ounce chicken breast,
   skinned, boned, and
   tendons removed
3 tablespoons minced shallots
½ teaspoon salt
1 tablespoon Aromat*
¼ teaspoon ground nutmeg
¼ teaspoon mace
½ teaspoon powdered sage
1 pinch each white pepper,
   cayenne pepper, ground
   cloves, and dried oregano,
   thyme, and rosemary
6 tablespoons brandy
2 eggs
2 tablespoons butter, softened

Soften the gelatin in ¼ cup cold water in the top pan of a double boiler, dissolve it over hot water, and set aside. Trim the chicken livers, cutting away any discolored spots. Cut the tofu and the chicken breast into medium chunks.

Put the chicken livers, tofu, chicken meat, shallots, and all the seasonings into the container of a food processor and, using the standard steel blade, process into a paste. Add the brandy, eggs, and the reserved gelatin. Continue processing until the mixture is smooth. Alternatively, put all the heavier ingredients through a meat grinder twice, using the finest blade, and then beat in the lighter ingredients by hand.

Generously butter a 9-by-5-inch loaf pan. Pour the liver mixture into the pan and bake in a preheated 400° oven 25 minutes. Remove the pâté from the oven, cool, and chill in the refrigerator several hours. Serve with buttered rye bread. *Serves 6 to 10.*

*Aromat is a liquid seasoned with herbs. It may be omitted.

ITALIAN PICKLED ZUCCHINI
Contributed by Roland Petersen

8 medium zucchini
½ cup olive oil, or more
   if necessary
3 cups red-wine vinegar, or
   more if necessary
6 cups dry red wine, or more
   if necessary
8 cloves garlic
6 bay leaves
1 teaspoon salt

Wash the zucchini very thoroughly and cut off the stem ends. Cut zucchini into ¼-inch-thick lengthwise slices.

Heat the oil in a large, heavy skillet over fairly high heat until very hot but not smoking. Fry the zucchini slices, a few at a time, until lightly browned on both sides. Use more oil if necessary. As slices are done, spread them out on a platter. Do not drain on paper towels.

Put the vinegar, red wine, garlic, bay leaves, and salt in a large heavy pot over medium heat and bring just to a boil. Add all the zucchini slices and cook 5 minutes. Drain in a colander over a bowl and reserve the liquid.

Pack the zucchini in jars, interspersing the garlic and bay leaves from the cooking liquid, until the jars are ¾ full. Fill the jars with the cooking liquid, using more wine and vinegar if necessary. Store in the refrigerator 1 week. Serve cold. *Serves 6 to 8.*

SALADS

Three-Bean Salad ❧ Arthur Nelson

Beet and Daikon Salad with Orange Vinaigrette ❧ Joanne Rruff

Beet and Egg Salad ❧ Paul Wonner

California Sun Salad ❧ Karl Benjamin

Crab, Shrimp, and Macaroni Salad ❧ Ralph Maradiaga

One-Cup Fruit Salad ❧ Arthur Nelson

Layered Salad ❧ Judy Chicago

Peanut-Cabbage Slaw ❧ Bella Feldman

Shrimp Salad ❧ Frank Hamilton

Strawberry-Roquefort Salad ❧ Judith Golden, for Van Deren Coke

Tofu Salad ❧ Gerald Gooch

Irma Cavat. *Cornucopia on Prince Street*. 1980. Courtesy Kennedy Galleries, New York

THREE-BEAN SALAD
Contributed by Arthur Nelson

1 16-ounce can cut green
    beans, drained
1 16-ounce can red kidney
    beans, drained
1 16-ounce can garbanzos
    (chickpeas), drained
1 7¼-ounce can pitted ripe
    olives, drained
1 medium red onion, thinly
    sliced
1 small green pepper, cored,
    seeded, and minced
⅓ cup salad oil
⅓ cup red-wine vinegar
⅓ cup red Burgundy
⅓ cup sugar
½ teaspoon mixed dried salad
    herbs
¼ teaspoon garlic powder
1 teaspoon salt, or more
    to taste
Freshly ground pepper to taste

Toss all ingredients thoroughly together in a salad bowl. Chill in the refrigerator at least 6 hours, stirring frequently. *Serves 6 to 8.*

Beth Van Hoesen. *Daikon.* 1979. Aquatint

BEET AND DAIKON SALAD
WITH ORANGE VINAIGRETTE*
Contributed by Joanne Rruff

12 young medium beets
2 10- to 12-inch daikons
    (Japanese white radishes)
Grated rind of 2 oranges
    (no white part)
½ cup olive oil
Salt
Freshly ground pepper
2½ tablespoons sherry
    vinegar
⅓ cup chopped cilantro
    (fresh coriander leaves)

Trim off all but 2 inches of the stems of the beets and boil the beets until barely tender in a large quantity of lightly salted water. The cooking time will depend on the age and size of the beets. If very young, begin testing them for doneness with a sharp-pointed knife after 15 minutes. Older, larger beets can take 1 hour. When barely tender, drain them and put in a bowl under very cold running water 3 or 4 minutes. Still under running water, rub the beets with your fingers. The stems and skins should come off easily. Cut the beets in ¼-inch julienne strips.

Trim the daikons and scrub with a vegetable brush.

Grate them through the larger holes of a grater. Wring out excess water by squeezing between the hands. Store in the refrigerator until needed.

Put the beets in a bowl with the grated orange rind and a generous tablespoon of the oil. Season to taste with salt and pepper and toss lightly. Make a vinaigrette from the remaining oil and the vinegar, seasoned to taste with salt and pepper. Pour over the beets and toss thoroughly.

Pile the beets in the center of a platter, surround with a ring of the grated daikon, and garnish with the chopped cilantro. The salad may be served at room temperature or chilled. *Serves 6.*

*Recipe by Shelley Handler, as prepared at Chez Panisse, Berkeley.

BEET AND EGG SALAD
Contributed by Paul Wonner

10 young medium beets
3 hard-cooked eggs, coarsely chopped
6 scallions, trimmed and thinly sliced, including some of the green tops
1 clove garlic, minced
2 tablespoons chopped fresh dill, or ½ teaspoon dried
¼ pound Swiss cheese, cut in ¼-inch dice
½ cup mayonnaise, or more to taste
½ teaspoon Dijon-type prepared mustard
Salt
Freshly ground pepper

Trim and cook the beets as in the preceding recipe and cut in ½-inch dice. Toss in a bowl with the eggs, scallions, garlic, and dill. Chill in the refrigerator 1 hour or longer. Just before serving, add the cheese, mayonnaise, and mustard. Season to taste with salt and pepper and toss thoroughly. *Serves 6.*

Paul Wonner

CALIFORNIA SUN SALAD
Contributed by Karl Benjamin

3 large heads salad greens, such as romaine, escarole, chicory, or Boston lettuce (a combination may be used)

½ pound sharp cheddar cheese, cut in ¼-inch julienne strips

1 large green pepper, cored, seeded, and cut in thin strips

2 stalks celery, thinly sliced

½ cup salad oil

½ cup wine vinegar

½ teaspoon dry mustard

¼ cup sugar

2 teaspoons dried minced onion

Salt

Freshly ground pepper

4 oranges, peeled, seeded, and cut in bite-size pieces

1 avocado, peeled, pitted, and thinly sliced

3 tablespoons sesame seeds, toasted

Trim and wash the salad greens thoroughly, tear into bite-size pieces, and dry between paper towels, or use your own drying method. Toss in a bowl with the cheese, green pepper, and celery. Chill in the refrigerator at least 1 hour.

Beat together in a small bowl the oil, vinegar, mustard, sugar, dried onion, and salt and pepper to taste. Chill in the refrigerator at least 1 hour.

Pour the dressing over the salad and toss thoroughly. Add the orange pieces and avocado, sprinkle with the sesame seeds, and toss lightly. Serve at once.
Serves 10.

Basket of salad greens in the photographer's kitchen

CRAB, SHRIMP, AND MACARONI SALAD
Contributed by Ralph Maradiaga

½ pound elbow macaroni
1 8-ounce can small new peas,
    drained
2 4½-ounce cans crabmeat,
    rinsed and drained
1 4½-ounce can shrimp,
    rinsed and drained
¼ cup minced parsley
¼ teaspoon garlic salt
½ cup mayonnaise, or more
    to taste
Salt
Freshly ground pepper
1 hard-cooked egg, sliced

Cook the macaroni in a very large pot of boiling salted water about 9 minutes, or until barely tender. Drain, rinse thoroughly with cold water, and shake excess water from the macaroni. Put the macaroni in a salad bowl. Add the peas, crabmeat, shrimp, parsley, garlic salt, and mayonnaise. Toss lightly and season to taste with salt and pepper. Chill in the refrigerator at least 2 hours. Just before serving, garnish with the egg slices.
Serves 6.

ONE-CUP FRUIT SALAD
Contributed by Arthur Nelson

1 chilled cup each:
    White seedless grapes
        (peeled, if desired)
    Pineapple chunks (fresh or
        canned; if canned, drain)
    Mandarin-orange sections
        (fresh or canned; if
        canned, drain)
    Miniature marshmallows
    Shredded coconut
        (preferably fresh)
    Sour cream

Toss all ingredients lightly together in a salad bowl and serve at once.   *Serves* 6 *to* 8.

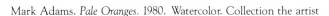

Mark Adams. *Pale Oranges.* 1980. Watercolor. Collection the artist

31

LAYERED SALAD
Contributed by Judy Chicago

2 large onions, sliced
2 tablespoons butter
½ pound spinach leaves,
  trimmed, washed, and dried
¼ pound mushrooms,
  trimmed, cleaned, and
  thinly sliced
2 apples or peaches, peeled,
  cored or pitted, and sliced
1 large cucumber, peeled and
  thinly sliced
1 16-ounce jar artichoke
  hearts, drained
½ pound cheddar cheese, cut
  in ¼-inch julienne strips
1½ cups leftover chicken or
  beef, shredded or thinly sliced
4 hard-cooked eggs, thinly sliced
1 16-ounce can garbanzos
  (chickpeas)
½ pound blue cheese,
  crumbled
1½ cups bottled health-food
  Italian salad dressing

Saute the onions in the butter until soft but not brown. Put the spinach in the bottom of a large salad bowl, spread the onions on top, and add a layer of each of the remaining ingredients (except the dressing), ending with the blue cheese. Pour the dressing over the salad, but do not toss. Spoon deep into the bowl and serve a cross section of the layers.
Serves 10.

Judy Chicago

PEANUT-CABBAGE SLAW
Contributed by Bella Feldman

½ small cabbage, cored
  and shredded
¼ cup sour cream
¼ cup mayonnaise
1 teaspoon grated onion
¼ small green pepper, cored,
  seeded, and minced
½ small cucumber, peeled,
  seeded, and finely chopped
Salt
¼ cup peanuts, chopped or
  crumbled with a rolling pin

Toss the cabbage in a bowl and chill in the refrigerator at least 1 hour. Mix the sour cream, mayonnaise, onion, green pepper, and cucumber in a small bowl. Season to taste with salt. Chill in the refrigerator at least 1 hour. Just before serving, toss the cabbage with the dressing and sprinkle the peanuts on top.
Serves 4.

SHRIMP SALAD
Contributed by Frank Hamilton

1½ pounds medium shrimp
¼ cup brandy or bourbon
¼ cup minced cilantro (fresh
    coriander leaves)
2 tablespoons chili sauce
6 tablespoons mayonnaise
1 bunch watercress, trimmed,
    washed, and dried

Put the shrimp in a saucepan with lightly salted water to cover, bring to a boil over medium heat, boil 1 minute, and drain. When cool enough to handle, peel the shells from the shrimp, score the back sides with a sharp knife from head to tail, and remove the intestinal veins.

Mix the brandy or bourbon, cilantro, chili sauce, and mayonnaise in a bowl. Add the shrimp and coat them thoroughly. Marinate in the refrigerator 4 to 6 hours, stirring occasionally. Serve the shrimp on beds of watercress on chilled plates.
Serves 4.

Mark Adams. *Big Green Pepper.* 1980. Watercolor. Collection the artist

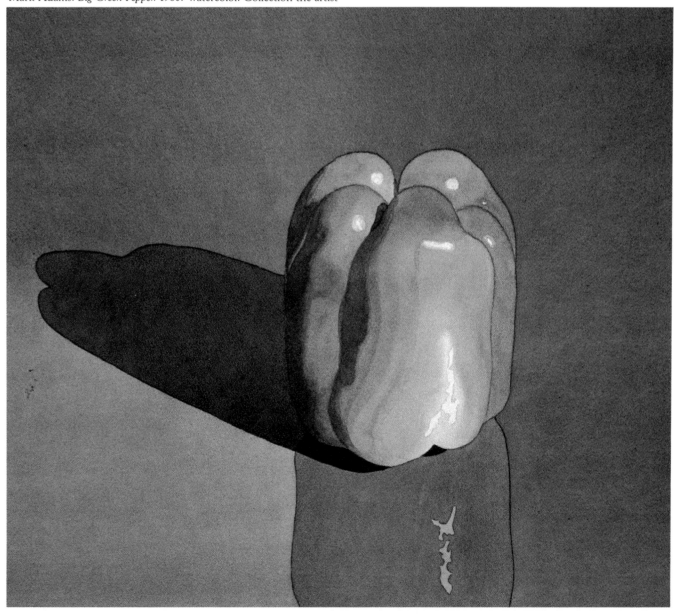

STRAWBERRY-ROQUEFORT SALAD

Contributed by Judith Golden for Van Deren Coke

¼ cup Roquefort cheese, at
    room temperature
½ cup plain yogurt
1 tablespoon lemon juice
1 tablespoon vegetable oil
1 pint strawberries
1 large head Boston lettuce,
    or 4 heads Bibb lettuce

Mash the cheese to a paste in a small bowl with a fork. Gradually add the yogurt and then the lemon juice and oil, stirring until the dressing is smooth and creamy. Chill in the regrigerator.

Wash and hull the strawberries. Reserve a few of the most perfect and slice the remainder. Chill in the refrigerator.

Tear the lettuce in bite-size pieces and wash and dry. Chill in the refrigerator.

At serving time, toss the sliced berries lightly with the greens in a salad bowl, garnish with the whole berries, and pour the dressing over the center. Mix lightly again at the table. *Serves 4.*

Contributor's note: This salad is ideal with Greek Chicken (page 110).

TOFU SALAD
Contributed by Gerald Gooch

1 pound compressed tofu,
  crumbled

2 stalks celery, minced

1 medium green pepper,
  cored, seeded, and minced

1 medium red onion, minced

1 cup sprouted sunflower
  seeds (see *Note*)

¼ cup sesame oil

½ cup cider vinegar

¼ cup lemon juice

2 teaspoons sea salt, ground

1 tablespoon honey

2 tablespoons prepared
  mustard

3 dill pickles, finely chopped

⅔ cup pitted olives, finely
  chopped

Lettuce (optional)

Put the crumbled tofu and the celery, green pepper, and red onion in a bowl and toss lightly. Chill in the refrigerator 1 hour.

Put the sunflower seeds, sesame oil, vinegar, lemon juice, sea salt, honey, and mustard in the container of a food processor and, using the standard steel blade, process until they form a smooth emulsion. Alternatively, use a blender or beat by hand. Pour this dressing over the chilled salad, add the pickles and olives, and toss thoroughly. If you like, serve on crisp lettuce.
Serves 6.

Note: Hulled sunflower seeds (nontreated, purchased at a health-food store) may be sprouted in a jar. Cover them with water, tying several thicknesses of cheesecloth over the top of the jar, and then pour off the excess water. The seeds should be only moist, not soaking. After 24 hours, add fresh water and drain again. Repeat this process until the seeds have sprouted, usually in 4 or 5 days.

Opposite page:
Judith Golden and Van Deren Coke

Mark Adams. *Onion and Spoon.*
1979. Watercolor.
Collection the artist

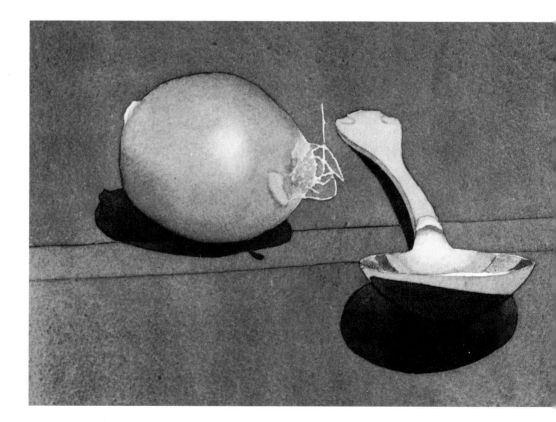

SOUPS

Judy Chicago. *Hildegarde of Bingen* (detail of place setting from *The Dinner Party*). 1979. Mixed medium.
Collection of Through The Flower Corporation, Santa Monica

Cream of Carrot and Cider Soup ❧ Joanne Rruff

Ty's Clam Chowder ❧ Tyrone Head

Caribbean Conch Chowder ❧ Frederick Eversley

Exotic Soup ❧ Richard and Margaret Mayer

Garlic Soup ❧ Frederick Eversley

Cream of Lettuce Soup ❧ Beth Van Hoesen

Herbed Lentil Soup ❧ Dona and Stephen De Staebler

Sea Breeze Soup ❧ Richard and Margaret Mayer

AA's Sorrel Soup ❧ Ansel Adams

Mast Va Kair (Cold Lentil Soup) ❧ Marian Clayden

CREAM OF CARROT AND CIDER SOUP*

Contributed by Joanne Rruff

24 young carrots, peeled
4 tablespoons sweet butter
3 medium onions, thinly
  sliced
1 liter French cider
4 cups heavy cream
Salt
Freshly ground pepper
2 tablespoons minced cilantro
  (fresh coriander leaves)

Cut the carrots in ½-inch slices. There should be about 5 cups. Melt the butter over low heat in a large saucepan, add the carrots and onions, stir briefly, and cover the pan tightly with a lid. Let them stew, or "sweat," about 15 minutes, stirring occasionally. The onions should be soft and translucent but not brown. Remove cover, add ½ cup of the cider, raise the heat, and stir until the cider has nearly evaporated. Add the remaining cider and the cream. Simmer uncovered over moderate heat 20 minutes, or until the carrots are very tender.

Pour the soup through a strainer into a bowl. Put the drained carrots and onions with 1 cup of the liquid into the container of a food processor and, using the standard steel blade, process until very smooth. Alternatively, press the carrots and onions through the strainer with the back of a wooden spoon.

Return the puréed vegetables and the liquid to the saucepan, season to taste with salt and pepper, and simmer covered 5 minutes, or you may keep the soup over very low heat until ready to serve. Garnish each serving with a little of the cilantro.
Serves 6.

*Recipe by Shelley Handler, as prepared at Chez Panisse, Berkeley.

Mark Adams. *Carrots*. 1978. Watercolor. Courtesy John Berggruen Gallery, San Francisco

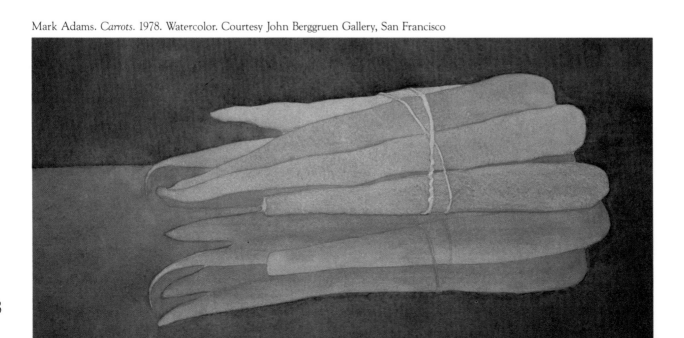

A shelf of dried beans, grains, and legumes in Priscilla Birge's kitchen

TY'S CLAM CHOWDER
Contributed by Tyrone Head

4 slices bacon, cut in 1-inch
  pieces
3 scallions, trimmed and
  thinly sliced, including the
  green tops
5 medium potatoes, peeled
  and quartered
½ small green pepper, cored,
  seeded, and finely chopped
1 stalk celery, thinly sliced
1 carrot, peeled and thinly
  sliced
1 clove garlic, minced
  and mashed
Salt
Freshly ground pepper
1 teaspoon Worcestershire
  sauce
4 drops Tabasco
3 dozen clams, shelled
  (reserving their juice)
⅔ cup heavy cream
1⅓ cups half-and-half

Sauté the bacon in a large, heavy, preferably enameled-iron pot over medium heat until crisp. Add the scallions, potatoes, green pepper, celery, carrot, garlic, and 2 cups of water. Season with the salt (very lightly; the bacon will salt the soup), freshly ground pepper, Worcestershire sauce, and Tabasco. Bring to a boil, cover tightly, and simmer over medium heat 15 minutes, or until the potatoes are barely tender. Mash the potatoes slightly, or, if you prefer a thick soup, mash them thoroughly into the liquid.

Strain the clams over a small saucepan. Chop the clams coarsely, add them to their juice, and heat 3 minutes over a moderate flame.

Add the clams and their juice, the cream, and the half-and-half to the soup pot, season with salt and pepper, if necessary, and bring just to a simmer. Do not boil or it will curdle.   *Serves 4.*

CARIBBEAN CONCH CHOWDER
Contributed by Frederick Eversley

8 large conchs, skinned
½ pound salt pork, cut in
 ¼-inch dice
2 medium onions, coarsely
 chopped
4 cloves garlic, minced
1 large green pepper, cored,
 seeded, and finely chopped
1 28-ounce can peeled
 tomatoes, drained
1 6-ounce can tomato paste
10 bay leaves
2 teaspoons barbecue sauce
1 teaspoon poultry seasoning
1 teaspoon dried oregano
1 tablespoon white vinegar
3 pounds new potatoes,
 peeled and cut in half
Salt
Freshly ground pepper

Force the conchs through a meat grinder, using the coarse blade, and set aside. Saute the salt-pork dice in a heavy saucepan over medium heat until they render most of their fat and are golden. Add the onions, garlic, and green pepper. Stir over medium heat about 5 minutes, or until the onions are soft but not brown. Add the tomatoes, tomato paste, and the 4 seasonings. Cook over medium heat, stirring frequently, for 15 minutes, or until well blended.

Bring 2 quarts of water and the vinegar to a boil in a large, heavy, preferably enameled-iron pot. Add the conch and the tomato mixture. Simmer covered 30 minutes, add the potatoes, season to taste with salt and pepper, and simmer 30 minutes longer, or until the potatoes are very tender.
Serves 10 to 12.

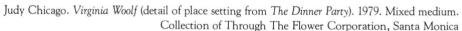

Judy Chicago. *Virginia Woolf* (detail of place setting from *The Dinner Party*). 1979. Mixed medium.
Collection of Through The Flower Corporation, Santa Monica

EXOTIC SOUP
Contributed by Richard and Margaret Mayer

3 cloves garlic, quartered
1 large onion, quartered
3 large ripe tomatoes, peeled,
    seeded, and quartered
3 tablespoons soybean oil
2 tablespoons tarragon wine
    vinegar
1 cup beef broth
1½ teaspoons salt
1 teaspoon cracked pepper
1 cup vodka, chilled
1 large cucumber, peeled,
    seeded, and coarsely
    chopped
1 large green pepper, cored,
    seeded, and coarsely
    chopped
1 large onion, coarsely
    chopped
6 slices day-old French bread,
    cut in ½-inch cubes

Put the garlic, quartered onion, and tomatoes in the container of a food processor and, using the standard steel blade, process until very smooth. Pour the mixture into a bowl and add the oil, vinegar, and beef broth. Season with the salt and pepper, stir until well blended, and chill in the refrigerator at least 2 hours. Just before serving, stir in the chilled vodka.

Serve the soup in bowls that have been frosted in the freezer. Pass separate bowls of the cucumber, green pepper, chopped onion, and bread cubes.
Serves 4.

GARLIC SOUP
Contributed by Frederick Eversley

18 cloves garlic
½ teaspoon dried thyme
1 bay leaf
½ teaspoon dried sage
¼ teaspoon dried rosemary
6 sprigs parsley
3 whole cloves
7 tablespoons olive oil
Salt
Freshly ground pepper
3 egg yolks
1 cup grated Parmesan cheese

Put the garlic, herbs, cloves, 4 tablespoons of the oil, and 2 quarts of water in a large, heavy pot, bring to a boil, and simmer over medium heat 30 minutes. Season the broth to taste with salt and pepper and keep hot.

Put the egg yolks in a soup tureen and beat with a whisk until thick. Slowly beat in the remaining oil by droplets, forming an emulsion. Pour the broth through a fine strainer into a saucepan and discard the solid ingredients. Reheat the broth, if necessary. Very gradually pour it into the egg mixture, beating constantly. Serve at once. Pass the grated cheese separately.
Serves 6.

CREAM OF LETTUCE SOUP
Contributed by Beth Van Hoesen

2 heads salad greens, such as
    romaine, escarole, chickory,
    or Boston lettuce
A few spinach or watercress
    leaves (optional)
1 10-ounce can condensed
    chicken broth plus 1
    10-ounce can water
3 tablespoons butter
3 tablespoons flour
1½ cups milk, heated
1 cup half-and-half
Salt
Freshly ground pepper

Trim, wash, and shred the salad greens and optional spinach or watercress leaves. There should be about 8 loosely packed cups.

Bring the chicken broth and water to a boil in a large saucepan over high heat. Add the greens, cover tightly, and steam about 10 minutes, stirring occasionally. Pour the broth through a fine strainer into a bowl and reserve. Put the strained greens in the container of a food processor and, using the standard steel blade, process until puréed and smooth. Alternatively, force the strained greens through a food mill.

Melt the butter in a large saucepan over medium heat, add the flour, and stir with a whisk until the mixture bubbles. Add the hot milk all at once and stir until the mixture thickens. Add the puréed greens, the reserved chicken broth, and the half-and-half. Stir gently but thoroughly and season to taste with salt and pepper. Heat just until very hot, but do not boil. Serve at once or keep over very low heat until serving time. *Serves 4.*

Note: Escarole or chickory will provide a more robust—even pungent or slightly bitter—flavor than romaine or Boston lettuce.

Beth Van Hoesen

42

HERBED LENTIL SOUP
Contributed by Dona and Stephen De Staebler

½ pound lentils
½ cup butter
4 cardamon pods, seeds
  removed and crushed
2 bay leaves
1 sprig fresh mint, minced, or
  ¼ teaspoon dried
2 teaspoons ground cumin
¼ teaspoon ground ginger
¼ teaspoon ground fenugreek
1 clove garlic, minced
2 tablespoons minced parsley
1 teaspoon salt
¼ teaspoon freshly ground
  pepper
¼ cup heavy cream
½ cup yogurt

Put all the ingredients (except the cream and yogurt) in a heavy saucepan. Add water to cover by 4 inches. Bring to a boil over high heat, stir briefly, reduce the heat, and simmer uncovered 45 minutes. Stir in the cream and yogurt. Simmer over very low heat about 15 minutes longer. Remove bay leaves before serving.   *Serves 6.*

Richard Mayer

SEA BREEZE SOUP
Contributed by Richard and Margaret Mayer

3 10-ounce cans condensed
  cream of celery soup
¾ cup dry white wine
3 4¼-ounce cans flaked
  crabmeat, rinsed and
  drained
3 scallions, trimmed and very
  thinly sliced
2 small tomatoes, peeled,
  seeded, and chopped
Grated rind of 1 lemon
Salt
Freshly ground pepper

Put the soup, 3 cups of water, and the wine in a large saucepan and bring just to a boil over medium heat, stirring occasionally. Add the crabmeat, scallions, tomatoes, and lemon rind, and season to taste with salt and pepper. Stir gently just until the soup is very hot. Or allow the soup to cool, chill in the refrigerator 2 hours, and serve cold.   *Serves 6.*

Ansel Adams: portrait of a self-portrait   *Opposite page:* Marian Clayden

AA'S SORREL SOUP
Contributed by Ansel Adams

4 tablespoons butter
1 medium onion, minced
5 cups coarsely chopped fresh
   sorrel leaves
4 tablespoons flour
6 cups homemade chicken
   stock, heated
1 cup plain yogurt
1 cup heavy cream
Salt
Freshly ground pepper

Melt the butter in a large, heavy, preferably enameled-iron pot over medium heat. Add the onion and cook about 10 minutes, or until soft and translucent but not brown. Stir in the sorrel leaves, reduce the heat, and simmer until wilted and tender, about 5 minutes. Sprinkle the flour over the sorrel and cook 5 minutes longer, stirring often. Stir in the chicken stock, raise the heat slightly, and cook 10 minutes longer, stirring often.

Pour the mixture, half at a time, into the container of a food processor and, using the standard steel blade, purée. Alternatively, use a food mill.

Return the mixture to the pot and stir in the yogurt and heavy cream. Season to taste with salt and pepper. Heat just until very hot; do not boil. *Serves 6.*

MAST VA KAIR (COLD YOGURT SOUP)
Contributed by Marian Clayden

1 hard-cooked egg, chopped
½ cup yellow raisins, soaked
   in hot water 5 minutes and
   drained
3 cups plain yogurt
½ cup light cream, or ¼ cup
   heavy cream and ¼ cup
   half-and-half
1 medium cucumber, peeled,
   seeded, and chopped
¼ cup coarsely chopped fresh
   mint
½ cup chopped scallions,
   including the green tops
1 teaspoon lemon juice
½ cup finely chopped walnuts
6 ice cubes
2 teaspoons salt
Freshly ground pepper
4 fresh mint sprigs

Put all the ingredients, except the mint sprigs, in a large bowl and stir until well blended. Cover the bowl and chill in the refrigerator at least 3 hours; overnight is preferable. Mix the soup thoroughly again before serving in individual chilled bowls. Garnish each with a sprig of mint. *Serves 4.*

PASTA
AND RICE

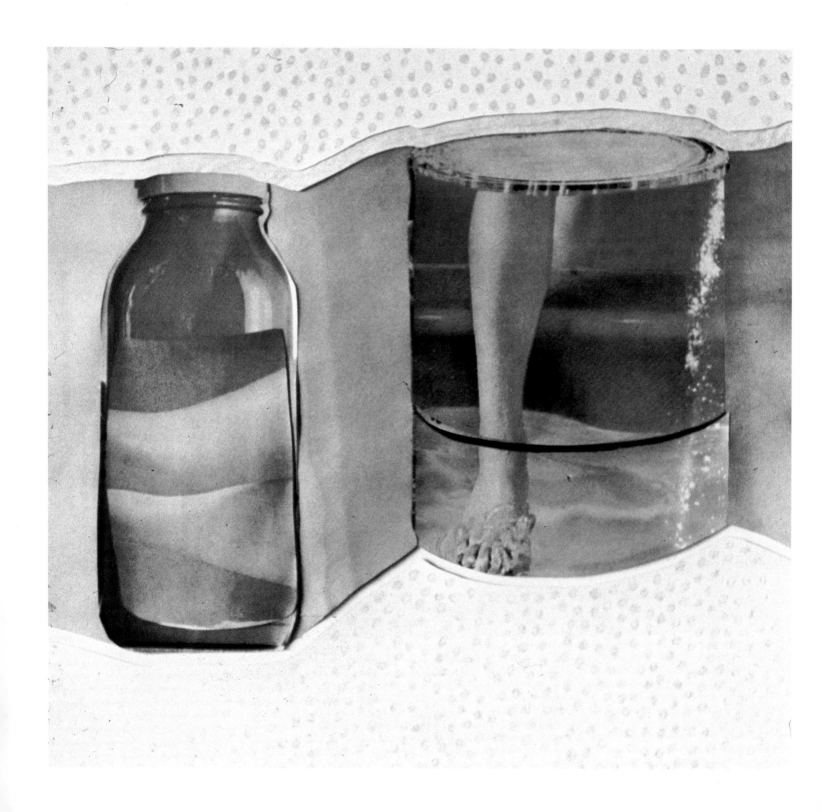

Fettuccine Fantastico ❧ Barnaby Conrad

Linguini with Red Clam Sauce ❧ Garner Tullis

Pasta with White Clam Sauce ❧ Al Farrow

Penne Strascicate (Pasta with Tomato-and-Crème-Fraîche Sauce) ❧ Rooney O'Neill

Rice and Bulgur Wheat with Peas ❧ Fred Reichman

Rice and Mushroom Ring ❧ Hans Burkhardt

Rice with Spicy Mushrooms ❧ Priscilla Birge

Shireen Polo (Sweet Rice) ❧ Marian Clayden

Spaghetti Carbonara ❧ Tony Costanzo

Spaghetti with Mizitra Sauce ❧ Wayne Thiebaud

Vegetable Spaghetti ❧ Patricia Tavenner

Vermicelli with Caviar ❧ Ann Thornycroft

Taglierini with Tomatoes and Basil ❧ K. Lee Manuel

Vermicelli Ring ❧ Hans Burkhardt

Wild Rice with Pistachios ❧ K. Lee Manuel

Priscilla Birge. *It's that Way Every Day.* © 1973. Montage. Collection the artist

FETTUCCINE FANTASTICO
Contributed by Barnaby Conrad

1 pair sweetbreads, about ¾ pound

3 tablespoons butter

½ large chicken breast, skinned, boned, and tendons removed

¼ pound mushrooms, cleaned and thinly sliced

Besciamella sauce:
   6 tablespoons butter
   5 tablespoons flour
   1 tablespoon curry powder, or more to taste
   3 cups milk, heated
   1 cup heavy cream, or more as needed
   Salt
   Freshly ground pepper
   Freshly grated nutmeg

1½ pounds fettuccine, or similar flat noodles

Salt

¼ cup pâté de foie gras, diced (optional)

½ cup freshly grated Parmesan cheese

¼ cup butter, melted

Soak the sweetbreads in ice water 1 hour to whiten them and soften the tissue surrounding them. Cover with fresh cold water in a saucepan over medium heat, bring to a boil, cover the pan, lower the heat, and simmer 25 minutes. Remove the sweetbreads from the pan and immediately plunge them in cold water. Let them soak again 20 minutes, changing the water often, or let them sit in a bowl under a trickle of running cold water. Remove them and pull off all the encasing and connective tissue. Wrap the sweetbreads in paper towels to dry. Set aside.

Heat the 3 tablespoons of butter in a large, preferably enameled-iron pot over medium heat until its foam subsides. Add the sweetbreads, chicken breast, and mushrooms. Stir briefly to coat with the butter, cover the pot tightly, lower the heat, and simmer 4 minutes. Uncover and stir briefly with a wooden spoon, turning the sweetbreads and chicken over. Re-cover and simmer 4 minutes longer. Remove the pot from the heat. Remove the sweetbreads and chicken and cut in ¼-inch dice. Return them to the pot, stirring them into the mushrooms and juices, and set aside.

Melt the 6 tablespoons of butter in a large, heavy saucepan over medium heat, add the flour and curry powder, and stir until the flour is bubbly but not browned. Add the milk all at once and whisk until the mixture is very thick and smooth. Gradually add 1 cup of cream and season to taste with salt, pepper, and nutmeg. Reduce the heat to very low and let the sauce sit, stirring it occasionally, while you cook the fettuccine.

Boil the fettuccine in lightly salted water as described for linguine on facing page, but leave it underdone, slightly more crunchy than *al dente*. Drain thoroughly and add to the pot with the sweetbreads and chicken. Add the pâté, if desired, and toss lightly.

Whisk the besciamella sauce vigorously. It should not be too thick. Thin it if necessary with a little more heavy cream and then pour over the fettuccine. Toss very thoroughly and taste for seasoning. Pour the fettuccine into a very large shallow buttered baking dish, sprinkle with the cheese, and drizzle with the melted butter. Bake in a preheated 400° oven about 15 minutes, or until the top is golden brown. Serve immediately.   *Serves 8 to 10.*

LINGUINI WITH RED CLAM SAUCE
Contributed by Garner Tullis

5 tablespoons olive oil
1 large onion, coarsely
   chopped
4 cloves garlic, minced
⅓ cup minced parsley
½ teaspoon dried dill
2 teaspoons dried basil
½ teaspoon dried thyme
4 tablespoons butter
1 28-ounce can whole ground
   tomatoes
1 15-ounce can tomato sauce
1 16-ounce can whole peeled
   tomatoes, drained
1 6-ounce can tomato paste
Salt
Freshly ground pepper
1½ pounds linguini
2 6½-ounce cans minced
   clams, undrained

Put the olive oil in a large, heavy, preferably enameled-iron pot over medium heat and add the onion, garlic, and parsley. Stir about 5 minutes, or until the onion is soft and translucent but not brown. Add the dried herbs and the butter and stir just until the butter is melted. Add the whole ground tomatoes, tomato sauce, whole tomatoes, and tomato paste. Season to taste with salt and pepper. Cook uncovered over medium heat, stirring frequently, about 30 minutes, or until much of the liquid has evaporated and the whole tomatoes are well blended into the sauce. Reduce the heat to very low.

Bring at least 6 quarts of lightly salted water to a rolling boil in a very large pot over high heat. Add the linguini and 1 tablespoon of the tomato sauce, which keeps the water from boiling over, and cover loosely with a lid. After 1 minute, uncover, and stir the linguini to be sure it is not sticking together. Replace lid loosely, and after another 8 minutes begin tasting for doneness by removing a single strand and biting into it. When the pasta is still slightly chewy, or *al dente*, drain in a very large colander.

About 2 minutes before the linguini is cooked, add the minced clams with their juice to the tomato sauce and reheat the sauce briefly over medium heat. Serve the linguini in large bowls and top with a generous amount of the sauce.   *Serves 6 to 8.*

Note: The addition of some tomato sauce to the pasta cooking water adds acidity, which diminishes or even eliminates the foam that would be produced if the pot were covered. Covering the pot loosely ensures a fast rolling boil at all times. Both these procedures are optional, however, and may be omitted.

Al Farrow

PASTA WITH WHITE CLAM SAUCE
Contributed by Al Farrow

1 pound pasta, such as
  spaghetti, linguini, noodles,
  or shells
½ cup olive oil
5 cloves garlic, minced
2 6½-ounce cans minced
  clams (or whole baby
  clams), undrained
1 cup minced parsley
Salt
Freshly ground pepper

Cook the pasta as described in preceding recipe. The timing will depend on the type of pasta.

While the pasta is cooking, put the oil in a saucepan over medium heat, add the garlic, and stir about 5 minutes, or until the garlic is barely golden. About 2 minutes before the pasta is done, add the clams and their juice and the parsley to the olive oil and garlic. Reheat briefly just until the clams are very hot. Season the sauce very lightly with salt and generously with pepper. Spoon the sauce over the drained pasta in a large serving bowl or in individual bowls. *Serves 3 or 4.*

Contributor's note: Sometimes I work twenty hours at a stretch and don't have time to prepare meals. So when cooking pasta or rice, I make extra. I toss a pound of leftover unsauced pasta with 2 tablespoons of olive oil and then refrigerate it. At mealtime I just dump it in the heated sauce and toss it around until it has heated through.

I use the same method for rice, but refrigerate it without the oil. To make easy and delicious stir-fried rice I heat it up in a skillet with oil, a mashed clove or two of garlic, and a chopped onion, and then toss in cheese or leftover meat or vegetables or any combination. Then I add ½ teaspoon sesame oil and red-pepper flakes and soy sauce to taste. For 1 cup of cooked rice, use ¼ to 1 cup of leftovers. Be creative.

PENNE STRASCICATE
(PASTA WITH TOMATO-AND-CRÈME-FRAÎCHE SAUCE)
Contributed by Rooney O'Neill

3 large cloves garlic
3 whole fresh hot peppers, seeded, or 3 dried hot red peppers, or 1 scant teaspoon red-pepper flakes
½ cup olive oil
1 28-ounce can whole Italian plum tomatoes, drained
Salt
Freshly ground pepper
1 pound penne, or other tubular pasta, such as small rigatoni
1 10-ounce container *crème fraîche* (see *Contributor's note*)

Rooney O'Neill

Bruise the garlic cloves by pressing slightly with the flat side of a knife. Put them with the fresh or dried hot peppers, or the pepper flakes, and the oil in a large, heavy, preferably enameled-iron (*not* aluminum) pot over medium heat. Cook clowly at least 5 minutes, stirring frequently. Adjust the heat so that the oil is very hot but not smoking. The garlic should color but not brown. The oil should become heavily flavored with the garlic and the hot peppers.

Add the tomatoes and season to taste with salt and pepper. Cook slowly, stirring frequently, over medium heat (about 30 minutes), or until much of the liquid has evaporated and the sauce is thickened and fairly smooth. If desired, the garlic and whole peppers may now be discarded.

While the sauce is simmering, cook the pasta in a large quantity of lightly salted water until barely tender, or *al dente*, as described for linguine on page 49.

Just before the pasta is done, add the *crème fraîche* to the tomato sauce and simmer only until heated through; do not allow it to boil. Drain the pasta and add to the pot. Stir it gently in the sauce for 4 or 5 minutes and serve immediately in 4 hot bowls or on plates. Do not serve grated cheese with this pasta. If you have not discarded the garlic cloves and whole peppers, be sure to warn guests.   *Serves 4.*

Contributor's note: This is another recipe, like Pollo o Tacchino Steccato (page 115), Vitello Tonnato (page 99), and Crostata di Frutta (page 172), that comes from my sister and her Florentine husband. The first time I prepared it, three people made it vanish, and one of them had already dined. *Strascicate*, incidentally, means "dragged" or "stirred." In Italy the cream for this recipe would be a *panna di cucinare* ("cooking cream"). *Crème fraîche* is becoming more and more available in America and makes a fine substitute.

RICE AND BULGUR WHEAT WITH PEAS
Contributed by Fred Reichman

¼ pound capelli d'angeli or
  taglierini (very fine
  spaghetti)
3 tablespoons butter
2 cups long-grain rice
1 cup Bulgur wheat (Burghul)
3 tablespoons safflower oil
⅓ cup pine nuts (pignoli)
6 cups chicken broth, or
  more if necessary
¼ teaspoon powdered saffron,
  dissolved in ¼ cup water
Salt
Freshly ground pepper
2 pounds peas, shelled (or 1
  10-ounce box frozen tiny
  peas)

Cook the capelli d'angeli or taglierini as described for linguini on page 49, but test for doneness after 4 minutes. Drain very thoroughly. Melt the butter in a skillet over medium heat. When it is golden but not brown, add the pasta and brown very lightly, tossing often. Remove from the heat and set aside.

Put the rice, Bulgur wheat, and oil in a large, heavy, preferably enameled-iron pot over medium heat and stir until the grains begin to turn golden, about 5 minutes. Add the pine nuts and stir briefly. Add the chicken broth, saffron, and salt and pepper to taste. Stir well, bring to a boil, reduce the heat to very low, and cover the pot tightly. Cook gently without stirring about 30 minutes. Add the pasta and the peas, tossing them lightly into the grains. If the mixture seems dry, add a little more chicken broth; if there is excess liquid, raise the heat and cook briefly uncovered. Then re-cover the pot and cook about 15 minutes longer, or until the peas are tender (frozen peas will cook in less time). *Serves* 6.

RICE AND MUSHROOM RING
Contributed by Hans Burkhardt

1 pound mushrooms,
  trimmed, cleaned, and cut
  in quarters
6 tablespoons butter
3 cups cooked rice
Salt
Freshly ground pepper
2 pounds peas, shelled
  (or 1 10-ounce box frozen
  tiny peas)
Boiling water
½ cup slivered almonds

Put the mushrooms in the container of a food processor and, using the standard steel blade, mince finely. Alternatively, put them through a meat grinder, using the coarse blade, or mince finely by hand.

Melt 2 tablespoons of the butter in a saucepan over medium heat, add the mushrooms, and stir about 5 minutes. Add the rice and season to taste with salt and pepper. Stir the mixture over the heat 5 minutes longer.

Grease a 9-inch ring mold with a tablespoon of the butter and spread the rice mixture evenly in the mold, pressing it down slightly. Place the mold in a larger flat pan containing 2 inches of boiling water and bake in a preheated 350° oven 30 minutes.

Cook the peas in lightly salted boiling water to cover

for 5 to 8 minutes, or until tender, and drain. (If using frozen peas, follow package directions.) Melt the remaining butter in a skillet over medium heat, add the almonds, and stir until they are golden. Add the drained peas, season to taste with salt and pepper, and heat just until very hot.

Unmold the rice ring onto a heated serving dish and put the peas in the center of the ring.   *Serves 4.*

Note: Other fillings may be substituted if desired.

RICE WITH SPICY MUSHROOMS
Contributed by Priscilla Birge

2 pounds mushrooms, trimmed and cleaned
10 tablespoons butter
1 medium onion, minced
2 green peppers, cored, seeded, and finely chopped
½ cup brown sugar, tightly packed
1 tablespoon Dijon-type mustard
2 tablespoons Worcestershire sauce
¾ cup dry red wine
Salt
Freshly ground pepper
2 cups long-grain rice
Juice of ½ lemon
½ cup sour cream or plain yogurt (optional)

Thinly slice the mushrooms by hand or push them through the thin-slicing blade of a food processor. Set aside.

Melt 8 tablespoons of the butter in a large, heavy saucepan over medium heat. Add the onion and stir 5 minutes, or until soft and translucent but not brown. Add the green pepper and stir 2 minutes longer. Remove from heat, add the mushrooms, and set aside.

In a bowl, mix the brown sugar, mustard, and Worcestershire sauce until they form a paste. Gradually add the red wine and season lightly with salt and pepper. Add this mixture to the mushroom mixture, stirring it in well. Simmer over low heat 45 minutes, or until it thickens, stirring frequently.

While this sauce is cooking, prepare the rice. Melt the remaining 2 tablespoons of butter in a heavy saucepan over medium heat, add the rice, and stir constantly with a wooden spoon until the rice is opaque and milky-looking, about 3 minutes. Add 3 cups of cold water, the lemon juice, and 1 teaspoon of salt, or more to taste. Bring to a boil, stir well, and cover tightly. Reduce the heat to very low and simmer 20 minutes without stirring.

If desired, add the sour cream or yogurt to the sauce and heat just until it is very hot, but do not boil or it will curdle. Turn the hot rice onto a serving dish and top with the sauce.   *Serves 6.*

SHIREEN POLO (SWEET RICE)
Contributed by Marian Clayden

Rind of 2 oranges (no white
   part), cut in julienne strips
Salt
3 medium carrots, peeled and
   cut in 1-inch julienne strips
½ cup butter
1 large onion, finely chopped
1 teaspoon powdered saffron
1 cup slivered almonds
1 cup light brown sugar
4 cups freshly cooked long-
   grain rice

Blanch the orange strips in simmering water 5 minutes. Drain, pat dry with paper towels, and set aside.

Bring 2 cups of lightly salted water to a boil in a small saucepan, add the carrot strips, and simmer about 5 minutes, or until barely tender. Drain and set aside.

Melt the butter in a large, heavy skillet over medium heat. Add the onion and stir about 2 minutes, or until soft and translucent but not brown. Add the saffron, almonds, orange rind, and carrots. Stir about 1 minute and add the brown sugar. Continue stirring until the sugar has melted and is well blended with the other ingredients. Remove skillet from the heat and cover loosely until the rice is ready.

At serving time reheat the sugar mixture until bubbly, pour over the hot rice on a large platter, and mix well. *Serves 4.*

Contributor's note: This is an ideal accompaniment for Jujeh Kebabs (Chicken Kebabs—page 110). It will also go well with broiled chicken or broiled or roast lamb.

SPAGHETTI CARBONARA
Contributed by Tony Costanzo

1 pound spaghetti
4 eggs, lightly beaten
½ cup grated Parmesan
   cheese
½ cup minced parsley
5 tablespoons butter
5 tablespoons olive oil
½ pound lean salt pork, cut
   in ¼-inch dice
1½ tablespoons cracked or
   crushed peppercorns

Cook the spaghetti as described for linguini on page 49. While the spaghetti is cooking, lightly beat together the eggs, cheese, and parsley in a bowl. Set aside.

Heat the butter and oil in a skillet over medium heat, add the salt-pork dice, and cook until the fat is rendered out of the salt pork and dice are golden. Do not allow the butter and oil to burn. Do not drain.

Drain the spaghetti when it is *al dente* and turn out onto a large platter. Immediately pour the egg mixture over it and toss lightly. Pour the salt-pork dice with all the fat in the skillet over it, sprinkle with the pepper, and very quickly toss again. The hot fat will cook the eggs. Season with additional pepper, if desired. *Serves 4.*

SPAGHETTI WITH MIZITRA SAUCE

Contributed by Wayne Thiebaud

1 pound spaghetti
¼ pound sliced bacon, cut in
   1-inch pieces
¼ cup olive oil
1 medium red onion, thinly
   sliced
¼ pound prosciutto, sliced
   paper thin and cut in short
   strips
4 tablespoons butter, melted
½ cup chicken broth, heated
   to boiling point
4 egg yolks, lightly beaten
½ cup minced parsley
2 cups grated dry Mizitra
   cheese*
Freshly ground pepper
Salt

*Mizitra cheese is made in both dry
and soft forms. It may be obtained
in Greek specialty stores.

Cook the spaghetti as described for linguini on page 49. Have all the sauce ingredients ready in advance, so that the spaghetti can be sauced as soon as it is *al dente*. While the spaghetti is cooking, sauté the bacon until crisp in a skillet over medium heat. While the bacon is cooking, put the oil in a large, heavy pot over medium heat, add the onion, and stir until soft and translucent but not brown. Add the prosciutto and stir 2 minutes longer. Using a slotted spoon, transfer the crisp bacon to the pot. Reduce the heat to very low.

When the spaghetti is *al dente*, drain thoroughly in a colander and transfer to the pot containing the onion, prosciutto, and bacon. Add the melted butter and boiling chicken broth, raise the heat, and toss briefly. Remove the pot from the heat, immediately add the egg yolks, and toss lightly. Sprinkle with the parsley and 1 cup of the cheese. Season generously with pepper and only if necessary with salt (the bacon, prosciutto, and cheese will salt the sauce). Toss again and transfer to a serving dish. Pass the remaining cheese separately.
Serves 4.

Wayne and Betty Jean Thiebaud

VEGETABLE SPAGHETTI
Contributed by Patricia Tavenner

¼ cup olive oil
1 medium onion, finely chopped
¼ pound mushrooms, trimmed, cleaned, and minced
2 cups mixed diced raw vegetables, such as zucchini, carrots, and string beans
1 28-ounce can whole peeled tomatoes, drained
1 6-ounce can tomato paste
3 cloves garlic, minced
2 tablespoons minced parsley
1 tablespoon dried basil
1 tablespoon dried oregano
Salt
Freshly ground pepper
1 pound pasta, such as spaghetti, linguini, noodles, or shells

This sauce improves by resting at least 24 hours. If possible, prepare it a day in advance and refrigerate overnight or longer. It also freezes well.

Heat the oil in a large, heavy, preferably enameled-iron pot over medium heat. Add the onion and stir about 5 minutes, or until the onion is soft and translucent but not brown. Add the mushrooms and cook, stirring frequently, 10 minutes, or until all the mushroom juices have evaporated. Add the diced vegetables and stir over fairly high heat 2 or 3 minutes, coating them well with the oil. Add the tomatoes, tomato paste, garlic, and herbs, and season to taste with salt and pepper. Reduce the heat and simmer uncovered, stirring frequently, about 20 minutes, or until the tomatoes are well blended into the sauce. Remove from the heat, cool, and store in a covered container in the refrigerator.

About 30 minutes before serving, reheat the sauce gently over low heat, stirring occasionally. Cook and drain the pasta as described for linguini on page 49. Transfer it to 4 large serving bowls and top with a generous amount of the sauce.
Serves 4.

VERMICELLI WITH CAVIAR
Contributed by Ann Thornycroft

½ pound vermicelli
4 tablespoons sweet butter, melted
2 tablespoons lemon juice
4 tablespoons coarsely chopped Italian parsley
4 tablespoons fresh Beluga caviar
2 lemon wedges, seeded

Cook the vermicelli as described for linguini on page 49, but test for doneness after 4 minutes. Drain thoroughly. Divide into 2 hot serving bowls. Combine the butter and lemon juice, stir briefly, and pour over the vermicelli. Sprinkle with the parsley and toss lightly. Top each portion with 2 tablespoons of the caviar and garnish each with a lemon wedge. Provide salt and a pepper mill, preferably containing white peppercorns, at the table. Serve immediately with a good dry chilled champagne.
Serves 2.

TAGLIERINI WITH TOMATOES
AND BASIL
Contributed by K. Lee Manuel

4 tablespoons olive oil

8 large very ripe tomatoes, peeled, seeded, and coarsely chopped

½ cup tomato juice

2 tablespoons tomato paste

Salt

Freshly ground pepper

1 pound taglierini

1 loosely packed cup fresh basil leaves, coarsely chopped

1 cup grated Parmesan cheese

The simple perfection of this dish can only be achieved with dead-ripe tomatoes and fresh basil.

Heat the oil in a large, heavy, preferably enameled-iron saucepan over medium heat, add the tomatoes, and stir about 5 minutes, or until much of the juice has evaporated and the tomatoes are soft. Add the tomato juice and tomato paste, and season to taste with salt and pepper. Simmer uncovered 5 minutes longer, stirring frequently.

Cook the taglierini as described for linguini on page 49, but test for doneness after 5 minutes. Drain. Divide into 4 large serving bowls. Add the basil to the hot tomatoes, stirring it in well, and put a generous amount of the sauce, topped with grated cheese, over each serving. *Serves 4.*

Ann Thornycroft

K. Lee Manuel

Below: A kitchen still-life
at K. Lee Manuel's

VERMICELLI RING
Contributed by Hans Burkhardt

½ pound vermicelli
1 cup heavy cream, whipped
½ cup canned sweet red
    peppers (pimientos),
    drained and coarsely
    chopped
1 cup minced parsley
Salt
Freshly ground pepper
2 tablespoons butter, melted
Boiling water

Cook the vermicelli as described for linguini on page 49, but test for doneness after 4 minutes. Drain in a colander and turn into a bowl. Add the whipped cream, peppers, and parsley, and season to taste with salt and pepper. Toss thoroughly.

Brush a 9-inch ring mold with the butter, spread the vermicelli evenly in the mold, and set the mold in a larger flat pan containing 2 inches of boiling water. Bake in a preheated 350° oven for about 20 minutes, or until the top is golden.

Unmold the ring onto a hot serving dish. If desired, the center of the ring may be filled with cooked vegetables or sauced meat or fish.
Serves 4.

WILD RICE WITH PISTACHIOS
Contributed by K. Lee Manuel

2 tablespoons butter
¼ cup chopped pistachios
1 scallion, trimmed and
    very thinly sliced
1 tablespoon cognac
1 cup wild rice
1 teaspoon salt
Freshly ground pepper

Melt the butter in a heavy saucepan over medium heat, add the pistachios and scallion, and stir about 5 minutes, or until the scallion is soft but not brown. Add the cognac, the wild rice, 2 cups of cold water, the salt, and pepper to taste. Stir well, bring to a boil, cover tightly, reduce the heat to very low, and simmer without stirring about 45 minutes. Test after 30 minutes; if the liquid has evaporated, add a little more water. Serve at once, or keep warm on an asbestos pad over low heat.
Serves 4.

SEAFOOD

Wayne Thiebaud. *Fish*. 1970. Collection the artist

Abalone Sauté ❧ Cole Weston

Crabmeat au Gratin ❧ Pamela Kroner

Tibetan Curry ❧ Ynez Johnston

Fish and Noodle Casserole ❧ Joan Brown

Fish Pudding ❧ Hans Burkhardt

Aunt Sophie's Fish Pudding ❧ Sonya Rapoport

Fish Stew for Bob Arneson ❧ Sandra Shannonhouse

Gumbo ❧ Frederick Eversley

Italian Red Snapper ❧ Garner Tullis

Mussels in Saffron-Garlic Cream ❧ Joanne Rruff

Paella ❧ Nancy Genn

Salmon Dave Barbecue Buffet ❧ Barbara Foster

Salmon on a Plank ❧ William Wiley

Paupiettes de Sôle ❧ Richard and Margaret Mayer

Salmon Quenelles ❧ Frank Hamilton

Stuffed Squid with Beurre Blanc ❧ Laddie John Dill

Squid Vinaigrette ❧ Tony DeLap

Satsuma Tuna Patties ❧ Joseph Goldyne

Oriental Seafood with Vegetables ❧ Joseph Raffael

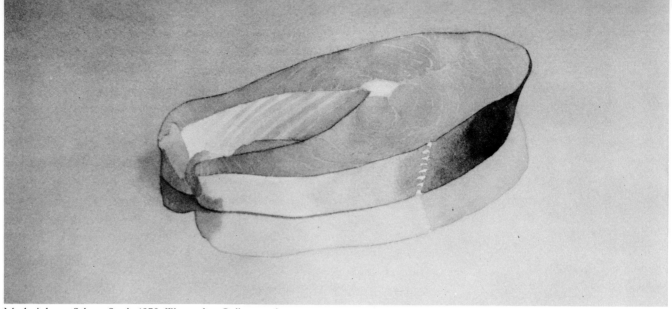

Mark Adams. *Salmon Steak*. 1978. Watercolor. Collection the artist

ABALONE SAUTÉ
Contributed by Cole Weston

My brother Neil and I often arose at 4 A.M. to gather these evasive creatures snuggled in tight crevices in the freezing Pacific Ocean. Reds, being the largest, were the ones we were after. Stillwater Cove in Pebble Beach was our favorite place to dive. We called it our own special deep freeze. We used abalone irons, which are like tire irons with a bend, for prying off the shells. After we shucked the abalone with the iron, we trimmed and pared them with a very sharp knife and sliced them into smaller pieces. In those days we used a wooden stump outdoors and pounded the pieces with a heavy wooden mallet until they were tender. Then we sautéed them in butter in a heavy black skillet for just a minute on each side and ate them with a squeeze of lemon.

Note: Several species of abalone live along the Pacific coast, but, because of the dwindling supply, California does not allow abalone to be canned, or to be shipped fresh or frozen out of the state. Thus it is rare to find fresh abalone anywhere in the United States except on the West Coast, although very occasionally frozen Mexican abalone will be found in markets. Canned abalone, usually Japanese, is available and can be cooked by Cole Weston's method without trimming and pounding, but one cannot expect it to match the unique quality of fresh abalone.

CRABMEAT AU GRATIN
Contributed by Pamela Kroner

White sauce:
  3 tablespoons butter
  3 tablespoons flour
  2 cups milk, heated
  1 teaspoon salt
  White pepper
  Freshly grated nutmeg

⅛ teaspoon cayenne pepper
½ cup brandy
½ cup minced parsley
4 tablespoons butter, softened
2 cups cooked white rice
3 cups fresh crabmeat, picked
  over, or substitute canned,
  rinsed and drained
½ cup grated Parmesan
  cheese
½ pound sharp white cheddar
  cheese, coarsely grated
¼ cup thinly sliced blanched
  almonds

Prepare the white sauce first. Melt the butter in a saucepan over medium heat. Stir in the flour with a whisk, and stir constantly about 1 minute, but do not allow the flour to color. Add the milk all at once and stir with the whisk until the mixture comes to a boil. Season with the salt and then with pepper and nutmeg to taste. Reduce the heat and simmer, stirring occasionally, about 10 minutes. This last cooking will eliminate the floury taste. Season additionally with the cayenne, brandy, and half the parsley, mixing well, and set aside.

Grease an 8-cup casserole with 2 tablespoons of the softened butter. Spread the rice in the bottom and then make alternate layers of half each of the crabmeat, sauce, and the 2 cheeses mixed together. Repeat with another 3 layers. Sprinkle the top layer of cheese with the almonds and the remaining parsley, and dot with the remaining butter. Bake in a preheated 350° oven about 25 minutes, or until the sauce is bubbly and the top is golden. Serve from the casserole.
Serves 6.

Sketch by the artist

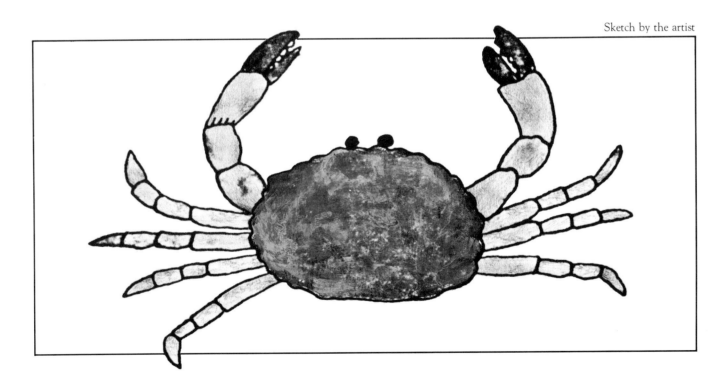

TIBETAN CURRY

Contributed by Ynez Johnston

3 tablespoons butter
2 cups long-grain rice
Juice of 1 lemon
Salt
Freshly ground pepper
1 cup orange juice
½ cup red wine
2 tablespoons olive oil
2 tablespoons soy sauce
1 teaspoon dried tarragon
¼ teaspoon anise seeds
½ teaspoon dried dill
2 tablespoons curry powder
1 carrot, peeled and very
   thinly sliced
1 cup shredded cooked
   chicken meat
½ medium green pepper,
   cored, seeded, and minced
¼ pound mushrooms,
   trimmed, cleaned, and
   thinly sliced
4 scallions, trimmed and
   thinly sliced
2 cloves garlic, minced
½ cup pitted green olives,
   sliced
¼ cup white raisins
1 cup melon balls, such as
   cantaloupe or honeydew
1 banana, sliced
1 medium apple, cored,
   peeled, and coarsely
   chopped
12 oysters, shucked
12 medium shrimp, shelled
   and deveined
12 clams, scrubbed

Melt the butter in a large, heavy, preferably enameled-iron casserole over medium heat, add the rice, and stir until the rice is opaque and milky-colored. Add 4 cups of water and the lemon juice. Season to taste with salt and pepper, bring to a boil, stir briefly, and cook uncovered until the liquid has evaporated or been absorbed. Remove from the heat and stir the rice lightly. It will be only partly cooked. Set aside.

Put the orange juice, red wine, olive oil, soy sauce, dried herbs, curry powder, and carrot in a saucepan over medium heat, bring to a boil, and simmer 5 minutes. Remove from the heat and set aside.

Add all the remaining ingredients to the casserole and toss them lightly but thoroughly. Pour the orange-juice mixture over, season lightly with salt and pepper, and toss again. Cover the casserole tightly with a lid or foil and bake in a preheated 375° oven 25 minutes, or until the rice is tender and the clams have opened. Serve from the casserole. *Serves 6 to 8.*

Joan Brown and friend

FISH AND NOODLE CASSEROLE
Contributed by Joan Brown

1 pound ½-inch-wide noodles
2 cups white sauce (page 63)
2 tablespoons sherry
1 cup cooked and flaked
    nonoily fish, such as cod,
    halibut, or sole, or
    substitute canned salmon or
    tuna, drained
Salt
Freshly ground pepper
2 tablespoons butter, softened
1 pound Monterey Jack
    cheese, thinly sliced
1 7-ounce can pitted black
    olives, sliced
½ cup grated Parmesan cheese
Paprika

Cook the noodles as described for linguini on page 49, but test for doneness after 6 minutes.

While the noodles are cooking, heat the white sauce in a very large saucepan over medium heat, add the sherry and fish, and stir lightly to avoid breaking up the fish flakes. Cook just until hot and remove from heat.

When the noodles are done, drain thoroughly in a colander, pour into saucepan with the fish sauce; toss lightly but thoroughly. Add salt and pepper to taste.

Grease a large casserole with the butter and spread about half the noodle mixture in the bottom. Arrange about half the Monterey Jack slices over the noodles and sprinkle with half the sliced olives and half the Parmesan. Repeat with another layer of each and sprinkle a little paprika over the top. Cover the casserole with a lid or foil and bake in a preheated 350° oven about 30 minutes. Serve from the casserole. *Serves 6.*

FISH PUDDING
Contributed by Hans Burkhardt

⅓ pound fresh halibut
1 egg white
Salt
White pepper
Cayenne pepper
Cracked ice
½ cup heavy cream, very cold
1 tablespoon butter, softened
Boiling water

Put the fish in the container of a food processor and, using the standard steel blade, purée. Alternatively, force through a meat grinder twice, using the finest blade. Put the purée in a bowl and, using a wooden spoon, work the egg white into the fish until the mixture is smooth. (If ground in meat grinder, force the mixture through a wire strainer into a bowl.) Season to taste with salt, pepper, and cayenne. Set the bowl in a larger one containing cracked ice and gradually work in the chilled cream, a few teaspoons at a time.

With the butter, grease an oven-proof glass bowl or dish just large enough (2–2½-cup capacity) to hold the fish mixture, spread the mixture evenly in the dish, and set the dish in a pan containing 2 inches of boiling water. Bake in a preheated 325° oven 30 minutes. Unmold the pudding onto a serving dish and top with any desired sauce, such as creamed shrimp or lobster or a mushroom sauce. *Serves 2.*

AUNT SOPHIE'S FISH PUDDING
Contributed by Sonya Rapoport

2 pounds raw boneless
   nonoily fish, such as red
   snapper, cod, or flounder
¾ cup matzo meal
3 cups milk
4 eggs, lightly beaten
1 medium onion, minced
½ cup butter, melted
Salt
Freshly ground pepper
Sugar
2 tablespoons butter, softened

Put the fish in the container of a food processor and, using the standard steel blade, purée. Alternatively, force the fish through a meat grinder twice, using the finest blade. Put the fish in a large bowl and add the matzo meal, milk, eggs, onion, and butter. Mix thoroughly until well blended. Season to taste with salt, pepper, and sugar, mixing in well.

Grease a 9-by-12-inch glass baking dish with the butter, spread the fish mixture evenly in it, and bake in a preheated 350° oven 1 hour, or until an inserted knife comes out clean.

Serves 6.

FISH STEW FOR BOB ARNESON
Contributed by Sandra Shannonhouse

2 pounds assorted boneless
    nonoily white fish, such as
    sea bass, halibut, cod, or
    shark
1 pound scallops
1 pound shrimp
12 mussels or clams (optional)
3 tablespoons butter
2 large onions, finely chopped
5 cups bottled clam juice
3 cups dry white wine
½ lemon, seeded
Bouquet garni:
    ¼ cup parsley stems
    ½ cup mushroom stems
    ⅛ teaspoon fennel seeds
    1 teaspoon dried thyme
⅛ teaspoon powdered saffron
3 tablespoons Pernod
4 medium ripe tomatoes,
    peeled, seeded, and coarsely
    chopped
Salt
Freshly ground pepper
¼ cup minced fresh chervil or
    parsley

Cut the fish in 1-inch cubes, removing any bones. If using sea scallops, cut in quarters; leave bay scallops whole. Shell and devein the shrimp, reserving the shells. Tie the shells in a bag of cheesecloth and set aside. If the shrimp are very small, leave whole; otherwise cut in bite-size pieces. Set all the seafood aside.

If using mussels or clams, steam as described in Mussels in Saffron-Garlic Cream on page 69, being careful not to overcook them. Remove them from their shells and set aside in a small bowl. Strain and reserve their juices and cooking liquid.

Melt the butter in a very large, preferably enameled-iron (*not* aluminum) pot over medium heat. Add the onion and saute until soft and translucent but not brown. Add the clam juice, wine, lemon, the bouquet garni tied securely in cheesecloth, and the reserved bag of shrimp shells. Raise the heat and boil until the liquid is reduced to about 6 cups. Remove the shrimp shells and the bouquet garni, pressing the bags against the inside of the pot to extract their juices. Discard the lemon. If desired, the broth may be removed from the heat until just before serving. If you wish to wait several hours, leave the broth uncovered, but refrigerate the fish.

About 10 minutes before serving, add the saffron, Pernod, tomatoes, and any mussel or clam juices to the broth. Bring to a boil over high heat, add all the seafood, and stir gently. Let the liquid return to a boil, then immediately reduce the heat and simmer 2 minutes. Sprinkle with the chervil or parsley and serve at once from the pot or ladle carefully into a tureen.

Serves 6 as a main course or 12 as a soup course.

GUMBO
Contributed by Frederick Eversley

6 tablespoons butter
1 large onion, coarsely
   chopped
½ pound lean veal, cut in
   ¼-inch cubes
½ pound uncooked ham, cut
   in ¼-inch cubes
½ cup flour
1 pound okra, trimmed and
   cut in ½-inch slices
8 scallions, trimmed and cut
   in ¼-inch slices
2 cloves garlic, minced
¼ cup minced parsley
1 bay leaf
½ teaspoon dried thyme
¼ teaspoon ground cloves
Salt
Freshly ground pepper
2 pounds medium shrimp,
   shelled and deveined
1 tablespoon filé powder

Melt the butter in a large, heavy, preferably enameled-iron pot over fairly high heat. Add the onion and stir constantly until lightly browned. Add the veal and ham and continue stirring until lightly browned. Sprinkle with the flour and mix it in well. Add 2 quarts of water, and whisk until it comes to a boil. Reduce the heat and add the okra, scallions, garlic, parsley, bay leaf, thyme, and cloves. Season to taste with salt and pepper. Simmer covered 1 hour, stirring occasionally. Add the shrimp, mixing them in well, and simmer 30 minutes longer. If the gumbo seems too thick, add a little water.

Just before serving, correct the seasoning and sprinkle with the filé powder. Stir briefly and remove from the heat. Serve over rice on individual plates.
Serves 6 to 8.

ITALIAN RED SNAPPER
Contributed by Garner Tullis

3 tablespoons butter, softened
4 large red-snapper fillets
Salt
Freshly ground pepper
1 28-ounce can whole ground
   tomatoes
⅓ cup minced parsley
⅔ cup grated Parmesan
   cheese
3 tablespoons butter, melted

Smear the softened butter over an oven-proof, preferably stainless-steel serving platter. Lay the fish fillets on it and season with salt and pepper. Spoon the whole ground tomatoes over the fish and season again lightly with salt and pepper. Sprinkle with the parsley and cheese, and drizzle with the melted butter.

Bake uncovered in a 350° oven about 15 minutes, or until the fish flakes easily. Serve on the platter.
Serves 4.

MUSSELS IN SAFFRON-GARLIC CREAM*

Contributed by Joanne Rruff

Cream sauce:
    4 cups heavy cream
    ¼ teaspoon powdered
        saffron
    6 cloves garlic, very finely
        minced
    Salt
    Freshly ground pepper

2 tablespoons olive oil
1 medium onion, thinly sliced
½ cup dry white wine or
    water
32 mussels, scrubbed, beards
    removed, and soaked 3
    hours in cold water
Rind of 1 orange (no white
    part), cut in fine julienne
    strips

Put the cream in a very large, heavy, preferably enameled-iron saucepan over fairly high heat. A 6-quart-capacity pan is the smallest that should be used, because cream will boil over very quickly in a smaller pan. Bring cream to a boil and cook uncovered until reduced by about half and the consistency is that of a white sauce. Watch carefully and stir frequently, particularly when it begins to thicken, to prevent any scorching on the bottom of the pan. It will take about 20 minutes to reduce. When the cream is thickened, lower the heat and stir in the saffron, garlic, and salt and pepper to taste. Keep warm over the lowest possible heat.

Heat the oil in a very large, preferably stainless-steel or enamel (not aluminum) pot over medium heat. Add the onion and stir until soft and translucent but not brown. Add the wine or water, raise the heat, and bring just to a boil. Add the mussels and cover the pot tightly. Steam the mussels about 5 minutes, shaking the pot back and forth over the heat, or until the shells have opened. Discard any unopened mussels. Pour the mussels into a colander over a bowl. Shuck them, allowing their juice to drip into the bowl.

Add the mussels to the cream sauce in the saucepan and reheat very briefly. If the sauce seems too thick, thin with a little of the mussel juices, strained, saving the rest for another use. Spoon the mussels and sauce into hot soup bowls and sprinkle the orange rind over each. *Serves 4.*

*Recipe by Shelley Handler, as prepared at Chez Panisse, Berkeley.

PAELLA
Contributed by Nancy Genn

2 tablespoons olive oil

4 tablespoons butter

1 2½- to 3-pound frying
    chicken, cut in pieces

2 cups long-grain rice

½ teaspoon powdered saffron

5 cups light chicken stock, or
    more if necessary, heated

Salt

Freshly ground pepper

1 1½-pound live lobster

12 shrimp, shelled and
    deveined

12 medium mussels, scrubbed,
    beards removed, and
    soaked 3 hours in cold
    water

12 small clams, scrubbed

1 chorizo (Spanish sausage),
    cut in ½-inch slices

½ cup canned pimientos,
    drained and cut in pieces

Heat the olive oil and 2 tablespoons of the butter in a large, heavy skillet until very hot but not smoking. Arrange the chicken in the skillet and saute over fairly high heat about 10 minutes, or until the pieces are well browned on all sides. Remove the chicken from the pan and set aside. Add the rice to the butter and oil remaining in the pan and cook, stirring, about 5 minutes, or until lightly colored. Stir the saffron into 4 cups of the hot chicken stock, pour over the rice, season to taste with salt and pepper, and cook the rice uncovered over medium heat about 10 minutes, or until all the liquid has evaporated or been absorbed. Remove the skillet from the heat and set aside.

Cut the lobster in half lengthwise, using a sharp knife or kitchen shears, and twist off both claws from the body. Remove the intestinal sac that is just behind the eyes. Cut both halves in half crosswise. Crack the claws slightly, using a mallet or nutcracker.

Grease a large, heavy, preferably enameled-iron casserole with the remaining 2 tablespoons of butter and put half the lobster pieces in the bottom. Around them arrange half the chicken pieces and half the shrimp, mussels, clams, chorizo, and pimiento. Cover these with half the rice and then repeat the process. Pour the remaining cup of stock into the casserole, cover tightly, and bake in a preheated 350° oven 15 minutes. Remove the lid; if the rice seems dry, add a little more stock. Bake uncovered about 15 minutes longer, or until the rice is tender and the mussels and clams have opened. Serve from the casserole. *Serves 6 to 8.*

Nancy Genn

SALMON DAVE BARBECUE BUFFET
Contributed by Barbara Foster

½ cup butter

1 medium onion, coarsely chopped

1 clove garlic, minced

⅔ pound mushrooms, trimmed, cleaned, and coarsely chopped

½ cup coarsely chopped parsley

1 tablespoon chopped fresh sage, or 1 teaspoon dried

⅔ pound flaked fresh crabmeat

1 cup fresh bread crumbs

½ cup thinly sliced blanched almonds

¾ pound very small shrimp, shelled and deveined

Salt

Freshly ground pepper

2 6- to 8-pound silver salmon, cleaned, heads and tails intact

2 small trout, cleaned, heads and tails intact

Oil

2 pounds cherry tomatoes

Parsley sprigs

Melt 4 tablespoons of the butter in a skillet over medium heat, add the onion and garlic, and stir about 5 minutes, or until the onion is soft and translucent but not brown. Add the mushrooms and stir another 5 minutes, or until the mushroom juices have evaporated. Stir in the parsley and sage and remove from the heat.

Melt 2 tablespoons of the butter in each of 2 skillets. Put half the mushroom mixture in each skillet. To the first skillet add the crabmeat and half the bread crumbs and sliced almonds. Season lightly with salt and pepper, and stir gently over medium heat about 5 minutes. Remove from the heat and set aside. To the second skillet add the shrimp and the remaining bread crumbs and sliced almonds. Season with salt and pepper, and stir gently over medium heat about 5 minutes. Remove from the heat and set aside.

Season the cavities of the salmon lightly with salt. Stuff one salmon with the crabmeat mixture, saving a little for the trout, and stuff the other with the shrimp mixture, likewise saving a little. Sew up the cavities securely, using butcher's string and a trussing needle. Wrap each fish completely in lightly oiled heavy-duty aluminum foil, crimping to seal it securely. Stuff and wrap the trout in the same manner as the salmon.

Place both salmon on a grill over a bed of hot coals about 1 hour and 15 minutes. Turn over after 30 minutes and again after another 30 minutes. Put the trout on the grill for the last 15 minutes. Turn once.

Unwrap the salmon carefully so as not to lose any juices. Put each on a platter. Garnish with cherry tomatoes and parsley sprigs. Unwrap the trout and put one in each salmon's mouth. Put a cherry tomato in each trout's mouth. *Serves 18 to 24.*

SALMON ON A PLANK
Contributed by William Wiley

1 6- to 8-pound salmon,
   cleaned, head and tail
   removed
Salt
Freshly ground pepper
¾ cup butter, melted

Bone the salmon, or have your fishmonger do it, so there are 2 large fillets. Do not remove the skin.

Staple aluminum foil over a piece of plywood slightly larger than the 2 fillets. Using small nongalvanized nails, tack the fillets to the board, skin side down. Run light-gauge wire back and forth over the fillets, twisting it around the nails, so that the fillets are held securely in place.

Sketches by the artist

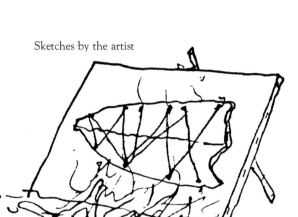

Build a long, low fire and prop the fillets near it. Season the flesh with salt and pepper and baste occasionally with the butter. Turn the board occasionally, so that the fish cooks evenly. The smoke and heat will glaze the outer flesh but keep the fillets moist and tender. Timing will depend on the thickness of the fillets. They are done when the flesh flakes easily.

Serves 8.

PAUPIETTES DE SÔLE
Contributed by Richard and Margaret Mayer

4 tablespoons butter
½ pound mushrooms,
   trimmed, cleaned, and
   thinly sliced
4 teaspoons lemon juice
1½ cups canned shrimp
   bisque
½ cup dry sherry
Salt
Freshly ground pepper
6 large fillets of sole
1 cup cooked small shrimp,
   coarsely chopped
1 cup flaked cooked crabmeat

Melt 2 tablespoons of the butter in a skillet over medium heat, add the mushrooms and 1 teaspoon of the lemon juice, and stir lightly about 5 minutes, or until the mushroom juices have evaporated. Add the shrimp bisque, sherry, and salt and pepper to taste. Stir until the mixture is very hot. Remove from the heat.

Season the sole fillets lightly with salt and pepper and sprinkle with the remaining lemon juice. Top each fillet with the shrimp and crabmeat and roll up lengthwise.

Grease a shallow oven-proof dish with the remaining butter, arrange the fillets in the dish, and spoon the sauce over the fillets. Bake in a preheated 350° oven about 25 minutes. Transfer the fillets to a hot serving dish. Stir the sauce remaining in the baking dish and spoon it over the fillets.

Serves 6.

SALMON QUENELLES
Contributed by Frank Hamilton

1 cup fresh sourdough bread
   crumbs
1 cup milk, heated
Freshly grated nutmeg
Salt
Freshly ground white pepper

Sauce:
   4 tablespoons butter
   2 tablespoons flour
   3 cups canned lobster
      bisque
   2 tablespoons sherry

1 pound salmon, boned,
   skinned, and cut in chunks
1 cup plus 2 tablespoons
   butter, softened
2 eggs, plus 4 yolks, lightly
   beaten
Boiling water
¼ cup sour cream
2 tablespoons Madeira

Kitchen still-life at the photographer's

Mix thoroughly the bread crumbs and milk in a bowl. Season with a very little nutmeg, and salt and pepper to taste. Chill this panada in the refrigerator 2 hours.

Prepare the sauce while the panada is chilling. Melt the butter in a saucepan over medium heat, stir in the flour with a whisk, and stir until bubbly but not colored. Add the lobster bisque and sherry, reduce heat; simmer 10 minutes, stirring often. Remove from heat and cover loosely.

When the panada has chilled, put the salmon in the container of a food processor and, using the standard steel blade, purée. Alternatively, force the salmon through a meat grinder twice, using the finest blade, and then force it through a wire strainer, pressing with the back of a wooden spoon. Put the salmon purée in a bowl and, either with an electric beater or by hand, beat in the chilled panada and then 1 cup of the butter and the eggs and yolks. Season to taste with nutmeg, salt, and pepper.

Grease 2 large shallow pans or skillets with the remaining butter. Using a large metal kitchen spoon dipped into hot water from time to time, form the salmon mixture into oval quenelles and, using another hot-water-dipped kitchen spoon, ease them into the pans. They should not be crowded in the pans. Set over low heat and immediately add boiling water to cover. Carefully and gently slide a spatula under each quenelle to make sure it is not sticking to the bottom of the pan. Simmer 10 minutes. Remove the quenelles with a slotted spoon and drain very briefly on a cloth towel.

Reheat the sauce over medium heat and stir briskly with a whisk to incorporate any film that has formed on the top. Stir in the sour cream and Madeira. Correct the seasoning. Heat just until very hot; do not boil or the sauce will curdle. Spoon the sauce over the quenelles on hot individual serving plates, or the quenelles may be reheated in the sauce pans and then served.
Serves 6.

Note: The quenelles may be frozen, defrosted 4 hours at room temperature, and gently reheated in the sauce.

STUFFED SQUID WITH BEURRE BLANC

Contributed by Laddie John Dill

12 small squid (*Loligo opalescens*)

Stuffing:
2 tablespoons butter
1 large onion, coarsely chopped
2 cloves garlic, minced
2 cups dry white wine
6 large ripe tomatoes, peeled, seeded, and coarsely chopped
3 bay leaves
1 teaspoon dried thyme
Salt
Freshly ground pepper

Flour
3 tablespoons vegetable oil
2 cups butter
3 tablespoons minced shallots
2 cups white-wine vinegar
Salt
White pepper

Separate the bodies and the tentacles of the squid and discard the spines. Peel off the skin and pull off the 2 side fins. Pull off the heads and discard them along with the innards and the ink sacs. Wash the bodies and the tentacles thoroughly in running cold water. Pat dry with paper towels and set aside.

Prepare the stuffing. Melt the butter in a large skillet over medium heat, add the onion and garlic, and stir until the onion is soft and translucent but not brown. Add the wine, raise the heat, and boil until the wine has reduced to about ¼ cup. Add the tomatoes, bay leaves, thyme, and salt and pepper to taste. Stir over fairly high heat until most of the liquid has evaporated and the mixture is quite thick. Remove from the heat, discard the bay leaves, and cool.

Spoon the stuffing into the cavities of the squid's bodies and, if possible, tie the bodies tightly closed with the tentacles. If this is too difficult, reserve the tentacles for another use and tie the bodies closed with butcher's string. Dredge the squid in flour.

Heat the oil in a very large skillet over fairly high heat. It should be very hot but not smoking. Sauté the stuffed squid, turning several times, about 6 minutes, or until golden on all sides. Remove with a slotted spoon and keep warm while preparing the sauce.

Melt 2 tablespoons of the butter in a heavy saucepan over medium heat, add the shallots, and stir about 2 minutes. Add the vinegar, raise the heat, and boil until the vinegar has reduced to about ⅓ cup. Reduce the heat to low. Cut the remaining butter into 1-inch pieces and, a piece at a time, whisk into the liquid remaining in the pan. The sauce will gradually form a creamy emulsion, about the consistency of a light hollandaise. It must be stirred continuously. It must not boil and it cannot be re-

Opposite: Wayne Thiebaud. *Fish Circle.* 1970. Collection the artist

heated or it will separate. Remove from the heat and continue to stir about 15 seconds to cool it slightly. Season to taste with salt and white pepper.

Transfer the squid to 6 hot serving plates, 2 squid to a plate, and spoon the sauce over them. Serve immediately. *Serves* 6.

Note: the sauce is also delicious over steamed or poached fish.

SQUID VINAIGRETTE
Contributed by Tony DeLap

2 pounds small squid
4 tablespoons olive oil
6 scallions, trimmed and
    thinly sliced
4 cloves garlic, minced
Salt
Freshly ground pepper

Vinaigrette:
    ⅔ cup olive oil
    ⅓ cup red-wine vinegar
    ½ teaspoon dry mustard
    2 tablespoons chopped fresh
       tarragon
    ¼ cup chopped parsley
    ¼ cup chopped cilantro
       (fresh coriander leaves)
    Salt
    Freshly ground pepper

Clean the squid as described in the preceding recipe. Separate the bodies from the tentacles. Cut the bodies in strips about 3 inches long and ½ inch wide. Cut the tentacles in 3-inch pieces. Dry the squid with paper towels and set aside.

Heat the olive oil in a large, heavy skillet over medium heat, add the scallions and garlic, and stir 2 minutes. Add the squid and sauté about 5 minutes, or until milky white and tender. Season lightly with salt and pepper. Remove the skillet from the heat, cool, and transfer the squid to a bowl.

Mix the vinaigrette ingredients in a small bowl, seasoning to taste with salt and pepper. Pour over the squid and toss lightly. Chill in the refrigerator 2 hours. Toss again before serving. *Serves 6.*

Joseph Goldyne. *Dirty Dish*. 1979. Hand-colored monotype (proof). Courtesy John Berggruen Gallery, San Francisco

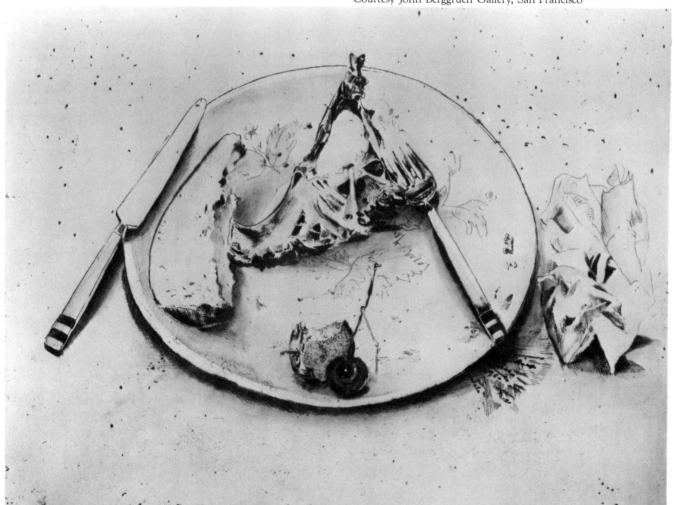

SATSUMA TUNA PATTIES
Contributed by Joseph Goldyne

Tuna patties:

    4 7-ounce cans white
      (albacore) tuna, drained

    1 medium onion, grated

    4 eggs, lightly beaten

    ¾ cup cornflake crumbs

    ¼ teaspoon paprika

    ¼ teaspoon lemon-pepper
      seasoning

    ½ teaspoon salt, or more to
      taste

    ½ teaspoon dried dill

    1 medium banana, finely
      chopped

    1 heaping tablespoon
      Satsuma plum jam, or
      substitute Damson plum
      jam

Vegetable oil

Dill sauce:

    2 cups sour cream

    ⅓ cup chopped fresh dill,
      or 2 tablespoons dried

    2 teaspoons lemon juice

    Salt

    White pepper

Mix all the tuna-patty ingredients in a large bowl with a wooden spoon until well blended. With moistened hands, form into patties about 1 inch thick and 3 inches in diameter. Chill in the refrigerator at least 1 hour.

Pour vegetable oil to a depth of ½ inch into a large, heavy skillet set over medium heat. When the oil is very hot but not smoking, fry the patties a few at a time about 4 minutes on each side, or until golden brown. As they are done, drain on paper towels and gently blot the tops with more paper towels. When all are done, let them cool to room temperature and then chill, covered, in the refrigerator at least 4 hours.

Whisk the dill-sauce ingredients in a bowl, seasoning to taste with salt and pepper. Chill in the refrigerator at least 3 hours.

Serve the patties well chilled with the dill sauce on the side.

Makes about 15 patties.

Contributor's note: Since these patties keep well in the refrigerator for several days, it is well worth making a large batch of them to serve as a handy quick appetizer or lunch.

Above: Joseph Goldyne preparing his Satsuma Tuna Patties

ORIENTAL SEAFOOD WITH VEGETABLES

Contributed by Joseph Raffael

Seafood:

2 tablespoons sesame or
  peanut oil
2 cloves garlic, minced
1 tablespoon minced fresh
  ginger
4 large shrimp, shelled and
  deveined
4 large sea scallops
1 fillet of red snapper or
  similar fish, such as sole
  or flounder, cut crosswise
  in 1-inch slices
½ cup dry white wine
1 teaspoon Chinese chili
  paste
½ pound tofu, cut in
  ½-inch cubes
1 cup fresh or canned bean
  sprouts
3 scallions, trimmed and cut
diagonally in ½-inch slices,
  including the green tops
1 tablespoon tamari or soy
  sauce
1 tablespoon finely chopped
  cilantro (fresh coriander
  leaves)

Broccoli:

1 tablespoon peanut oil
1 clove garlic, minced
½ teaspoon salt
2 cups broccoli flowerets
2 tablespoons chicken broth

Spinach:

1 pound fresh spinach
  leaves, very thoroughly
  washed
1 tablespoon soy sauce
1 tablespoon sesame seeds,
  toasted

Heat the 2 tablespoons of oil in a wok over fairly high heat. Add the garlic and ginger and stir a few seconds without letting them brown. Add all the seafood and stir-fry 2 minutes, coating thoroughly with the oil. Add the wine and chili paste, bring to a boil, and stir gently about 3 minutes. Add the tofu, bean sprouts, and scallions. Stir slowly and lightly about 3 minutes longer, or until the wine has nearly evaporated and the mixture is very hot. Do not overcook. Stir in the tamari or soy sauce and immediately transfer the mixture to a hot platter. Sprinkle with the chopped cilantro and keep warm.

Heat the 1 tablespoon of oil in a clean wok over fairly high heat, add the garlic and salt, and stir a few seconds.

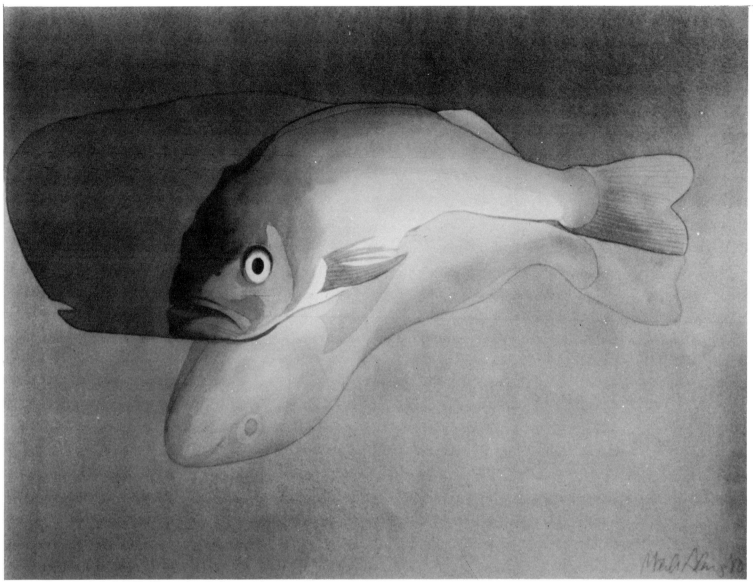

Mark Adams. *Rock Cod*. 1980. Watercolor. Collection the artist

Add the broccoli and stir-fry 2 minutes. Add the chicken broth, cover the wok, and cook 3 minutes. Remove the cover and stir lightly until the broth has nearly evaporated. The broccoli should be tender but still crunchy. Transfer to a hot serving dish and keep warm.

Put the freshly washed spinach in a clean wok over high heat, cover tightly, and cook about 4 minutes, stirring occasionally. Remove the cover, add the soy sauce, and stir lightly about 1 minute, or until barely tender. Remove the spinach from the wok with 2 spoons, pressing lightly to remove excess liquid, and transfer to a hot serving dish. Sprinkle with the sesame seeds.
Serves 2.

MEATLESS
MAIN DISHES

Mark Adams. *Three Potatoes* (detail). 1978. Watercolor. Courtesy John Berggruen Gallery, San Francisco

Green Chile Casserole ❧ Mary Heebner

Chile Rellenos ❧ Taffy Dahl

Millet Soufflé ❧ Hans Burkhardt

No-Meat Meatballs ❧ Hans Burkhardt

Parmesan Tofu ❧ Victor Bergeron ("Trader Vic")

Tabbouli ❧ Frederick Eversley

Tofu-and-Vegetable Kebabs ❧ Karen Breschi

Vegetable Sauté ❧ Bella Feldman

GREEN CHILE CASSEROLE
Contributed by Mary Heebner

2 tablespoons butter, softened
1 23-ounce can Ortega-brand
    hot peppers (Jalapeño
    chilies)
½ pound Longhorn cheese,
    coarsely grated
½ pound Monterey Jack
    cheese, coarsely grated
9 eggs
Salt

Spread the butter on the sides and bottom of an 8-cup casserole. In it make 3 alternate layers of the chilies and the 2 cheeses mixed together, ending with a layer of the cheeses. Beat the eggs lightly in a bowl with salt to taste and slowly pour into the casserole. Poke gently with a 2-pronged fork to allow the eggs to run between the chilies and cheese without disturbing the layers. Bake in a preheated 350° oven 30 minutes. The top should be golden and an inserted knife should come out clean. Serve from the casserole. *Serves 6.*

CHILE RELLENOS
Contributed by Taffy Dahl

16 fresh medium Anaheim
    chilies, or 1 27-ounce can
    Ortega-brand whole roasted
    peppers
3 tablespoons olive oil
1 large onion, minced
2 cloves garlic, minced
1 28-ounce can whole
    tomatoes, drained
1 cup chicken stock
½ teaspoon dried oregano
Salt
Freshly ground pepper
1 pound Monterey Jack
    cheese
Flour
5 eggs
Vegetable oil

If using fresh chilies, puncture the top of each near the stem with a sharp knife to allow steam to escape when they are roasted. Set them a few at a time on a rack directly over a high gas flame and char completely on all sides, turning as necessary with tongs. After each is completely blackened, hold it under running cold water and rub off the charred outer skin with your fingers or scrape off any stubborn bits with a dull knife. Cut out and discard the stems. Then slit each chili slightly and remove all the seeds. If using canned peppers, drain them, slit them slightly, and remove the seeds. Drain the peppers on several thicknesses of paper towels while making the tomato sauce.

Heat the olive oil in a heavy saucepan over medium heat, add the onion and garlic, and stir about 2 minutes, or until the onion is soft and translucent. Add the tomatoes, chicken stock, and oregano. Cook about 15 minutes, stirring frequently, until the liquid has evaporated slightly but the sauce is still runny. Season to taste with salt and pepper. Divide into 2 large skillets and set aside.

Pat the outside and inside of the chilies as dry as possible with paper towels. Slice the cheese ¼ to ⅓ inch thick and shape the slices so they will fit snugly inside the chilies; the cheese should be completely covered. Dust the

Mary Heebner

outside of each cheese-filled chili thoroughly with flour and set aside.

Separate the eggs. Beat the whites in a bowl with an electric mixer or a whisk until stiff but not dry. Continue beating while adding the yolks one at a time and about 1 teaspoon of salt. Set aside.

Add oil to a depth of ¾ inch to a large, very heavy skillet set over high heat. When it is smoking hot, dip the stuffed chilies one at a time in the egg batter, coating them generously, and drop into the hot oil. Do not crowd them in the skillet. Cook about 2 minutes on one side and then turn them over. After another 2 minutes they should be golden brown and slightly puffed. As they are done, transfer to a rack covered with paper towels. After frying, they may rest an hour or even longer.

Just before serving, heat the 2 skillets of tomato sauce until bubbling. Carefully slide 8 of the chilies into each skillet and heat about 5 minutes. They should puff up again slightly. Transfer to a platter or 4 individual plates and spoon a little sauce over each.

If desired, serve with refried beans (page 121).
Serves 4.

Taffy Dahl

MILLET SOUFFLÉ
Contributed by Hans Burkhardt

1 cup millet meal
1 cup milk
4 egg yolks, well beaten
1 small onion, grated
2 tablespoons chopped chives
  (optional)
Salt
5 egg whites
¼ pound sharp cheddar
  cheese, coarsely grated
2 tablespoons butter, softened

Bring 4 cups of lightly salted water to a boil in the top pan of a double boiler over fairly high heat. Slowly add the millet and stir 2 minutes, making sure there are no lumps. Set the pan over the double-boiler bottom pan containing 2 inches of boiling water, cover tightly, and steam over medium heat 15 minutes, stirring occasionally.

Scrape the cooked millet into a large bowl, add the milk, and stir until well blended. Add the egg yolks, onion, optional chives, and salt to taste. Mix thoroughly. Beat the egg whites until stiff but not dry with a whisk or an electric beater. Gently fold them into the millet mixture, sprinkling in the cheese as you fold.

Grease an 8-cup soufflé dish with the softened butter, pour in the millet mixture, and bake in a preheated 350° oven 45 minutes. Serve from the dish.
Serves 6.

NO-MEAT MEATBALLS
Contributed by Hans Burkhardt

1 tablespoon olive oil
½ cup buckwheat groats
  (kasha)
1½ cups boiling water
½ teaspoon salt
2 tablespoons butter
1 large onion, finely chopped
½ cup shelled chestnuts,
  finely chopped
Whole-wheat or rice flour
Oil for deep frying

Heat the olive oil in a saucepan over medium heat, add the groats, and stir about 5 minutes, or until lightly browned. Add the boiling water and the salt, cover the pan tightly, reduce the heat, and steam about 20 minutes. Remove the cover and continue cooking, stirring occasionally, until the water has been absorbed. Set aside.

Melt the butter in a skillet over medium heat, add the onion, and stir about 5 minutes, or until the onion is soft and translucent but not brown. Remove from the heat.

Scrape the groats into a bowl; add the onion, chestnuts, and about ¼ cup of the flour; mix thoroughly. Add more flour if necessary to make the mixture thick enough to form into 1½-inch balls. Roll each ball in whole-wheat or rice flour and fry the balls, about a dozen at a time, in 375° deep fat about 2 minutes, or until golden brown.
Serves 4.

PARMESAN TOFU

Contributed by Victor Bergeron ("Trader Vic")

Sauce:
- 2 tablespoons butter
- 1 large shallot, minced
- 1 large ripe tomato, peeled, seeded, and coarsely chopped
- 1 tablespoon flour
- 1 cup chicken stock
- ½ cup dry white wine
- 1 tablespoon dried basil
- 1 teaspoon dried oregano
- ½ teaspoon garlic powder
- Salt
- Freshly ground pepper

4 ½-pound compressed tofu cakes
Salt
Few drops lemon juice
Few drops Worcestershire sauce
Flour
2 eggs, lightly beaten
2 cups grated Parmesan cheese
4 tablespoons butter, or more if necessary
¼ pound cooked ham, cut in 3-inch julienne strips

Prepare the sauce a little in advance. Melt the butter in a heavy saucepan over medium heat. Add the shallot and stir 1 minute. Add the tomato and stir about 5 minutes, or until the tomato juices have evaporated. Sprinkle with the flour and stir briefly. Add the chicken stock, wine, herbs, garlic powder, and salt and pepper to taste. Cook uncovered, stirring frequently, about 20 minutes, or until the sauce has thickened slightly. Cover and keep hot over a very low flame.

Cut the tofu cakes in half to form rectangles about ½ inch thick. Season lightly with salt and sprinkle with a few drops of lemon juice and Worcestershire sauce. Dredge the tofu pieces in the flour, dip them in the beaten eggs, and then dredge them in the Parmesan cheese, coating them thoroughly.

Melt the butter in a large skillet over medium heat and sauté the tofu until golden brown on both sides. Do not crowd the pieces in the skillet. Sauté in 2 batches if necessary. Transfer the tofu to a platter or plates, top each piece with a little ham, and coat with the sauce.
Serves 4 to 8.

Victor Bergeron ("Trader Vic")

85

TABBOULI
Contributed by Frederick Eversley

1½ cups Bulgur wheat
    (Burghul)
8 cups boiling water
1 cup minced parsley
8 scallions, trimmed and
    finely sliced, including the
    green tops
½ cup lemon juice
4 medium ripe tomatoes,
    peeled, seeded, and
    coarsely chopped
½ cup currants
½ cup olive oil
Salt
Freshly ground pepper
½ cup chopped fresh mint

Put the Bulgur wheat in a large bowl and pour the boiling water over. Let sit 20 minutes. Drain into a large sieve, and let sit in the sieve another 20 minutes. Shake the Bulgur in the sieve until very dry.

Put the Bulgur in a serving bowl and add all the ingredients except the mint, seasoning to taste with salt and pepper. Chill in the refrigerator at least 1 hour. Just before serving, stir in the chopped mint.
Serves 6.

TOFU-AND-VEGETABLE KEBABS
Contributed by Karen Breschi

1 pound tofu
1 cup soy sauce
3 medium tomatoes,
    quartered
1 large green pepper, cored,
    seeded, and cut in 12
    1-inch squares
12 medium mushrooms,
    trimmed and cleaned
6 small white onions, cut in
    half
2 medium zucchini, cut in 12
    1-inch slices
Vegetable oil
Salt
¼ cup sesame seeds

Cut the tofu in 12 evenly sized cubes. Put them in a bowl, add the soy sauce, and marinate 1 hour, turning occasionally.

Alternate 3 pieces each of the tofu and the vegetables on 4 skewers. Brush lightly with vegetable oil, season lightly with salt, and sprinkle with the sesame seeds. Broil in a preheated medium broiler about 15 minutes, turning occasionally so that the vegetables cook evenly. Transfer to a serving dish or, if desired, serve on a bed of brown rice.
Serves 4.

Opposite page:
Paul Wonner. *Dutch Still-life with Flowers and Fish* (right panel of diptych). 1981. Acrylic on canvas. Courtesy John Berggruen Gallery, San Francisco

VEGETABLE SAUTÉ
Contributed by Bella Feldman

1 medium eggplant, peeled
   and cut in 1-inch cubes
1 large onion, coarsely chopped
2 large ripe tomatoes, peeled,
   seeded, and coarsely chopped
¼ cup minced cilantro (fresh
   coriander leaves)
1 tablespoon curry powder
Salt
Freshly ground pepper

Put all the ingredients in a heavy saucepan or skillet, seasoning to taste with salt and pepper. Stir very frequently over medium heat until the eggplant is tender, about 10 minutes. There should be enough liquid in the tomatoes so that no other liquid is necessary. Transfer to a serving dish or, if desired, serve on a bed of rice.
Serves 4 to 6.

MEAT

Marianne Boers. *Safeway Meats.* 1973. Courtesy John Berggruen Gallery, San Francisco

Chili Verde ❧ Larry Bell

Entrecôte Dijonnais ❧ Fletcher Benton

Hamburger Stroganoff ❧ Taffy Dahl

Gourmet Meat Balls ❧ Hans Burkhardt

Meat-and-Vegetable Loaf ❧ Ray Holbert

Oxtail Ragout ❧ Hans Burkhardt

Pork Chops Orange-Rosé ❧ William Dole

Rabbit Braised with Rosemary ❧ Jerrold Davis

Rattlesnake Marcalibre ❧ Robert Freimark

Steak au Poivre ❧ William Brice

Steak-and-Kidney Pie Ma Belle ❧ Paul Wonner

Cable Car Veal ❧ Christopher Lane

Veal Marengo ❧ Fletcher Benton

Vitello Tonnato (Cold Veal with Tuna Sauce) ❧ Rooney O'Neill

Venezuelan Hallacas ❧ Lee Mullican and Luchita Hurtado

Beef Tenderloin Bordelaise ❧ Charles Arnoldi

CHILI VERDE
Contributed by Larry Bell

4 tablespoons olive oil
6 large onions, thinly sliced,
   and the slices cut in half
5 cloves garlic, thinly sliced
3 27-ounce cans Ortega-brand
   whole green chilies, drained
1 teaspoon cinnamon
½ teaspoon ground cloves
6 lemons
6 pounds pork shoulder,
   boned, trimmed of excess
   fat, and cut in 2-inch cubes
Salt
3 bay leaves
Sour cream

Heat the oil in a very large, heavy, preferably enameled-iron pot over medium heat. Add the onions and stir thoroughly. Reduce the heat to very low, cover the pot, and steam the onions about 20 minutes, stirring occasionally. They should be very soft and translucent but not brown. Stir in the garlic, chilies, cinnamon, cloves, and the juice of 4 lemons. Raise the heat slightly and simmer uncovered 45 minutes, stirring occasionally.

Lay the pork cubes on top of the chilies, squeeze the juice of the remaining 2 lemons over the pork, and push the rinds of the 2 lemons down into the mixture. Simmer covered 1 hour. Stir the pork cubes into the chilies, season to taste with salt, add the bay leaves, and simmer covered 3 hours over very low heat.

Chili Verde is best if allowed to rest a full day before serving. Do not refrigerate but keep in a cool place with the lid slightly ajar. It may also be frozen.

Reheat gently, discard the lemon rinds and bay leaves, and serve with separate bowls of sour cream.
Serves 12.

ENTRECÔTE DIJONNAIS
Contributed by Fletcher Benton

4 round steaks, cut from the
   upper leg, ½ inch thick
12 peppercorns, crushed
Salt
Flour
4 tablespoons clarified butter
¼ cup minced shallots
½ cup dry white wine, or
   more if necessary
2 tablespoons Dijon-type
   mustard
½ pound mushrooms,
   trimmed, cleaned, and
   thinly sliced

Rub both sides of the steaks with the pepper, season to taste with salt, and dredge in flour. Heat the butter in a large, heavy skillet over high heat until very hot but not smoking. Sear the steaks, 2 at a time to keep from crowding, about 1 minute on each side, or until nicely browned. As they are done, remove from the skillet to a warm platter.

Add the shallots to the skillet and stir 1 minute. Add the wine and bring to a boil. Push the shallots to one side of the skillet. Smear both sides of the steaks with the mustard and return them to the skillet, overlapping if need be. Spoon the wine and shallots in the skillet over them and sprinkle the mushrooms on top. Cover the skillet tightly, reduce the heat to low, and simmer 30 minutes, or until the steaks are tender. Add more wine

Fletcher Benton

only if the liquid in the skillet evaporates. Transfer the steaks to a hot platter and spoon all the shallots, mushrooms, and pan juices over them. Serve at once.
Serves 4.

HAMBURGER STROGANOFF
Contributed by Taffy Dahl

2 tablespoons butter
1 medium onion, coarsely
   chopped
1 clove garlic, minced
1 pound sirloin or top round,
   ground
Salt
Freshly ground pepper
3 tablespoons flour
1 cup evaporated milk
1 10½-ounce can concentrated
   beef consommé, or more if
   necessary
3 tablespoons tomato paste
1 tablespoon A-1 or
   Worcestershire sauce
1½ cups buckwheat groats
   (kasha), cooked according
   to package directions

Melt the butter in a heavy pot or skillet over fairly high heat, add the onion and garlic, and stir about 3 minutes, or until golden. Add the beef, crumble it with a 2-pronged fork, and stir with the fork about 5 minutes, or until the meat loses its red color. Season very lightly with salt (the consommé is salted) and generously with pepper. Sprinkle the flour over the beef and stir in thoroughly. Add the evaporated milk, consommé, tomato paste, and A-1 or Worcestershire sauce. Stir very thoroughly. Bring to a boil, reduce the heat, and simmer partly covered 20 minutes, stirring frequently. If the mixture becomes too dry, add a little more consommé (or water). Add more salt if necessary. Serve over cooked groats.
Serves 4.

GOURMET MEAT BALLS
Contributed by Hans Burkhardt

1 pound sirloin or top round,
   finely ground
1 medium onion, grated
½ cup heavy cream
Freshly grated nutmeg
Salt
Freshly ground pepper
Flour
8 tablespoons clarified butter
½ pound mushrooms,
   trimmed, cleaned, and
   thinly sliced
Juice of ½ lemon
2 fresh black truffles, minced
   (optional)

Put the beef, onion, and cream in a bowl, mix thoroughly with a 2-pronged fork, and season to taste with nutmeg, salt, and pepper. Sprinkle a generous amount of flour over a pastry board. Form the beef mixture into 1-inch balls, dropping a dessertspoonful at a time onto the flour and rolling the balls in the flour with the palm of your hand. As they are formed, set them aside on a sheet of wax paper.

Heat 2 tablespoons of the butter in a skillet over medium heat. Add the mushrooms, lemon juice, and optional truffles. Shake the skillet over the heat about 5 minutes, or until much of the liquid has evaporated. Season lightly with salt and pepper. Remove from the heat and set aside.

Heat the remaining butter in another skillet over high heat until very hot but not smoking. Sauté the beef balls, about a dozen at a time, in the butter about 2 minutes, or until golden brown. As they are done, remove with a slotted spoon to a hot platter and keep warm.

Reheat the mushrooms over high heat 1 minute, or until most of the liquid they have released has evaporated. Spoon them over the meatballs and serve at once. *Serves 4.*

MEAT-AND-VEGETABLE LOAF
Contributed by Ray Holbert

1 pound chuck, ground
1 10-ounce package frozen
  spinach, cooked according
  to package instructions,
  well drained, and chopped
1 large carrot, peeled and
  coarsely grated
¼ cup minced parsley
1 medium red onion, finely
  chopped
1 green pepper, cored, seeded,
  and finely chopped
1 4-ounce can pitted black
  olives, rinsed, drained, and
  sliced
2 eggs
4 tablespoons soy or
  Worcestershire sauce
1 teaspoon dried basil
1 teaspoon salt
½ teaspoon freshly ground
  pepper
2 tablespoons butter, softened

Put all the ingredients, except the butter, in a large bowl and mix very thoroughly with a two-pronged fork.

Grease a 9-by-6-inch glass or metal loaf pan with the softened butter.

Lightly press the beef mixture into a mass. Lift it out of the bowl, pack it in the pan, and bake in a preheated 375° oven 1 hour. *Serves 4.*

Manuel Neri's kitchen

OXTAIL RAGOUT
Contributed by Hans Burkhardt

3 pounds oxtails, trimmed of
　excess fat and cut in pieces
　at the joints
Flour
6 tablespoons butter
1 large onion, coarsely
　chopped
1 large carrot, peeled and
　thinly sliced
2 cups beef broth, or more if
　necessary
2 cups dry red wine, or more
　if necessary
Salt
Freshly ground pepper
½ pound medium
　mushrooms, trimmed,
　cleaned, and quartered

Dredge the oxtails in flour. In a heavy, preferably enameled-iron pot in which the oxtails will fit in one layer, melt the butter over fairly high heat and brown the oxtails, a few at a time, on all sides. As they are browned, transfer them temporarily to a platter. Add the onion and carrot to the butter remaining in the pot and brown lightly. Return the oxtails to the pot and add the broth and wine. The liquid should barely cover the oxtail pieces; add a little more if necessary. Season to taste with salt and pepper. Bring to a boil and spoon off any scum from the surface. Reduce the heat, cover the pot tightly, and simmer 3 hours. About 15 minutes before the oxtails are done, stir the mushrooms into the pot. Transfer the ragout to a serving dish or platter.
Serves 6.

PORK CHOPS ORANGE-ROSÉ
Contributed by William Dole

4 loin pork chops, 1½ inches
　thick
3 tablespoons butter
Salt
Freshly ground pepper
1 teaspoon powdered dried
　sage
½ teaspoon dried oregano
1 large seedless orange, peeled
　and thinly sliced
2 cups vin rosé, or more if
　necessary
1 bunch watercress, trimmed,
　washed, and dried

Trim off almost all the fat from the pork chops, leaving only a thin layer around the loin side. Heat the butter in a large heavy skillet over fairly high heat until golden and sauté the chops about 3 or 4 minutes on each side. Season to taste with salt and pepper, rub a little of the herbs on each chop, and lay the orange slices on top. Add the wine, which should come about halfway up the sides of the chops, bring to a boil, reduce the heat, cover the skillet, and simmer 35 minutes. Check occasionally to see if the liquid has evaporated, adding more wine if necessary. Remove the cover, raise the heat, and reduce the liquid until slightly syrupy. Transfer the chops to a platter, spoon the pan juices over them, garnish with watercress, and serve at once.
Serves 4.

RABBIT BRAISED WITH ROSEMARY
Contributed by Jerrold Davis

1 4-pound rabbit, cut in
  pieces for frying
2 cloves garlic, minced
3 tablespoons chopped fresh
  rosemary, or 3 teaspoons
  dried
Juice of 1 lemon
1½ cups dry white wine
2 tablespoons butter
2 tablespoons olive oil
2 tablespoons minced shallots
2 medium onions, finely
  chopped
2 cups homemade chicken
  stock, or more if necessary
1 bay leaf
Salt
Freshly ground pepper
½ pound medium
  mushrooms, trimmed,
  cleaned, and quartered
About 3 tablespoons *beurre
  manié* (3 tablespoons each
  butter and flour blended
  together to a smooth paste)
¼ cup chopped parsley

Lay the rabbit pieces in a shallow glass baking dish. Mix together in a bowl the garlic, 2 tablespoons of the fresh rosemary (or 2 teaspoons of the dried), the lemon juice, and ½ cup of the wine. Pour this marinade over the rabbit pieces, stirring to coat well, and marinate at least 1 hour, stirring occasionally. Remove the pieces from the dish, saving the marinade, and pat dry with paper towels. Strain the marinade through a fine sieve into a bowl and set aside.

Heat the butter and oil in a large, heavy, preferably enameled-iron pot over fairly high heat until it is very hot but not smoking. Brown the rabbit pieces, a few at a time, on both sides, removing them to a platter as they are done. Add the shallots and onions to the butter remaining in the pot, reduce the heat slightly, and stir about 5 minutes, or until the onions are soft and translucent but not brown. Return the rabbit to the pot and mix well with the onions.

Pour the stock over the rabbit and add the remaining 1 cup of wine, the reserved marinade, the remaining 1 tablespoon of fresh rosemary (or the 1 teaspoon of dried), and the bay leaf. Season to taste with salt and pepper and mix well. Bring to a boil, cover tightly, reduce the heat, and simmer 30 minutes. Turn the rabbit pieces over, spooning the sauce and onions over them, and simmer covered another 30 minutes. About 15 minutes before the rabbit is done, stir the mushrooms into the pot.

Transfer the rabbit pieces to a hot serving platter. Using a slotted spoon, lay the mushrooms and onions over them. Keep the rabbit warm while preparing the sauce.

Whisk enough of the *beurre manié* into the liquid in the pot to thicken it (about 1 tablespoon of the *beurre manié* per cup of liquid). Raise the heat, whisk the sauce about 5 minutes, and correct the seasoning. At serving time, spoon the sauce over the rabbit pieces and sprinkle with the parsley. *Serves* 6.

RATTLESNAKE MARCALIBRE
Contributed by Robert Freimark

Rattlesnake can be a delicious treat for special guests—particularly Europeans, who seem to take delight in our rugged culinary vivacity.

Rattlesnake must be very fresh. A rattler should be at least 3 feet long to be worth cooking. Decapitate well below the head to avoid the poison sack, and then peel off the skin as you would a nylon stocking. Save the skin and rattle, if you like, for a wall memento or a hat band.

Gut the rattler with a very sharp knife. Rattlers clean very readily. Wash the meat thoroughly with cold water, pat dry with paper towels, and cut crosswise into steaks about ⅜ inch thick.

Brush the steaks with melted butter and lay them on a grill over a bed of hot coals. Sear quickly about 3 minutes on each side. The meat becomes flaky and white, a little firmer than whitefish.

Season lightly with salt, pepper, and paprika. Serve piping hot, garnished with lemon quarters and chopped fresh dill.

STEAK AU POIVRE
Contributed by William Brice

2 tablespoons black peppercorns
1 sirloin or porterhouse steak, 1 inch thick
2 tablespoons clarified butter
2 tablespoons olive oil
Salt
¼ cup strong beef bouillon
3 tablespoons cognac
½ teaspoon arrowroot

Crack or coarsely grind the peppercorns in a stone mortar with a pestle, or put them on a chopping board and roll the bottom of a heavy pan over them.

Trim off almost all the fat from the steak, leaving only a thin layer around the sides. With the heel of your hand, imbed the cracked pepper in both sides of the steak. Let the steak rest at room temperature at least 1 hour.

Heat the butter and oil in a heavy skillet over high heat until almost smoking hot. Sear the steak 1 minute on each side and then continue cooking until done to your taste of rareness. Transfer the steak to a hot platter and salt to taste.

Stir the bouillon, cognac, and arrowroot together in a small bowl. Pour into the butter and oil remaining in the skillet and stir with a wooden spoon 1 minute. Pour over the steak and serve at once. *Serves 2.*

STEAK-AND-KIDNEY PIE MA BELLE
Contributed by Paul Wonner

Pastry:
  1½ cups unbleached
     all-purpose flour
  ½ teaspoon salt
  6 tablespoons cold butter
  2 tablespoons lard or Crisco
  1 egg, lightly beaten
  4 tablespoons cold milk

4 tablespoons butter
1 pound mushrooms,
    trimmed, cleaned, and cut
    in ¼-inch slices
6 tablespoons flour
2 teaspoons salt
½ teaspoon freshly ground
    pepper
1 teaspoon mixed dried herbs
    (basil, sage, oregano,
    rosemary, etc.)
3 pounds sirloin, trimmed of
    fat and cut in 1-inch cubes
1 pound lamb or veal
    kidneys, trimmed of fat and
    cut in 1-inch pieces
¼ cup dry red wine
1 egg, lightly beaten

Prepare the pastry well in advance. Mix the flour and salt by hand in a bowl. Slice the butter and lard (or Crisco) and drop the slices into the bowl. Using a pastry blender or 2 knives, or simply your fingertips, work the butter and lard into the flour until it resembles coarse meal. Add the egg and milk, stir quickly with a 2-pronged fork just until the mixture forms a mass, roll into a ball, wrap in wax paper, and let rest in the refrigerator at least 1 hour.

While the pastry is resting, melt the 4 tablespoons of butter in a large skillet over medium heat. Add the mushrooms and sauté about 3 minutes. Remove the skillet from the heat and set aside.

Mix together the flour, salt, pepper, and herbs in a small bowl. Put the beef cubes and kidney pieces in a larger bowl, sprinkle with the flour mixture, and toss thoroughly. Transfer to an 8-cup baking dish or casserole, interspersing the mushrooms with the meat. Pour into the dish any liquid the mushrooms have released and the wine. Cool to room temperature.

Roll the chilled pastry out on a lightly floured board into a shape slightly larger than the baking dish. Lay the pastry over the dish, cut off the excess, moisten the underside of the pastry all around its edge with cold water, and press it firmly against the inside rim of the dish. Prick the surface with a fork in several places to allow steam to escape. If desired, cut any scraps of pastry into leaf shapes, moisten their undersides with water, and decorate the top with them. Brush the surface with the beaten egg.

Bake in a preheated 350° oven 1 hour. Check toward the end of the baking time; if the crust is becoming too brown, cover very loosely with foil. After 1 hour insert a larding needle through the crust into the meat. If it is not fully tender, bake a little longer. Serve from the baking dish. *Serves 6.*

CABLE CAR VEAL
Contributed by Christopher Lane

1 4-pound veal shoulder
   roast, boned and rolled
8 small sprigs fresh rosemary,
   or 1 tablespoon dried
Salt
Freshly ground pepper
2 cups sweet vermouth
Oil
3 cups seedless white and red
   grapes, mixed

With a small, sharply pointed knife, make deep incisions all over the roast. Insert the rosemary, pushing it well into the meat. Rub the surface with salt and pepper. Put the roast in a large bowl and pour the vermouth over it. Marinate 3 hours, turning frequently.

Drain the roast and place in a well-oiled brown paper bag large enough to allow space around the sides and top of the veal. Roll the bag tightly closed and fasten with paper clips. Place on a rack in a shallow roasting pan and roast in a preheated 350° oven 2 hours.

Carefully transfer the roast in its bag to a serving platter. Slit the bag open, allowing the juices to run onto the platter, and discard the bag. Carve the veal into slices and surround with the grapes. *Serves 6.*

VEAL MARENGO
Contributed by Fletcher Benton

3 tablespoons olive oil
2 cloves garlic, minced
½ cup dry white wine, or dry
   sherry or Madeira
2½ pounds veal shoulder,
   boned, trimmed of excess
   fat, cut in 1-inch cubes, and
   well dried on paper towels
3 tablespoons flour
4 cups homemade chicken stock
2 stalks celery, thinly sliced
Salt
Freshly ground pepper
2 tablespoons butter
24 fresh pearl onions or 18
   very small white onions
3 large ripe tomatoes, peeled,
   seeded, and coarsely chopped
½ pound small mushrooms,
   trimmed and cleaned
½ cup minced parsley

Heat the oil in a large, heavy, preferably enameled-iron pot over fairly high heat. Add the garlic and stir until golden, about 2 minutes. Add the wine and cook until it evaporates. Add the veal cubes and stir until lightly browned on all sides. Sprinkle the flour over the veal and stir well. Add the stock and bring to a boil, stirring constantly. Add the celery. Season to taste with salt and pepper. Reduce the heat, cover, and simmer 45 minutes, or until the veal is fork tender.

While the veal is cooking, melt the butter in a large skillet over medium heat, add the onions, stir to coat them with the butter, cover, reduce the heat, and simmer 10 minutes, shaking the skillet occasionally. Remove from the heat, remove the lid, and set aside.

After the veal has cooked 45 minutes, add the onions, tomatoes, and mushrooms and stir in well. Correct the seasoning, raise the heat slightly, and cook uncovered about 15 minutes longer, stirring occasionally. Transfer to a serving dish and sprinkle with the parsley.
Serves 6.

VITELLO TONNATO
(COLD VEAL WITH TUNA SAUCE)
Contributed by Rooney O'Neill

2½ pounds veal, cut from the upper leg in 1 piece
2 7-ounce cans Italian-style tuna (packed in oil), drained
6 anchovy fillets
1 medium onion, stuck with 2 cloves
1 stalk celery, cut in 1-inch pieces
2 carrots, peeled and cut in 1-inch pieces
1 bay leaf
6 parsley sprigs
1 cup dry white wine
3 cups homemade mayonnaise
2 lemons, thinly sliced and seeded
8 olives stuffed with pimiento, sliced
2 tablespoons capers
¼ cup minced parsley

Trim off all fat and membranes from the veal. Tie the meat very tightly with string so that it will hold its shape and slice easily after cooking.

Put the veal in a large, heavy, preferably enameled-iron pot with 1 can of the tuna, 2 anchovy fillets, the onion, celery, carrots, bay leaf, parsley sprigs, and wine. Add enough water to barely cover the veal. Bring to a boil over medium heat and skim off scum. Reduce the heat to low, cover the pot tightly, and simmer about 1½ hours. When done, the veal can be pierced easily with a fork, or an instant-register meat thermometer will read 170°. Uncover and let the veal cool to room temperature in the cooking liquid. Refrigerate 12 hours, making sure the veal is covered with liquid. Add water if necessary.

Several hours before serving, remove the veal. Boil the liquid until it is reduced by half and has a strong flavor. Strain through a fine sieve and let cool.

Remove the strings from the veal and slice it thinly. Arrange the slices, slightly overlapping, on a long, deep serving platter.

Put the remaining tuna, anchovy fillets, and ¼ cup of the cooking liquid in the container of a food processor fitted with the standard steel blade and process until smooth. Add the mayonnaise, process again until smooth, and gradually add enough of the cooking liquid so that the sauce is the consistency of heavy cream. Pour the sauce slowly over the veal, loosening the slices so it will run between them. Chill in the refrigerator 3 hours.

Remove the veal from the refrigerator about 20 minutes before serving. It should be chilled but not ice cold. Spoon the sauce again over and between the slices. Garnish with the lemon slices, olive slices, capers, and minced parsley. *Serves* 6.

Editors' note: As a variation substitute a 3-pound boned turkey breast for the veal. Prepare in the same manner, but simmer for only 30 minutes. In Tuscany especially, *tacchino tonnato* is considered more of a *piatto di gran lusso* than *vitello tonnato*.

VENEZUELAN HALLACAS*
Contributed by Lee Mullican and Luchita Hurtado

Dough or *masa* (see *Note*)

 6 cups Mexican dried corn
  kernels *(maiz de tostar)*
 1 cup lard or shortening,
  softened
 1 tablespoon salt
 2 tablespoons paprika

Filling:

 ½ cup lard or olive oil
 2 large onions, finely chopped
 2 cloves garlic, minced
 1 pound lean pork, cut in
  ¼-inch cubes
 1 15-ounce can whole
  tomatoes, drained
 2 medium green peppers,
  cored, seeded, and minced
 ¼ cup sugar
 1 teaspoon salt, or more to
  taste
 1 tablespoon ground cumin
 ½ cup wine vinegar
 3 cups cooked chicken meat,
  shredded (dark meat preferred)
24 pieces banana leaves (see
 Note), or parchment paper,
 cut in 12-by-14 inch rectangles

Garnish:

 4 hard-cooked eggs, each
  cut in 12 slices
 ¼ cup capers
 ⅓ cup raisins
 6 large canned pimientos,
  each cut in 8 strips
 48 whole almonds, blanched
  and skinned
 48 small stuffed green olives

Cover the corn kernels with 8 cups of cold water in a saucepan and bring to a boil over high heat. Reduce the heat and cook uncovered 30 minutes. Remove from the heat and let stand 24 hours. Rinse and drain the kernels several times, using cold water. While still wet, force them through a meat grinder several times, using the finest blade, until they are finely pulverized. Alternatively, use a food processor fitted with the standard steel blade. Put softened lard or shortening in a bowl with the salt and paprika and beat with an electric mixer until fluffy. Gradually add the ground corn and beat until smooth. Or, more simply, beat lard or shortening and seasonings with a wooden spoon until fluffy and knead in the ground corn by hand. Set aside. There should be about 6 cups of dough.

Heat the ½ cup of lard or oil in a large, heavy saucepan over medium heat. Add the onions and garlic and stir until very lightly browned. Add the pork cubes and continue stirring until they are lightly browned. Add the remaining filling ingredients (except the chicken) and mix thoroughly. Bring to a boil, reduce the heat slightly, and cook, stirring occasionally, about 30 minutes, or until much of the liquid has evaporated, the sauce has thickened, and the pork is tender. Add the chicken and simmer 10 minutes longer. Remove from the heat and let cool. There should be about 6 cups of filling.

If using banana leaves, soften each just before using by holding it briefly about 6 inches above the flame of a burner, being careful not to let the leaves scorch. Shape ¼ cup of the dough into a ball and place in the center of a banana leaf or sheet of parchment paper. Press the dough out with your hands into a 6-by-8-inch rectangle, leaving a 3-inch border of leaf or paper on all sides. Spread ¼ cup of the filling lengthwise down the center of the dough and garnish with 2 egg slices, a few capers and raisins, 2 pimiento slices, 2 almonds, and 2 olives. Lift the two longer sides of the leaf or paper and, pressing them together at the center, enclose the filling with the dough. Fold the borders of these two sides securely together so that they lie flat over the dough-wrapped filling, and then fold the two end borders toward the center, as you would wrap a package. Tie down both end flaps securely with string. Proceed in this manner until 24 packages are formed.

Bring 2 inches of water to boil in a very large pot fitted with a steaming rack (use 2 pots if necessary). Stack the packages flap side up loosely in the pot. Cover tightly, lower the heat slightly, and steam 1 hour, adding a little more boiling water occasionally if necessary.

Remove the strings from the packages before serving. Allow guests to unwrap their own *hallacas* at the table. *Serves 6.*

Note: Corn flour, or *masa harina,* available in Hispanic markets, may be used to make this dough. The flour should be mixed with an equal amount of water or light broth before beating or kneading in the lard or butter and seasonings.

Banana leaves are frequently available in Hispanic markets, but parchment paper is a perfectly acceptable substitute.

Smaller *hallacas* may fit more easily into a steamer. If desired, cut smaller pieces of banana leaves or parchment paper and proportionately reduce the amount of dough and filling for each.

Irma Cavat. *Mercato* (detail). 1975. Collection the artist

Hallacas are Venezuelan soul food. It is said that Simon Bolivar owed much of the success of his military campaigns to them. Serving *hallacas* on New Year's Day is traditional and brings good luck in the coming year.

BEEF TENDERLOIN BORDELAISE
Contributed by Charles Arnoldi

Stock:

　3 to 4 pounds veal bones,
　　including, if possible, a
　　calf's foot split in half
　3 large unpeeled onions,
　　coarsely chopped
　2 carrots, peeled and sliced
　3 stalks celery, sliced
　1 leek (white part only),
　　sliced lengthwise
　1 cup mushroom stems,
　　trimmed and cleaned
　4 large ripe tomatoes,
　　coarsely chopped
　1 bay leaf
　½ teaspoon dried thyme
　4 peppercorns
　6 sprigs parsley

2 tablespoons butter
¼ cup minced shallots
1 teaspoon minced fresh
　thyme, or ¼ teaspoon dried
3 cups very good dry red wine
1¼ cups sweet butter, softened

5-pound center-cut fillet of
　beef, at room temperature
Salt
Freshly ground white pepper
Watercress, trimmed, washed,
　and dried

Roast the veal bones in a shallow pan in a very hot oven about 15 minutes, or until well browned. Transfer to a very large pot, add all the remaining stock ingredients, cover generously with cold water, and bring to a boil over high heat. Reduce the heat to very low and cook uncovered at the barest simmer 24 hours. It is not necessary to skim. Strain the stock through a colander and discard the bones and vegetables. Strain again through a very fine sieve or through dampened cheesecloth. Chill in the refrigerator 24 hours and remove every particle of fat from the surface. Transfer the stock, discarding any sediment at the bottom, to a heavy saucepan. Bring to a boil and simmer slowly about 3 hours, or until reduced to 2 cups and slightly thickened. As it cooks, remove any scum that collects at the edge of the pan. During the last hour, stir frequently to prevent scorching. Remove from the heat and set aside.

Melt the 2 tablespoons of butter in a saucepan over medium heat. Add the shallots and thyme, and stir until the shallots are soft and translucent but not brown. Add the wine, bring to a boil, lower the heat slightly, and cook until reduced to about ½ cup. Pour through a very fine strainer into the reduced stock and set aside.

Spread about ¼ cup of the softened butter all over the beef and set it on the rack of a shallow roasting pan. Roast 25 minutes in a 500° oven for rare, or slightly longer for medium rare. As the meat cooks, baste frequently with the butter and juices in the pan. Transfer to a hot serving platter and let rest at least 5 minutes before carving.

Wayne Thiebaud. *Buffet*. 1975.
Collection the artist

While the beef is resting, reheat the reduced stock and wine to the barest simmer. Whisk in the remaining softened butter a tablespoon at a time, incorporating each before adding more. The butter will thicken the sauce and give it a high glaze. Do not let the sauce boil or it will separate. Season to taste with salt and pepper. If necessary, keep warm over barely hot water.

Carve the beef into generous slices and spoon a little of the sauce over them. Garnish with the watercress and serve at once. Pass the remainder of the sauce separately. *Serves 8.*

FOWL

Ballottine of Chicken ❧ Ray Saunders

Baked Chicken ❧ Toby Judith Klayman

Barbecued Chutney Chicken ❧ Ynez Johnston

Greek Chicken ❧ Judith Golden, for Van Deren Coke

Jujeh Kebabs (Chicken Kebabs) ❧ Marian Clayden

Cubist Chicken ❧ Irma Cavat

Chicken in Orbit ❧ Claire Falkenstein

Oriental Chicken with Mushrooms and Artichoke Hearts ❧ Nathan Oliveira

Indian Spiced Chicken (Murgh Jahl Frezi) ❧ Frederick Eversley

Chicken Renaissance ❧ Richard Diebenkorn

Oriental Lemon Chicken ❧ George Neubert

Pollo o Tacchino Steccato (Palisade of Turkey or Chicken Breasts) ❧ Rooney O'Neill

Chicken Tarragon ❧ David Gilhooly

Tofu-Herb Chicken ❧ Victor Bergeron ("Trader Vic")

Roast Wild Duck ❧ Henry T. Hopkins

Paul Wonner. *Dutch Still-life with Stuffed Birds and Chocolates.* 1981.
Acrylic on canvas. Courtesy John Berggruen Gallery, San Francisco

BALLOTTINE OF CHICKEN
Contributed by Ray Saunders

1 3- to 3½-pound chicken,
  with the giblets
½ teaspoon coriander seeds,
  freshly cracked or ground
2 teaspoons minced fresh
  thyme, or ½ teaspoon dried
Salt
1 medium carrot, scrubbed
  and coarsely sliced
1 medium onion, unpeeled
  and coarsely sliced
2 stalks celery, coarsely sliced
1 cup beef bouillon
1 bay leaf
¼ pound boiled fresh ham,
  cut in 1-inch pieces
2 shallots, minced
1 tablespoon minced fresh
  tarragon, or 1 teaspoon
  dried
¼ cup heavy cream
Freshly ground pepper
12 large leaves fresh spinach,
  or 6 leaves fresh Swiss
  chard, ribs removed
3 tablespoons butter
3 tablespoons olive oil

Cut off the neck of the chicken. Sever the wings from the body at the first joint down from the shoulder, and set aside with the neck and the giblets. Make a circular cut through skin and flesh about 2 inches up from the bottom of each leg.

Bone the chicken completely, leaving the flesh attached to the skin, which will serve as a covering for the chicken when it is stuffed. Use a very sharp knife with its cutting edge always slanted toward the bone, not toward the flesh. The skin should not be pierced except near the bottoms of the legs, down the back, and where the wings and legs are severed from the body. First, place the chicken on its breast and cut through the skin straight down the length of the backbone. Working downward and outward from the backbone, scrape and cut the bones from the flesh. Sever the thighs and wing joints from the carcass when you reach them, without cutting through the skin. Remove the carcass in one piece and reserve. Then bone the thighs, legs, and wings. Do not worry if pieces of the flesh fall free when you bone the thighs; put them to one side. Reserve all the bones with the neck, wing tips, giblets, and carcass.

Spread the chicken out flat, skin down. Pull off the 2 small fillets that are loose on the breast and lay them over the bare spots on the breast. Fill in any more bare spots with the loose pieces of flesh from the thighs. Sprinkle with the coriander, the thyme, and salt to taste. Cover loosely with foil and set aside.

Cut the carcass in several pieces and put them with all the giblets, bones, etc., in a large saucepan. Add the 3 vegetables, bouillon, bay leaf, and about 6 cups of water, or just enough to cover the bones. Bring to a boil and simmer covered over medium heat 2 hours. Strain the liquid into a bowl, discarding the vegetables, bones, giblets, etc., and then pour the broth into a pot that will be large enough to hold the chicken when it is stuffed and rolled. Season to taste with salt and set aside.

Put the ham in the container of a food processor and, using the standard steel blade, grind very fine. Alterna-

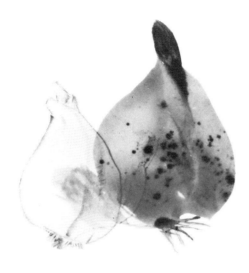

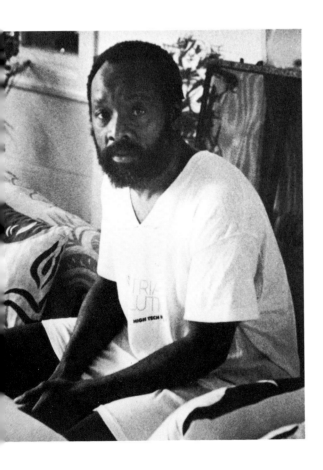

tively, force the ham through a meat grinder twice, using the finest blade. Transfer the ham to a bowl and stir in the shallots, tarragon, cream, and a few gratings of pepper. Set aside.

Wilt the spinach or chard leaves by dropping them for 30 seconds in a pot of boiling water. Drain, rinse with cold water to preserve their color, and pat dry with paper towels.

Spread the spinach or chard over the flesh of the chicken. Form the ham mixture into a long roll and lay it down the center of the chicken. To make the finished roll look neater, push the protruding wings and legs into the flesh side. Fold one side of the chicken over the ham roll and roll up fairly tightly, tucking in any loose pieces at the sides as you roll. Lay the roll on a length of cheesecloth and then roll up the chicken so that it is encased in 3 thicknesses of cloth. Tie both ends with butcher's string. Cut off any excess of cheesecloth and string. Tie strings at 1-inch intervals down the length of the roll so that it will keep its shape as it cooks.

Heat the butter and oil in a large, heavy skillet over fairly high heat. Add the roll and turn it gently so that the cloth absorbs the butter and oil on all sides.

Bring the reserved pot of broth to a boil, lower the chicken into it, and baste or turn the roll so that the cheesecloth is well soaked. Bring back to a boil, cover the pot, reduce the heat, and simmer about 45 minutes. Turn the roll over after about 20 minutes so that it cooks evenly. Remove the pot from the heat and let the chicken rest in the broth about 20 minutes, turning occasionally. Remove the roll from the pot, remove the strings, and unroll the chicken from the cheesecloth onto a serving platter.

The ballottine may be served hot, cut in crosswise slices; or it may be chilled, in which case it becomes a galantine, and then sliced.
Serves 6.

Ray Saunders

BAKED CHICKEN

Contributed by Toby Judith Klayman

3 tablespoons butter, softened
2 3-pound chickens, cut in
    pieces for frying
2 16-ounce cans tomato juice,
    or more if necessary
1 cup dry sherry
4 medium onions, coarsely
    chopped
10 medium carrots, peeled
    and thinly sliced
1 pound mushrooms,
    trimmed, cleaned, and sliced
3 cups broccoli florets, broken
    in pieces
4 green peppers, cored,
    seeded, and cut in 1-inch
    squares
½ cup coarsely chopped
    parsley
Garlic salt
Paprika
Salt
Freshly ground pepper

Grease a very large baking dish or shallow roasting pan with the butter. Arrange half the chicken pieces in the bottom and pour half the tomato juice and sherry over them. Sprinkle with half the vegetables and then with half the parsley. Season lightly with garlic salt, paprika, salt, and pepper. Add another layer of the chicken and vegetables and the remaining tomato juice, sherry, and parsley. Season lightly again.

Cover the baking dish tightly with foil and bake in a preheated 350° oven 1 hour. Loosen the foil at both ends of the dish to allow some of the liquid to evaporate and bake 1 more hour. If you like chicken that is falling from the bone, bake as long as a total of 4 hours, but check occasionally to make sure there is still liquid in the dish, adding more tomato juice if necessary. Serve from the baking dish.

Serves 8.

BARBECUED CHUTNEY CHICKEN

Contributed by Ynez Johnston

1½ cups mango chutney
3 tablespoons Grand Marnier
1 3-pound chicken, cut in
    pieces for frying
Oil
Salt

Finely chop the chutney in a blender. Alternatively, finely chop by hand. Put the chutney in a large bowl and stir in the Grand Marnier. Add the chicken pieces, stir to coat thoroughly, and marinate 6 hours, stirring occasionally.

Remove the chicken pieces from the marinade, brushing or scraping the marinade that clings to them back into the bowl. Reserve the marinade. Wipe the pieces fairly clean with paper towels, brush with oil, and season lightly with salt. Lay the pieces on a grill over a bed of very hot coals and brown about 5 minutes on each side. Raise the grill so that the heat is less intense and baste the pieces with the marinade. Basting frequently with the marinade, grill about 10 minutes on each side, or until the chicken is done to your taste. *Serves 2 to 4.*

CUBIST CHICKEN
Contributed by Irma Cavat

1 2½- to 3-pound frying chicken
1 medium onion, cut in half and thinly sliced, or 1 bunch scallions, trimmed and thinly sliced, including about 2 inches of the green part
3 slices fresh ginger root, peeled, or 1 teaspoon ground ginger
5 tablespoons soy sauce
4 tablespoons dry sherry
1 orange (or 2 small tangerines)
2 teaspoons sugar (or 1 overflowing tablespoon honey)
2 teaspoons white-wine vinegar (or rice vinegar)
3 or more grindings black pepper
Generous pinch cayenne pepper (optional)
6 tablespoons vegetable oil
1 tablespoon sesame oil (or sesame seeds)

Cut the chicken into sections. Discard (but save for stock pot) wing tips, leg tips, and back. With a cleaver or sharp poultry shears chop or cut the chicken parts into about 20 roughly cube-shaped pieces. Place in a bowl and add the onion, ginger, and 1 tablespoon each of the soy sauce and sherry. Turn the chicken pieces until well coated. Marinate the chicken 1 hour at room temperature, turning once or twice.

Peel the orange with a rotary peeler (do not include any white part). Cut the rind into julienne strips and set aside. Squeeze the orange and strain the juice into a bowl. Add the remaining soy sauce and sherry and the rest of the ingredients except the vegetable and sesame oils.

Pour the vegetable oil into a large skillet or wok and place over high heat until a light haze forms over the oil. Remove the chicken from the marinade and reserve the marinade. Sauté the chicken in the skillet 4 or 5 minutes, tossing and turning almost constantly. Remove chicken to a platter with a slotted spoon and pour off half the oil from the skillet. Add the reserved marinade, the orange-juice mixture, and the orange rind. Bring to a boil over high heat. Return the chicken to the skillet and cook 2 minutes, tossing and turning constantly. Pour the contents of the skillet into a shallow bowl or onto a deep platter. Sprinkle with the sesame oil and serve at once. *Serves 6.*

Note: This is marvelous served over white or brown rice or over pasta (homemade fettuccine, lightly buttered, is exceptionally good). An excellent accompaniment is a combination of stir-fried vegetables, such as broccoli florets, sliced zucchini, strips of sweet green or red peppers, strips of eggplant, mushrooms, sliced celery, or whatever is in season.

GREEK CHICKEN
Contributed by Judith Golden for Van Deren Coke

Juice of 2 lemons
1 tablespoon dried oregano
½ cup minced parsley
1 teaspoon salt
Freshly ground pepper
1 3-pound chicken, cut in
　pieces for frying
Oil

Preheat broiler element to medium or a thermostat setting of 350°.

Mix the lemon juice, oregano, parsley, salt, and a few gratings of pepper in a large bowl. Add the chicken and toss thoroughly. Lightly oil a baking dish large enough to hold the chicken pieces in one layer. Place the chicken skin down in the dish; leave any excess marinade in the bowl. Broil slowly 25 minutes, basting occasionally with the juices in the dish. Turn the pieces, spoon the remaining marinade over them, and broil another 25 minutes, basting occasionally. The chicken should be crisp and golden brown. *Serves 4.*

Contributor's note: Serve on a terrace overlooking the ocean or carry in a basket deep into a cool forest. Accompany the Greek Chicken with Strawberry-Roquefort Salad (page 34), crusty bread and cheese, and a very cold dry white wine.

JUJEH KEBABS (CHICKEN KEBABS)
Contributed by Marian Clayden

1 3-pound chicken

Marinade:
　½ cup lime or lemon juice
　½ cup chicken broth or
　　water
　1½ teaspoons salt
　½ teaspoon freshly ground
　　pepper
　1 tablespoon dried oregano
　½ teaspoon paprika
　1 medium onion, finely
　　chopped

½ cup butter, melted
Shireen Polo (Sweet Rice)
　(page 54)

Using poultry shears or strong kitchen scissors, cut along both sides of the backbone of the chicken, freeing it from the carcass; also cut off the wing tips. Using a cleaver or poultry shears and, when useful, a sharp knife, cut the chicken in 1½-inch pieces, reserving any trimmings, or pieces that are too thin, along with the backbone and wing tips, for making chicken stock. Alternatively, if you prefer boneless chicken, cut the flesh from the carcass (page 106) before cutting it in pieces.

Mix marinade in a bowl, add the chicken, and coat thoroughly. Marinate 4 hours, stirring occasionally.

Alternating pieces of light and dark meat, spear the chicken pieces on 4 long skewers. Brush generously with melted butter and broil under an oven broiler or, preferably, grill over charcoal about 10 minutes, turning and basting frequently with more melted butter.

Slide chicken from skewers onto a bed of Shireen Polo. *Serves 4.*

CHICKEN IN ORBIT
Contributed by Claire Falkenstein

1 3-pound chicken
Salt
Freshly ground pepper
1 teaspoon dried basil
1 teaspoon dried rosemary
½ teaspoon dried thyme
1 small Bermuda or Spanish
    onion, studded with 4 cloves
6 bananas, sliced ½ inch thick
6 carrots, peeled and sliced
    ¼ inch thick
2 cloves garlic, thinly sliced
6 tablespoons butter, melted

Rub the cavity of the chicken with salt and pepper and the herbs. Put the onion and a few of the banana and carrot slices in the cavity. Slide 1 or 2 fingers under the skin of the chicken to loosen it from the flesh, taking care not to pierce the skin. Push garlic slices between the skin and flesh, distributing them as evenly as possible all over the chicken.

Put the chicken in a shallow roasting pan. Brush the surface of the chicken with the butter, allowing it to dribble into the pan, and sprinkle lightly with salt. Spread the remaining carrots around the chicken, toss them lightly in the butter, and season them with salt and pepper. Cover the chicken loosely with foil and bake in a preheated 350° oven 45 minutes. Sprinkle the remaining banana slices over the carrots, seal the foil tightly around the edges of the pan, and bake about 20 minutes longer. Transfer the chicken to a platter and garnish with the carrots and bananas.
Serves 4.

Sketch by the artist

ORIENTAL CHICKEN WITH MUSHROOMS AND ARTICHOKE HEARTS
Contributed by Nathan Oliveira

1 3-pound chicken, cut in
    pieces for frying
½ cup soy sauce
2 cloves garlic, minced
Freshly ground pepper
½ pound mushrooms,
    trimmed, cleaned, and
    thinly sliced
8 canned artichoke hearts

Toss the chicken pieces with the soy sauce, garlic, and a few gratings of pepper in a shallow roasting pan. Arrange the pieces skin up and bake in a preheated 350° oven 20 minutes. Mix in the mushrooms, turn the chicken pieces over, and bake 25 minutes longer. Turn the pieces again, arrange the artichoke hearts around them, and bake 10 minutes longer. Transfer the chicken and vegetables to a hot platter and serve at once.
Serves 4.

INDIAN SPICED CHICKEN
(MURGH JAHL FREZI)
Contributed by Frederick Eversley

1½ cups plain yogurt
1 small onion, minced
1 teaspoon powdered cumin
1¼ teaspoons *garam masala**
1¼ teaspoons salt
¾ teaspoon powdered
   turmeric
¼ teaspoon minced fresh
   peeled ginger root
1½ pounds chicken wings
1½ pounds chicken thighs
4 tablespoons ghee, or
   clarified butter
2 large onions, thinly sliced
4 cloves garlic, minced
1 tablespoon tomato paste
1¼ teaspoons red-pepper
   flakes
6 cups boiled rice

Put ½ cup of the yogurt in a large bowl with the onion, cumin, *garam masala*, salt, turmeric, and ginger root. Mix thoroughly. Add the chicken parts and stir until well coated. Marinate 4 hours, stirring occasionally.

Heat the ghee, or clarified butter, in a large, heavy, preferably enameled-iron pan over fairly high heat. Add the onions and stir until golden brown. Push the onions to one side of the pan. Add the garlic and stir 1 minute. Add the tomato paste and stir thoroughly into the onions and garlic. Add the chicken pieces with their marinade to the pan and mix with the onions. Cook uncovered about 5 minutes. Lower the heat, cover the pot, and simmer 20 minutes. Add the remaining yogurt, sprinkle with the red pepper, and stir until well mixed. Simmer covered another 20 minutes. Transfer the chicken pieces to a platter and spoon the sauce and onions over them. Serve with boiled rice.
Serves 6.

* *Garam masala* is a powdered mixture of cardamom seeds, cinnamon, cloves, pepper, and nutmeg. It is available at Indian-food stores.

CHICKEN RENAISSANCE
Contributed by Richard Diebenkorn

3 chicken breasts, unboned
   and cut in half
Salt
Freshly ground pepper
6 tablespoons clarified butter
⅓ cup raspberry wine vinegar
⅔ cup homemade chicken stock
2 tablespoons minced shallots
3 cups seedless red grapes
   (Ribieros)
1 tablespoon arrowroot,
   dissolved in ½ cup chicken stock
¼ cup minced parsley

Season the chicken breasts lightly with salt and pepper. Heat the clarified butter in a large, heavy, preferably enameled-iron pot over fairly high heat until very hot but not smoking. Sauté the breasts about 2 minutes on each side, or until golden brown. Add the vinegar and stock, bring to a boil, reduce the heat to low, cover the pot tightly, and simmer about 10 to 15 minutes. When the breasts are springy (not firm) to the touch, they are done. Transfer to a serving platter and keep warm while preparing the sauce.

Add the shallots to the pot, raise the heat, and boil 2 minutes. Add the grapes and cook less than 1 minute, just until very hot. Add the arrowroot and stir just until

the liquid has thickened. Correct the seasoning if necessary. Spoon the grapes and sauce over the chicken and sprinkle with the parsley.
Serves 6.

Richard Diebenkorn

ORIENTAL LEMON CHICKEN
Contributed by George Neubert

1 pound skinless and boneless
   chicken breasts

Marinade:
   1 tablespoon cornstarch
   1 tablespoon cold water
   1 egg yolk
   ⅛ teaspoon freshly ground
      pepper
   ½ teaspoon salt
   ½ cup dry white wine
   ½ cup tamari or low-salt
      soy sauce

Seasoning sauce:
   1 tablespoon lemon juice
   1 tablespoon sugar
   1 tablespoon chicken broth
   ½ teaspoon salt
   2 teaspoons cornstarch
   1 teaspoon sesame oil

6 tablespoons cornstarch
3 tablespoons flour
Oil for deep frying
1 tablespoon vegetable oil
Yellow food coloring
   (optional)
1 tablespoon Chinese-style
   hot oil
1 lemon, thinly sliced and
   seeded
Parsley sprigs

Cut the chicken in 1-inch pieces with a very sharp knife. The chicken may be partly frozen to facilitate cutting.

Mix the marinade ingredients in a bowl. Add the chicken and toss thoroughly. Marinate 20 minutes, stirring occasionally.

Stir the seasoning-sauce ingredients in a small bowl until well blended. Set aside.

Mix the cornstarch and flour in a bowl. Remove the chicken pieces from the marinade with a slotted spoon and coat them with the flour and cornstarch by tossing quickly and lightly in the bowl with your fingers. Alternatively, they may be coated by shaking in a paper bag with the cornstarch and flour. Transfer them immediately to a rack to prevent their sticking together. Tap the rack lightly to shake off any excess starch.

Pour oil into a large, heavy saucepan to a depth of 4 inches and bring to 350° over medium heat. Put the chicken pieces in a frying basket or on a large Chinese mesh strainer and lower into the hot oil. Agitate the pieces slightly to make sure they do not stick together. Fry exactly 1 minute and remove briefly from the oil. Raise the heat and let the oil reach 375°. Reimmerse the chicken and fry 30 seconds longer. Remove from the oil and allow chicken to drain in the basket or on the strainer.

Heat the vegetable oil in a skillet over medium heat. Restir the seasoning sauce, add to the skillet, and stir until it thickens. Stir in the food coloring, if desired. Thin the sauce with a small amount of water to the desired consistency. Stir in the Chinese hot oil, which will make the sauce shiny. Add the chicken, toss 1 minute, and transfer to a platter. Garnish with the lemon slices and parsley. Serve immediately.
Serves 4.

POLLO O TACCHINO STECCATO (PALISADE OF CHICKEN OR TURKEY BREASTS)

Contributed by Rooney O'Neill

3 chicken breasts, cut in half, skinned, boned, and tendons removed; or 6 slices turkey breast, about ⅜-inch thick

18 fresh sage leaves

6 fresh rosemary sprigs

6 cloves garlic, minced

Salt

Freshly ground pepper

½ cup olive oil

½ cup dry white wine or dry white vermouth

Flatten the chicken breasts or turkey slices very slightly with the flat side of a cleaver. Lay them out on a board; if using chicken breasts, lay them smooth side down. Place 3 sage leaves and a sprig of rosemary on each, sprinkle generously with garlic, and season lightly with salt and pepper. Roll each and tie securely with string.

Heat the oil in a heavy skillet large enough to hold all the rolls without crowding. When the oil is very hot but not smoking, add the rolls and brown lightly and quickly on all sides. Reduce the heat and cook about 10 minutes longer, turning frequently; the exact time will depend on the thickness of the rolls. Transfer to a hot serving platter.

Add the wine to the skillet, raise the heat, and deglaze the skillet, scraping the bottom with a wooden spoon, until the wine is reduced by about half.

Remove the strings from the rolls and cut each roll in ½-inch slices. Pour the juices from the skillet over the slices and serve at once.

Serves 6.

Contributor's note: This recipe comes from my sister Ann, who lives in Florence with her Italian husband. She is the best cook I know, having learned much of her skill from her husband's family and friends. Her husband Gianni amusingly translated this dish as "Sticked Chicken or Turkey."

Editors' note: Steccato means "palisade" or "picket fence."

George Neubert

CHICKEN TARRAGON
Contributed by David Gilhooly

1 3-pound chicken
Salt
Freshly ground pepper
¼ cup minced fresh tarragon,
 or 2 tablespoons dried
8 tablespoons butter, softened

Season the cavity of the chicken with salt and pepper. Stir the tarragon into the butter in a bowl. Spread a little of the butter in the cavity and coat the outside of the chicken with the remainder.

Place the chicken on a rack in a shallow roasting pan and roast in a preheated 450° oven 10 minutes. Baste the chicken, reduce the heat to 350°, and roast about 45 minutes longer, basting frequently. Transfer the chicken to a platter and the pan juices to a sauce boat or a serving bowl. Spoon a little of the juices over each serving and pass the rest.   *Serves 4.*

TOFU-HERB CHICKEN
Contributed by Victor Bergeron ("Trader Vic")

1 pound tofu
¼ cup dry white wine
6 teaspoons dried basil
6 teaspoons dried thyme
4 large chicken thighs,
  skinned and boned
Salt
Freshly ground pepper
4 tablespoons butter
¼ pound mushrooms,
  trimmed, cleaned, and
  coarsely chopped
2 tablespoons minced shallots
¼ cup minced parsley

Cut the tofu in ½-inch cubes. Mix the wine and 4 teaspoons each of the basil and thyme in a bowl, add the tofu, and toss lightly. Cover the bowl and marinate 8 hours in the refrigerator, tossing occasionally.

Cut the chicken in ¾-inch cubes. To facilitate making neat cubes, the chicken may be partly frozen before cutting. Season the cubes with salt and pepper and sprinkle with the remaining basil and thyme.

Heat the butter in a shallow enameled-iron baking dish or an oven-proof skillet over fairly high heat until golden but not brown. Add the chicken and toss constantly about 3 minutes, or until lightly browned. Add the mushrooms and shallots and stir over the heat about 2 minutes longer. Add the tofu cubes, stir lightly, and remove from the heat. Put the baking dish or skillet in a preheated 475° oven and bake 5 minutes. Serve from the baking dish or transfer to a platter. Sprinkle with the parsley.   *Serves 4.*

ROAST WILD DUCK

Contributed by Henry T. Hopkins

2 2½-pound wild ducks, such as mallards,* plucked and drawn

Salt

Freshly ground pepper

2 small green cooking apples, cored and quartered but unpeeled

2 small onions, quartered

2 cups mayonnaise, or more as required

Oil

Season the cavities of the ducks with salt and pepper. Stuff each loosely with the apples and onions, and sew the cavities closed with a trussing needle and butcher's string, or close with skewers and string.

Slather mayonnaise about ¼ inch thick over both ducks and slide each carefully into a well-oiled brown paper bag large enough to leave 2 or 3 inches of room around the sides and breasts of the ducks. Roll the bags tightly closed and fasten with paper clips. Place on a rack in a large, shallow roasting pan and roast in a preheated 425° oven 40 minutes.

Carefully transfer the ducks in their bags to a large platter. Slit the bags open and discard, leaving the juices on the platter. Remove the strings, cut the ducks in half with poultry shears, and discard the apples and onions. Serve at once. *Serves 2 to 4.*

*If using smaller ducks, such as teal or muscovy, the roasting time should be reduced by 15 minutes.

Sketches by the artist

VEGETABLES

Beth Van Hoesen. *Carrots*. 1973. Aquatint

Stuffed Artichokes ❧ Gage Taylor

Bean Pot ❧ Nancy Genn

Refried Beans ❧ Taffy Dahl

Mom Fujii's Sautéed Burdock Root ❧ Ray Saunders

Carrot-and-Turnip Purée ❧ K. Lee Manuel

Broccoli with a Cheese Gratin ❧ Julia Huette

Champignons à la Provençale ❧ Paul Wonner

Eggplant Casserole ❧ Pamela Kroner

Easy Eggplant ❧ Coille Hooven

Steamed Eggplant ❧ Robert Hartman

Hoppin' John ❧ Eleanor Dickinson

Carolina Fried Okra ❧ Donna Mossholder

Augusta's Garlic-Toothpaste Potatoes ❧ Alberta Mayo

Stewed Tomatoes with Tofu ❧ Victor Bergeron ("Trader Vic")

Baked Summer Squash ❧ William Brice

STUFFED ARTICHOKES
Contributed by Gage Taylor

4 large artichokes
1 lemon, cut in half
2 tablespoons butter
2 scallions, trimmed and
    thinly sliced, including the
    green tops
¼ pound mushrooms,
    trimmed, cleaned, and
    minced
¼ pound cheddar cheese,
    finely grated
½ cup dry bread crumbs
¼ teaspoon dried chervil
2 eggs, lightly beaten
½ cup sour cream
1 teaspoon salt
Freshly ground pepper
4 tablespoons grated
    Parmesan cheese
Boiling water
1 cup butter, melted

Pull off the tough outer leaves around the bottom of the artichokes. Cut off the top third of each artichoke with a sharp knife and trim off the bottom so it will stand upright. Trim off the pointed ends of the leaves with scissors. Spread the center leaves apart and scoop out all the fuzzy choke with a melon-ball cutter or a grapefruit spoon. Be sure to remove every trace of the choke, as it can be unpleasant to eat. Rub all the cut parts of the artichokes with the cut side of the lemon.

Melt the 2 tablespoons of butter in a saucepan over medium heat, add the scallions, and stir about 5 minutes or until soft. Add the mushrooms and stir another 5 minutes, or until most of the mushroom juices have evaporated. Remove from the heat. Mix in a bowl with the cheddar cheese, bread crumbs, chervil, eggs, and sour cream. Season with the salt and freshly ground pepper to taste. Stuff the center cavity of the artichokes with this mixture and top each with Parmesan cheese. Set the artichokes in a baking dish containing 1 inch of boiling water, cover tightly with foil, and bake in a preheated 350° oven about 45 minutes, or until the outer leaves pull off very easily.

Transfer the artichokes to serving plates. Put the melted butter in small bowls for dipping the leaves.

Serves 4.

BEAN POT
Contributed by Nancy Genn

1 pound link pork sausages
8 tablespoons butter
2 large green peppers, cored,
    seeded, and coarsely chopped
4 large red onions, coarsely
    chopped
6 15-ounce cans kidney beans,
    drained
¾ cup brown sugar
Salt
Freshly ground pepper

Fry the sausages in a heavy skillet over medium heat until browned on all sides and well cooked. Remove with a slotted spoon and drain on paper towels. Cut in half and set aside.

Melt the butter in a large, heavy pot over medium heat, add the green peppers and onions, and stir about 5 minutes, or until the onions are soft and translucent but not brown. Add the kidney beans and sugar, season with salt and pepper to taste, and stir until the sugar is melted and the beans are very hot. Stir in the sausages. If the mixture seems dry, add a little water.

Pour into a large earthenware bean pot or casserole and bake in a preheated 350° oven 30 minutes. Serve from the pot. *Serves 8.*

REFRIED BEANS
Contributed by Taffy Dahl

½ pound pinto beans, or 2
  16-ounce cans
Salt
6 tablespoons bacon fat or
  lard

Recently picked beans require no soaking, but dried beans should be soaked overnight in cold water. Whichever you use, put the beans in a large, heavy, preferably earthenware pot, cover with cold water, and bring slowly to a boil over medium heat. Season very lightly with salt, reduce the heat, cover the pot, and simmer 1½ to 2 hours, or until tender. Check occasionally to make sure there is still liquid in the pot; it should not all be absorbed. Remove from the heat, cool, and store in the refrigerator at least 24 hours before frying. If using canned beans, drain them, reserving their liquid.

Heat the bacon fat or lard in a heavy skillet over medium heat and add about 1 cup of the beans. Mash them into the fat with a potato masher or any other convenient tool. Gradually add the remaining beans and a little of their liquid, mashing and stirring them constantly until they form a paste. Reduce the heat slightly and mash and stir the beans frequently with a wooden spoon about 10 minutes, or until the edges sizzle and the paste begins to come away from the skillet. Turn it out from the skillet like an omelet onto a hot serving dish and serve at once. *Serves 4.*

Paul Wonner. *Study for Still-life with Artichokes and Cherry Tomatoes*. 1981. Acrylic.
Courtesy John Berggruen Gallery, San Francisco

121

MOM FUJII'S SAUTÉED BURDOCK ROOT
Contributed by Ray Saunders

1 pound burdock roots
   (Japanese *gobō*)*
2 tablespoons sesame oil
1 tablespoon sugar
3 tablespoons soy sauce
⅛ teaspoon chili powder
1 tablespoon sesame seeds,
   toasted

*Available at Oriental-produce stores.

Scrub the burdock roots clean with a vegetable brush and trim off both ends. Cut the roots into 2-inch-long julienne strips, matchstick thin; as they are cut, drop immediately into a bowl of cold water to avoid discoloration. Soak 1 hour or longer, drain, and pat dry with paper towels.

Heat the sesame oil in a heavy skillet over medium heat and sauté the strips about 8 minutes, stirring and tossing frequently. Add the sugar, soy sauce, and chili powder. Stir until the liquid has evaporated and the strips are well coated with the seasonings. Transfer to a serving dish and sprinkle with the sesame seeds. May be served hot, at room temperature, or cold.   *Serves 4.*

CARROT-AND-TURNIP PURÉE
Contributed by K. Lee Manuel

3 medium turnips, peeled and
   quartered
6 medium carrots, peeled and
   cut in 2-inch lengths
3 tablespoons butter, softened
½ cup heavy cream
Salt
Freshly ground pepper

Cook the turnips in a saucepan of boiling lightly salted water 15 minutes; add the carrots and boil 15 minutes longer. Both vegetables should be very tender but not waterlogged. Drain thoroughly. Put the vegetables in the container of a food processor and, using the standard steel blade, purée while slowly adding the butter and cream. Season to taste with salt and pepper and process briefly again. Alternatively, use a blender or force the vegetables through a food mill and beat in the butter, cream, and seasonings by hand. Return the purée to the saucepan, stir briefly over medium heat, and transfer to a serving dish.   *Serves 4.*

Marianne Boers. *Radishes*. 1981. Watercolor. Courtesy John Berggruen Gallery, San Francisco

BROCCOLI WITH A CHEESE GRATIN
Contributed by Julia Huette

1 large bunch broccoli, about
   2 pounds
½ cup mayonnaise
¼ cup grated Parmesan
   cheese
2 tablespoons minced parsley
2 teaspoons lemon juice
2 egg whites
Salt
Freshly ground pepper

Cut off the tough bottom ends of the broccoli stalks and, if desired, peel the outer skins of the stalks with a sharp knife. Cut the flower-topped stalks into thin spears and steam in a tightly covered vegetable steamer about 5 minutes, or until barely tender. Arrange the spears in a shallow oven-proof dish.

Mix the mayonnaise, cheese, parsley, and lemon juice in a bowl. With a whisk or an electric mixer, beat the egg whites in another bowl until stiff but not dry and gently fold into the mayonnaise mixture. Spoon evenly over the broccoli. Set the dish under a preheated broiler about 5 minutes, or until the top is golden brown. Watch carefully so that it doesn't burn. Serve from the baking dish.

Serves 4.

CHAMPIGNONS À LA PROVENÇALE
Contributed by Paul Wonner

2 tablespoons butter
2 tablespoons olive oil
1½ pounds medium
   mushrooms, trimmed,
   cleaned, and quartered
Juice of ½ lemon
1 medium onion, finely
   chopped
3 cloves garlic, minced
3 medium ripe tomatoes,
   peeled, seeded, and coarsely
   chopped
1 teaspoon dried basil
¼ teaspoon fennel seeds
¼ teaspoon dried thyme
½ teaspoon paprika
Salt
Freshly ground pepper
¼ cup canned brown gravy
1 long loaf French bread

Heat 1 tablespoon each of the butter and oil in a large skillet over medium heat, add the mushrooms and lemon juice, and stir about 5 minutes, or until the mushrooms are barely tender and their juice has evaporated. Remove from the heat and set aside.

Heat the remaining butter and oil in a heavy saucepan over medium heat, add the onion and garlic, and stir about 5 minutes, or until the onion is soft and translucent but not brown. Add the tomatoes, herbs, paprika, and salt and pepper to taste. Stir 5 to 10 minutes, or until the tomatoes have softened and most of their juice has evaporated. Stir in the brown gravy and cook slightly longer, until the mixture is fairly thick. Add the reserved mushrooms and stir just until very hot. Remove from the heat and set aside.

Cut off the top of the French bread and hollow out the loaf with a fork so that it is boat shaped. Toast briefly in a preheated 350° oven.

Just before serving, reheat the mushroom mixture briefly and fill the loaf with it. Serve immediately and cut into 6 crosswise portions at the table.

Serves 6 as a side dish or appetizer.

EGGPLANT CASSEROLE
Contributed by Pamela Kroner

5 tablespoons olive oil

5 tablespoons butter

1 medium eggplant, peeled and cut in ½-inch-thick strips

3 scallions, trimmed and finely sliced

1 bulb fennel, finely chopped

2 cloves garlic, minced

¼ pound mushrooms, trimmed, cleaned, and thinly sliced

1 15-ounce can tomato sauce

12 pitted green olives, sliced

Salt

Freshly ground pepper

Oil

2 cups cooked brown rice

½ pound Tybo cheese (or substitute a soft white cheese such as fontina or Muenster), coarsely grated

½ pound Parmesan cheese, coarsely grated

¼ cup minced parsley

Heat 1 tablespoon each of the olive oil and butter in a large heavy skillet over high heat, add about ¼ of the eggplant strips, and sauté quickly until lightly golden. Transfer from the skillet to a plate and sauté the rest of the eggplant until all is done. Eggplant is very absorbent; try not to use an excess of oil and butter, as the strips will become logged with them. Turn the strips over almost immediately after adding them to the pan, so that their sides become coated very quickly, and you will not need more than 4 tablespoons each of the oil and butter. When all are done, set aside.

Heat the remaining 1 tablespoon each of the olive oil and butter in a heavy saucepan over medium heat and add the scallions, fennel, and garlic. Stir about 5 minutes, add the mushrooms, and cook about 5 minutes, until the mushroom juices have evaporated. Stir in the tomato sauce and the olives and cook about 5 minutes longer. Season to taste with salt and pepper and remove from the heat.

Lightly oil an 8-cup casserole. Spread the brown rice in the bottom and then make alternate layers of the eggplant, sauce, and the 2 cheeses mixed, ending with the cheeses. Sprinkle the parsley over the top, cover the casserole, and bake in a preheated 350° oven 35 minutes. Remove the cover and bake 10 minutes longer, or until the top is golden. Serve from the casserole.
Serves 6.

EASY EGGPLANT
Contributed by Coille Hooven

2 tablespoons butter
1 medium onion, coarsely
    chopped
3 cloves garlic, minced
1 eggplant, peeled, cut in
    1-inch cubes, and parboiled
    5 minutes in lightly salted
    water
3 medium zucchini, trimmed
    and sliced ¼ inch thick
2 stalks celery, thinly sliced
1 28-ounce can tomato sauce
½ pound cheddar cheese, cut
    in ½-inch dice
1 tablespoon brown sugar
1 tablespoon dried basil
1 teaspoon salt
4 grindings of pepper

Melt the butter in a saucepan over medium heat, add the onion and garlic, and stir about 5 minutes, or until the onion is soft and translucent but not brown. Scrape the onion and garlic into a large bowl and add all the remaining ingredients. Mix thoroughly and pour into a large casserole. Bake in a preheated 375° oven 50 minutes. Serve from the casserole.
Serves 6.

Coille Hooven

125

Mark Adams. *Eggplant*. 1978. Watercolor. Collection the Achenbach Foundation, San Francisco

Robert Hartman

STEAMED EGGPLANT

Contributed by Robert Hartman

1 medium eggplant
1 tablespoon safflower oil
2 garlic cloves, minced and crushed
1 tablespoon minced and crushed fresh ginger root
2 tablespoons cider vinegar
2 tablespoons soy sauce
1 tablespoon sugar
1 tablespoon sesame oil

Trim off the stem of the eggplant and cut the eggplant in half lengthwise. Cut deep crosshatched gashes with a sharp knife in the skin of each half, going about halfway through the flesh. Put the halves skin up on a heat-proof plate that will fit on the rack of a vegetable steamer. Put the plate and rack in the steamer over about 2 inches of boiling water, cover tightly, and steam 20 minutes, adjusting the heat so that the water does not evaporate. Test for doneness with a sharp-pointed knife; if necessary, steam a little longer. The exact time will depend on the thickness of the eggplant. Transfer the halves to a serving dish and cut crosswise in ½-inch slices. You may peel the eggplant or not, as you choose.

While the eggplant is steaming, prepare the sauce. Heat the safflower oil in a medium skillet over medium heat until very hot. Add the garlic and ginger and stir a few seconds. Add the vinegar, soy sauce, and sugar. Stir a few seconds and remove from the heat. Stir until the sugar is dissolved and add the sesame oil.

Spoon the sauce over the eggplant slices and let stand about 30 minutes, basting occasionally. The eggplant may be served warm or may be chilled in the refrigerator 4 hours or longer. *Serves 4.*

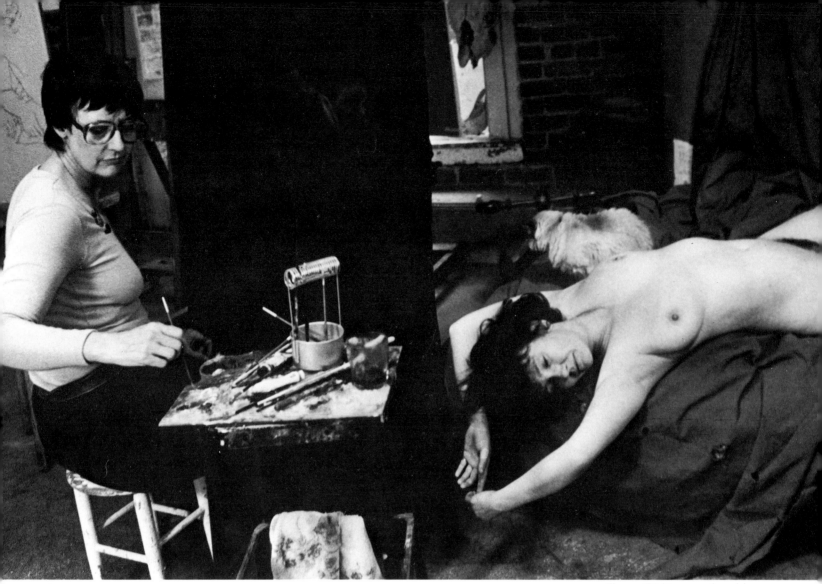

Eleanor Dickinson and model

HOPPIN' JOHN
Contributed by Eleanor Dickinson

½ pound dried black-eyed
   peas
¼ pound smoked country
   ham, cut in chunks (or
   substitute ¼ pound sliced
   bacon, cut in 1-inch pieces
   and fried)
3 cups cooked white rice
2 large onions, coarsely chopped
Salt
Freshly ground pepper

Put the peas in a saucepan with cold water that covers them by 2 inches. Bring to a boil over high heat and boil 2 minutes. Remove from the heat and let rest 2 hours. Drain, return to the saucepan with the ham (or bacon), add enough water to cover, bring to a boil, reduce the heat, and cook covered 30 minutes. Drain again, reserving the cooking liquid.

Put the peas in a bowl with the rice and onions. Season to taste with salt and pepper and moisten with a little of the cooking liquid. Pour into a 6- to 8-cup casserole and bake in a preheated 350° oven 20 minutes. Serve from the casserole. *Serves 4.*

CAROLINA FRIED OKRA

Contributed by Donna Mossholder

1 pound medium okra
⅔ cup flour
½ teaspoon salt
2 gratings pepper
½ teaspoon dried oregano
Vegetable oil

Trim off the stem ends of the okra and cut okra in ½-inch pieces. Place the pieces in a colander and wet thoroughly under running cold water.

Put the flour, salt and pepper, and oregano in a paper or plastic bag, add the wet okra, and shake vigorously so that the pieces are well coated.

Heat ¼ inch of oil in a large, heavy skillet over medium heat until very hot but not smoking. Shake excess flour from the okra in a colander, add the pieces to the skillet, and fry 5 minutes, stirring constantly. Reduce the heat, cover the skillet, and cook 5 minutes longer. Remove the okra with a slotted spoon to a serving dish. Serve immediately. *Serves 4.*

Sketch by the artist

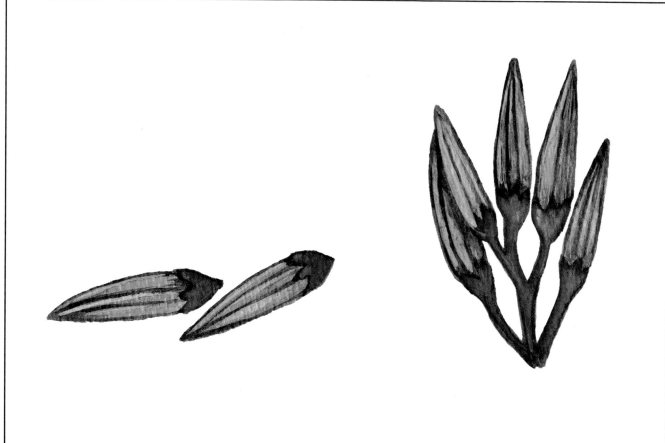

AUGUSTA'S GARLIC-TOOTHPASTE POTATOES

Contributed by Alberta Mayo

1 baking potato, well
  scrubbed
4 tablespoons butter, melted
Salt
Freshly ground pepper
3 cloves garlic, unpeeled

Cut the potato lengthwise into thirds and then cut each third into triangular French-fry size. Brush an oven-proof dish or pan lightly with some of the butter, spread the potato pieces evenly in the dish, and spoon the remaining butter over them. Season to taste with salt and pepper. Puncture each garlic clove with a toothpick and place in the dish.

Bake in a preheated 450° oven 20 minutes, or until the potato pieces are golden brown. Transfer to a plate and place the garlic cloves on the side. Eat by squeezing the garlic like a tube of toothpaste over the potatoes.
Serves 1.

Mark Adams. *Rainbow Glass.* 1979. Watercolor. Collection the artist

STEWED TOMATOES WITH TOFU
Contributed by Victor Bergeron ("Trader Vic")

1 16-ounce can stewed
  tomatoes
1 teaspoon butter
1 tablespoon dried onion
1 teaspoon brown sugar
1 bay leaf
1 teaspoon cornstarch
½ pound tofu, cut in ½-inch
  dice
Salt
Freshly ground pepper

Bring the tomatoes, butter, onion, brown sugar, and bay leaf just to a boil in an uncovered saucepan over medium heat. Mix the cornstarch with 2 tablespoons of water, pour into the tomatoes, reduce the heat, and stir until slightly thickened. Add the tofu, season to taste with salt and pepper, and simmer just until the tofu is very hot. *Serves 2.*

BAKED SUMMER SQUASH
Contributed by William Brice

3 medium-size yellow summer
  squash
½ cup butter
1 medium onion, coarsely
  grated
Salt
Freshly ground pepper

Cut the squash in half lengthwise and scoop out the seeds. Cut a thin slice from the bottom of each half so it will sit firmly. Grease a shallow baking dish with a little of the butter and arrange the squash in it.

Melt the remaining butter in a saucepan over medium heat. Add the onion and swirl 1 minute. Spoon the butter and onion into the hollows of the squash and season to taste with salt and pepper. Cover the baking dish tightly with foil and bake in a preheated 350⁰ oven 40 minutes. Transfer the squash to a dish and serve immediately. *Serves 6.*

SAUCES
AND RELISHES

Wayne Thiebaud. *Hot Dog* (detail). 1969. Collection the artist

Indian Apple Chutney ❧ Priscilla Birge

Lillian Jackson Duncan's Barbecue Sauce ❧ Ray Saunders

Cranberry Relish ❧ Priscilla Birge

Mayonnaise au Pistou ❧ John Peetz

Pineapple Vinegar ❧ Bella Feldman

Homemade Salsa ❧ Mary Heebner

Lupe's Salsa Verde ❧ Joan Brown

Sauce for Raw Vegetables, Cold Meat, or Salads ❧ Richard and Margaret Mayer

Creamy Sunflower Dressing ❧ Gerald Gooch

Vegetarian Sauce ❧ Mary Gould

INDIAN APPLE CHUTNEY
Contributed by Priscilla Birge

10 pounds tart green cooking apples, cored, peeled, and sliced
1 medium onion, minced
1 clove garlic, minced
2 quarts malt vinegar, or more if necessary
8 ounces kosher salt
4 ounces mustard seeds
4 pounds dark brown sugar
5 pounds raisins
3 ounces ground ginger
1 ounce cayenne pepper

Put the apples, onion, garlic, and about 1⅓ quarts of the vinegar in a very large, heavy, preferably enameled-iron (not aluminum) pot over fairly high heat and stir until the mixture is steaming. Cover the pot, reduce the heat, and cook, stirring very frequently to prevent any scorching on the bottom, about 20 minutes, or until the consistency is that of applesauce.

Very thoroughly stir in all the remaining ingredients. Bring the mixture back to a simmer, lower the heat slightly, and simmer about 30 minutes, stirring very frequently and adding more vinegar, as needed, to keep the mixture the consistency of applesauce.

Spoon the hot relish into hot, sterilized jars and seal with paraffin. *Makes about 8 quarts.*

Priscilla Birge

LILLIAN JACKSON DUNCAN'S
BARBECUE SAUCE
Contributed by Ray Saunders

1 cup strong espresso coffee
2 cups Worcestershire sauce
1½ cups ketchup
8 tablespoons butter
1 tablespoon salt
4 tablespoons sugar
2 tablespoons freshly ground
  pepper

Put all ingredients in a large, heavy, preferably enameled-iron pot over fairly high heat. Stir constantly until the mixture comes to a boil, lower the heat, and simmer uncovered about 30 minutes, stirring occasionally.

May be used as a sauce or for basting when grilling meat or chicken.

Makes about 4½ cups.

CRANBERRY RELISH
Contributed by Priscilla Birge

8 cups fresh cranberries,
  picked over and stems
  removed
1½ cups cider vinegar
⅔ cup water
6 cups sugar
2 tablespoons ground
  cinnamon
1 tablespoon ground cloves
1 tablespoon allspice

Mix all the ingredients in a large heavy saucepan (*not* aluminum) over high heat and stir constantly until the mixture begins to bubble. Reduce the heat, cover the saucepan, and simmer 45 minutes, stirring occasionally.

Pour or spoon the hot relish into hot, sterilized jars and seal with paraffin.

Makes about 1½ quarts.

MAYONNAISE AU PISTOU
Contributed by John Peetz

2 tablespoons heavy cream
2 ounces cream cheese
1 egg
¾ cup olive oil
½ cup fresh basil, lightly
  packed
½ small ripe tomato, peeled,
  seeded, and coarsely
  chopped
1 teaspoon salt
2 cloves garlic, coarsely
  chopped

Put all ingredients into the container of a food processor and, using the standard steel blade, process until very smooth. Alternatively, pound the basil, tomato, and garlic in a stone mortar with a pestle until they are a paste, add the remaining ingredients, and whisk until a smooth emulsion is formed.

Makes about 2 cups.

PINEAPPLE VINEGAR
Contributed by Bella Feldman

I was teaching in Uganda in the late sixties, and it was truly—before the rise and fall of Idi Amin—what Winston Churchill called it: "the pearl of Africa." There was an abundance of meat and fruit and vegetables, but the staples we take for granted were scarce. As a result, cooking took some inventive turns. This is a sample:

Cut the rind of a not overly ripe pineapple into chunks. Put them in a jar, cover with rainwater, and cover the jar with a lid. Let rest 3 weeks. Then strain the liquid into a pot, bring to a boil, cool, and store the vinegar in a corked bottle.

HOMEMADE SALSA
Contributed by Mary Heebner

6 fresh Anaheim or Poblano chilies

6 medium ripe tomatoes, peeled, seeded, and coarsely chopped

1 16-ounce can whole peeled tomatoes, drained

1 13-ounce can La Victoria-brand whole green tomatoes, drained

6 scallions, trimmed and thinly sliced

½ cup chopped cilantro (fresh coriander leaves)

2 teaspoons salt

½ teaspoon sugar

½ teaspoon ground cumin

½ teaspoon dried oregano

2 cloves garlic, minced and mashed

Juice of ½ lemon

Put the chilies on a rack directly over a medium-high gas flame and turn them with tongs until charred on all sides. Holding each chili under running cold water, scrape off the charred skin with a knife, or rub off with your fingers. If well charred, it should come off easily. Remove the core, seeds, and the inside ribs. Pat the chilies dry with paper towels, mince finely, and mash with the flat side of a chopping knife. Alternatively, place the chilies in a food processor and, using the standard steel blade, purée. Set aside.

Put the fresh and both the canned tomatoes in a bowl and mash with the hands until pulpy. Transfer to a heavy pot or saucepan, preferably of enameled iron (*not* aluminum), and place over fairly high heat. Add the mashed or puréed chilies and the remaining ingredients. Stir constantly until the mixture comes to a boil, reduce the heat, and simmer uncovered about 20 minutes, stirring occasionally. The mixture should reduce and thicken slightly.

Remove from the heat, cool, and chill in the refrigerator. Serve as a dip with corn Fritos or as a sauce for chile rellenos, eggs, etc.

Makes about 4 cups.

LUPE'S SALSA VERDE
Contributed by Joan Brown

2 13-ounce cans La Victoria-
   brand whole green
   tomatoes, drained
5 cloves garlic, minced and
   mashed
1 teaspoon white vinegar
¼ teaspoon crushed red
   pepper, or more to taste
⅓ teaspoon ground cumin
¼ cup minced cilantro (fresh
   coriander leaves)
1 teaspoon salt

Put the tomatoes in a bowl and mash with the hands until pulpy. Blend in well the remaining ingredients. Chill in the refrigerator at least 2 hours.

Excellent with hot tortillas stuffed with refried beans (page 121), cheese, and sliced fresh tomatoes.
Makes about 3 cups.

Joan Brown's bulletin
board and telephone

SAUCE FOR RAW VEGETABLES, COLD MEAT, OR SALADS
Contributed by Richard and Margaret Mayer

1 clove garlic, cut in half
2 cups mayonnaise
½ cup sour cream
Juice of ½ lemon
1½ teaspoons monosodium
   glutamate (optional)
1 teaspoon Spice Islands-
   brand Beau Monde
   seasoning
½ teaspoon dry mustard
1 teaspoon freshly ground
   pepper

Rub a serving bowl, preferably wood, with the cut sides of the garlic. Add the remaining ingredients, mix thoroughly, and chill in the refrigerator at least 2 hours.
Makes about 2¾ cups.

Flour, beans, and mortar and pestle in Priscilla Birge's kitchen

CREAMY SUNFLOWER DRESSING
Contributed by Gerald Gooch

½ cup lemon juice

1 cup rejuvelac,* or substitute water

¼ cup yellow raisins, soaked in ¼ cup warm water 1 hour

2 teaspoons sea salt

½ tablespoon Bragg's Aminos, or substitute Tamari sauce

1½ teaspoons dry mustard

½ teaspoon freshly ground pepper

1 small stalk celery, thinly sliced

¼ medium green pepper, cored, seeded, and cut in pieces

¼ cup minced parsley

1 small onion, cut in chunks

2½ cups sprouted sunflower seeds (p. 35)

2 cups safflower oil

Put all ingredients, except the sunflower seeds and safflower oil, in the container of a food processor and, using the standard steel blade, process until smooth and creamy. Add the sunflower seeds and process again. Add the oil in a slow drizzle, processing until the dressing forms a smooth emulsion. Alternatively, use a blender in the same manner. It will be more difficult to make this dressing by hand, but the more solid ingredients can be forced through a meat grinder, using the fine blade, and the liquid and powdered ones beaten in by hand, slowly adding the oil last.

Chill in the refrigerator or not, as desired. Use as a dressing with salads or over steamed vegetables.
Makes about 5 cups.

*Put ⅓ cup of spring-wheat kernels in a quart jar and fill the jar with water. After 24 hours, pour off the water, refill the jar with fresh water, and let sit another 24 hours. Repeat the process once more, and the strained liquid is rejuvelac. The process may be repeated twice more for additional rejuvelac.

VEGETARIAN SAUCE
Contributed by Mary Gould

3 tablespoons olive oil

1 medium onion, finely chopped

1 medium green pepper,
  cored, seeded, and finely
  chopped

1 clove garlic, minced

¼ pound medium
  mushrooms, trimmed,
  cleaned, and thinly sliced

½ cup pitted black olives,
  thinly sliced

¼ pound tofu, cut in ¼-inch
  cubes

1 15-ounce can tomato sauce

Juice of ½ lemon

¼ cup chopped fresh basil, or
  4 teaspoons dried

1 tablespoon Tamari sauce, or
  more to taste

Salt

Freshly ground pepper

Heat the oil in a heavy saucepan (*not* aluminum) over medium heat and add the onion, green pepper, and garlic. Stir about 5 minutes, or until the onion is soft and translucent but not brown. Add the mushrooms and stir about 3 minutes longer. Add the remaining ingredients, seasoning to taste with salt and pepper. Bring to a boil, reduce the heat, cover, and simmer about 15 minutes, or until well blended and slightly thickened.

Use as a sauce for Spider Bread (page 148) or over pasta or rice.

Makes about 3 cups.

Sketch by the artist

139

BREADS

Irma Cavat. *Vitrine Series: Boulangerie.* 1978. Collection the artist

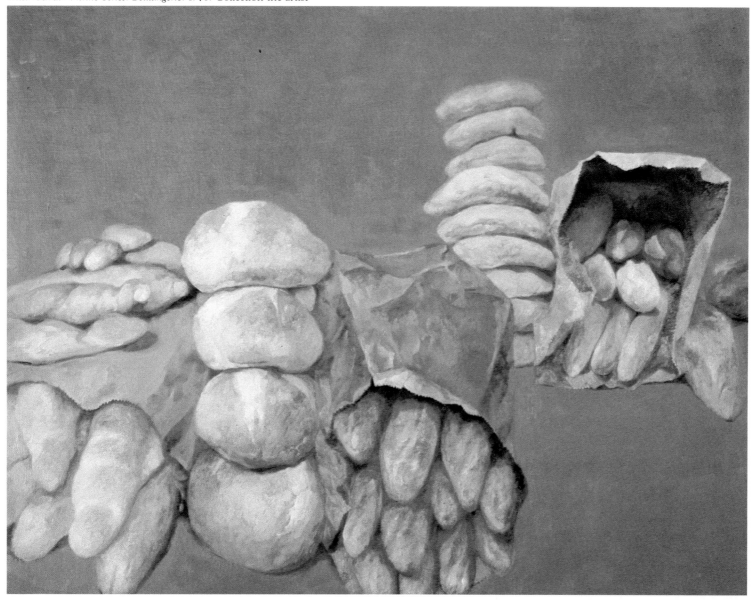

Banana Bread ❧ Toby Judith Klayman

Corn Spoon Bread ❧ Helen Lundeberg

Hamantashen Loaves ❧ Toby Judith Klayman

Easy French Bread ❧ Taffy Dahl

Manitoba Bread ❧ Alberta Mayo

Monkey Bread (Pull-Apart Bread) ❧ Charles Prentiss

Kathy's Pita Loaves ❧ Toby Judith Klayman

Spider Bread ❧ Mary Gould

Tennessee Spoon Bread ❧ Eleanor Dickinson

Menta Yeast Rolls ❧ Taffy Dahl

Our Daily White Bread ❧ Betty and Clayton Bailey

BANANA BREAD
Contributed by Toby Judith Klayman

1½ cups sifted unbleached
   all-purpose flour
1 cup sugar
1 teaspoon baking soda
½ teaspoon salt
2 large very ripe bananas
1 egg
4 tablespoons butter, melted
1 cup coarsely chopped
   walnuts
1 tablespoon butter, softened
¼ cup chopped candied
   citron
¼ cup walnut halves
¼ cup maraschino cherries,
   cut in half

Sift the flour, sugar, baking soda, and salt into a mixing bowl. Mash the bananas with a fork in another bowl, stir in the egg until well mixed, and then stir in the melted butter. Add this mixture and the chopped walnuts to the flour mixture and stir only until well blended.

Butter a 9-by-5-inch loaf pan, spread the batter evenly in the pan, and sprinkle the top with the citron, walnuts, and maraschino cherries. Bake in a preheated 350° oven 1 hour and 15 minutes. If using a low pan, check for doneness after 1 hour.

Makes 1 loaf, or serves 4 to 6.

Contributor's note: This recipe was originally by Belle Tarradash of Fall River, Massachusetts. It has been added to over years of experimentation and pleasure.

CORN SPOON BREAD
Contributed by Helen Lundeberg

3 cups milk
¾ cup yellow cornmeal
1 tablespoon sugar
1½ teaspoons salt
2 cups canned whole-kernel
   corn, undrained
5 tablespoons butter, melted
3 tablespoons safflower oil
½ medium green pepper,
   cored, seeded, and minced
¼ pound cooked ham, cut in
   ¼-inch dice
3 eggs, separated

Heat the milk in a large, heavy saucepan over medium heat until it reaches the boiling point. Gradually stir in the cornmeal and continue stirring until it is well blended with the milk and there are no lumps. Add the sugar, salt, and corn, stirring in well. Reduce the heat, cover the saucepan, and cook 10 minutes, or until the mixture has thickened, stirring occasionally.

Transfer the mixture to a large mixing bowl. Add 3 tablespoons of the butter and the safflower oil, green pepper, ham, and egg yolks. Mix thoroughly. Beat the egg whites until stiff but not dry and gently fold into the cornmeal.

Brush a 6-cup casserole with the remaining butter and pour the batter into it. Bake in a preheated 375° oven about 40 minutes, or until the center is firm and the top is nicely puffed and brown. Serve at once.

Serves 4 to 6.

HAMANTASHEN LOAVES
Contributed by Toby Judith Klayman

Filling:
    1 pound dried prunes
    3 cups orange juice
    1 pound walnuts, coarsely
    chopped
    2 cups apricot jam

Dough:
    5 cups sifted unbleached all-
        purpose flour
    1 cup sugar
    1 teaspoon salt
    2 teaspoons double-acting
        baking powder
    4 eggs
    ½ cup vegetable oil
    ½ cup orange juice
    (cooled prune cooking
    liquid can be used)

Flour
2 tablespoons butter, melted
3 egg whites, lightly beaten

Soak the prunes in the orange juice only if package directions specify soaking. Otherwise, put them in a saucepan with the orange juice over medium heat and simmer covered about 30 minutes, or until very soft. Drain, reserving the cooking liquid, and pit them. Put them in the container of a food processor with the walnuts and the apricot jam and, using the standard steel blade, process until smooth. Alternatively, pass the prunes and jam through a food mill, and grind the walnuts in a blender or nut grinder. If necessary, add a little of the cooking liquid to make the mixture easily spreadable but not runny. Set aside.

Sift the flour, sugar, salt, and baking powder into a large mixing bowl. Beat the eggs lightly in another bowl, stir in the oil and orange juice, and pour the mixture over the flour. Mix well with a wooden spoon. Press the dough down into the bowl and against the sides with your hands, turning it over several times, until it forms a cohesive ball.

Remove the dough and divide into quarters with a knife. Roll each quarter on a well-floured board with a rolling pin, or pat out with your hands, into a circle about 8 inches in diameter. Put ¼ of the prune filling in the center of each and spread it evenly, leaving 1 inch around the edge uncoated. Brush the uncoated edge with water and roll the circle up to form a loaf, pressing the edges lightly to keep the filling from escaping.

Brush a cookie sheet with the melted butter and dust with flour. Lay the 4 loaves on it seam side down and brush with the egg whites. Bake in a preheated 350° oven 1 hour. Cool on a rack before slicing and serving.
Makes 4 loaves, or serves about 16.

EASY FRENCH BREAD
Contributed by Taffy Dahl

1 package (¼ ounce) dry yeast
1 tablespoon sugar
1½ cups lukewarm (115°)
　water
3½ cups sifted unbleached all-
　purpose flour, and more as
　needed
2 teaspoons salt
2 tablespoons butter, melted
Cornmeal

Stir the yeast, sugar, and water in a large mixing bowl. Let sit 5 or 10 minutes, or until bubbles form on the surface. Sift the flour and salt into the bowl and stir or beat with a wooden spoon until the mixture is well blended. Do not knead. Set the bowl in a warm, draft-free place 1 hour, or until the dough has doubled in bulk.

Punch the dough down. Remove from the bowl and divide in half with a knife. Form each half into an elongated loaf on a well-floured board with floured hands. Brush a cookie sheet with the melted butter and sprinkle with the cornmeal. Lay the loaves on the sheet and snip several gashes on the top of each with scissors. Put the sheet in a warm place about 1 hour, or until the loaves have again doubled in bulk.

Bake in a preheated 400° oven 20 minutes, or until the crust is golden brown.
Makes 2 small loaves, or serves 4 to 6.

Note: For a crisper crust, toss 5 ice cubes into the bottom of the oven when you put in the bread.

MANITOBA BREAD
Contributed by Alberta Mayo

1 package (¼ ounce) dry yeast
1 tablespoon sugar
1 cup lukewarm (115°) water
1¾ cups sifted unbleached all-
　purpose flour, and more as
　needed
1¾ cups sifted whole-wheat
　flour
1½ teaspoons salt
½ teaspoon ground ginger
½ cup butter, melted and
　slightly cooled
3 tablespoons butter, softened

Stir the yeast, sugar, and ¼ cup of the water in a bowl. Let sit 5 or 10 minutes, or until bubbles form on the surface. Sift both flours, the salt, and the ginger into a large mixing bowl. Make a well in the center and add the yeast mixture, the remaining ¾ cup of water, and the melted butter. Mix with a 2-pronged fork, or with your hands, until the mixture forms a cohesive ball. Turn out onto a well-floured board and knead about 10 minutes, or until it is smooth and elastic and does not stick to your hands.

Grease a large mixing bowl with 1 tablespoon of the softened butter, put the dough in it, cover loosely with a clean dish towel, and set in a warm, draft-free place 1 hour, or until the dough has doubled in bulk. Punch it down in the bowl and then knead it briefly again on the floured board. Spread the remaining softened butter in a 9-by-5-inch loaf pan, put the dough in it, cover it again, and let it rise again in a warm, draft-free place until doubled in bulk.

Bake in a preheated 350° oven about 45 minutes. Test for doneness by inverting the loaf onto a rack; if the bottom sounds hollow when tapped with the fingers, the bread is done.

Makes 1 loaf, or serves 4 to 6.

Irma Cavat. *San Francisco Sourdough*. 1981. Collection the artist

MONKEY BREAD (PULL-APART BREAD)
Contributed by Charles Prentiss

2 packages (½ ounce) dry
　　yeast
⅓ cup sugar
¼ cup lukewarm (115°) water
½ cup butter, softened to
　　room temperature
¾ cup lukewarm (115°) milk
2 teaspoons salt
5 cups sifted unbleached all-
　　purpose flour, and more as
　　needed
3 eggs, lightly beaten
¾ cup butter, melted

Stir the yeast, 1 tablespoon of the sugar, and the water in a small bowl. Let sit 5 or 10 minutes, or until bubbles form on the surface.

Put the remaining sugar with the softened butter and the milk in a large bowl and stir until the butter is dissolved. Add the yeast mixture, the salt, about half the flour, and the eggs. Beat this thick batter with a wooden spoon until well blended. Cover the bowl with a clean towel and set in a warm, draft-free place 1 hour, or until doubled in bulk.

After rising, the batter-like dough will be very soft and spongy. Work in enough of the remaining flour with your hands to make a soft but workable dough. Turn it out onto a well-floured board and knead about 10 minutes, or until it no longer sticks to your hands or the board.

Grease a large bowl with a little of the melted butter. Add the dough and turn it to coat with the butter. Cover with a clean towel and set in a warm, draft-free place 1 hour, or until it has doubled in bulk again.

Punch the dough down in the bowl and then turn it out onto a well-floured board. Pat it out with your hands (rolling with a pin can make the dough overly elastic and difficult to handle) into a rectangle about ¼ inch thick. Using a sharp knife, cut the dough in a crisscross pattern to form diamonds about 2 inches wide and 3 inches long. Dip the diamonds in the remaining melted butter and arrange in layers in a 9-inch tube pan, such as a kugelhopf or a bundt mold. Cover with a clean towel and set in a warm, draft-free place 1 hour, or until the dough has doubled in bulk.

Bake in a preheated 375° oven about 35 minutes, or until golden brown on top. Unmold onto a platter. Serve while still warm, allowing guests to pull buttered sections from the whole loaf. *Serves* 6.

KATHY'S PITA LOAVES
Contributed by Toby Judith Klayman

1 package (¼ ounce) dry yeast
1¼ cups lukewarm (115°)
   water
1 teaspoon sugar
2 tablespoons olive oil
1 teaspoon salt
3 cups sifted unbleached all-
   purpose flour, and more as
   needed

Stir the yeast, sugar, and ¼ cup of the water in a large mixing bowl. Let sit 5 or 10 minutes, or until bubbles form on the surface. Add the remaining water, the olive oil, salt, and 1 cup of the flour. Stir thoroughly with a wooden spoon until well blended. Add enough of the remaining flour, ½ cup at a time, mixing with your hands, until the dough is no longer sticky. Try not to overmix and do not knead.

Turn the dough out onto a well-floured board and cut with a knife into 6 equal portions or lumps. Using well-floured hands or a rolling pin, pat or roll each into a circle about ¼ inch thick. As each circle is formed, push it to one side of the board. When all are formed, cover loosely with a towel or foil and let rest 30 minutes, or until they puff slightly. When all the circles are puffed, gather them, one at a time, lightly in the palm of your hand and squeeze gently into a ball to expel the air. Roll or pat each out again into a ¼-inch-thick circle.

Lay the circles of dough about 1 inch apart on an ungreased baking sheet and bake on the lowest rack of a preheated 500° oven 5 minutes. Quickly move the baking sheet to a higher rack in the oven and bake about 2 minutes longer, or until the circles are puffed and very lightly browned. Remove from the oven, cool, and store very soon in plastic bags to prevent a hard crust from forming. Each pita loaf should separate very easily into 2 layers, forming a pouch that can be filled as desired, with hamburger, sliced lamb, or vegetables, for instance.
Makes 6 pita loaves, or 6 servings.

SPIDER BREAD
Contributed by Mary Gould

1½ cups yellow cornmeal
½ cup unbleached all-purpose
   flour
⅓ cup sugar
1 teaspoon salt
2 teaspoons baking powder
1 cup unpasteurized sour
   milk, or buttermilk
1 teaspoon baking soda
2 eggs
2 cups milk
2 tablespoons butter

Sift the cornmeal, flour, sugar, salt, and baking powder into a mixing bowl. Mix the sour milk or buttermilk with the baking soda in a small bowl. Beat the eggs lightly in a third bowl and stir in 1 cup of the nonsour milk. Add both the milk mixtures to the dry ingredients and stir just until well blended.

Melt the butter in a 9-inch spider, or cast-iron skillet, over low heat. Remove from the heat and roll the skillet around so that the bottom and sides are well coated with the butter. Pour the batter into the skillet. Pour the remaining cup of milk over the batter but do not stir it in. Bake in a preheated 350° oven about 25 minutes.

Invert the skillet onto a serving dish. The bottom should be golden brown and the bread should have a custardlike consistency. Serve hot with Vegetarian Sauce (page 139).
Serves 4.

TENNESSEE SPOON BREAD
Contributed by Eleanor Dickinson

2 cups white or yellow
   cornmeal
1½ cups buttermilk
1 teaspoon baking soda
1½ teaspoons salt
8 tablespoons butter, melted
⅛ pound mild cheese, such as
   Monterey Jack, grated
2 eggs, lightly beaten

Bring 2½ cups of water to a rolling boil in a large, heavy saucepan over fairly high heat. Gradually stir in the cornmeal and continue stirring until the cornmeal is smooth and has no lumps. Remove from the heat and cool slightly.

Stir the buttermilk and baking soda briefly in a mixing bowl. Add the salt, 2 tablespoons of the butter, the cheese, and the eggs. Mix thoroughly. Add to the cornmeal and stir only until well blended.

Brush a large casserole with a little of the butter, pour the batter into it, and bake in a preheated 375° oven 40 minutes. Spoon the remaining butter over the top and serve at once.
Serves 6.

Judy Chicago. *Ishtar* (detail of place setting from *The Dinner Party*). 1979. Mixed medium.
Collection of Through The Flower Corporation, Santa Monica

MENTA YEAST ROLLS

Contributed by Taffy Dahl

Dough:
  2 packages (½ ounce) dry
    yeast
  ¾ cup sugar
  ¼ cup lukewarm (115°)
    water
  12 tablespoons butter
  1 teaspoon salt
  1 cup boiling water
  4 eggs, lightly beaten
  6 cups sifted unbleached all-
    purpose flour

Flour
3 eggs, lightly beaten
1 cup sugar, mixed with 2
  tablespoons cinnamon
1 cup raisins or currants
½ cup melted butter

Stir the yeast, 1 tablespoon of the sugar, and the luke-warm water in a small bowl. Let sit about 10 minutes, or until bubbles form on the surface.

Put the remaining sugar, the butter, and the salt in a large mixing bowl. Pour the boiling water over them and stir until the butter has melted and the mixture is luke-warm (115°). Add the 4 eggs and the yeast mixture and mix thoroughly. Add 3 cups of the flour and beat with a wooden spoon until well blended. Add the remaining flour and mix with your hands, pressing and turning the dough in the bowl until it forms a cohesive mass. Cover the bowl with wax paper and then with a dampened towel. Keep in the refrigerator at least 8 hours. It may be stored as long as a week, but the dough should be punched down occasionally if it rises over the top of the bowl, and the towel should be redampened when it dries out.

Turn the dough out onto a well-floured board. With floured hands or a rolling pin, pat or roll into a rectangle about 9 inches wide and 16 inches long. Brush the entire surface with the 3 beaten eggs and sprinkle the sugar-cin-namon mixture and the raisins evenly over it. Beginning at a longer edge, roll the rectangle up into a long roll. With a sharp knife, cut crosswise into 16 slices.

Brush 2 9-by-13-inch shallow baking pans with a little of the melted butter. Put 8 slices of the dough in each pan, spacing them slightly apart, and brush with the re-maining butter. Let rise about 25 minutes. Bake in a pre-heated 350° oven about 25 minutes, or until golden brown. Remove from the pans immediately, as the melted sugar may harden if the rolls are left on the pans, making them difficult or even impossible to remove. *Makes 16 pastries.*

Note: Dark or light brown sugar may be used in the filling.

OUR DAILY WHITE BREAD
Contributed by Betty and Clayton Bailey

6 cups white LaPiña flour, or substitute unbleached all-purpose flour

2 packages (½ ounce) dry yeast

2 teaspoons salt

2 teaspoons sugar

4 cups very hot, (200°) water

3 tablespoons butter, softened

Sift the flour into a large mixing bowl. Add the yeast, salt, and sugar. Mix very thoroughly. Gradually add the hot water, stirring constantly. Stir vigorously 3 minutes. Loosely cover the bowl with foil or a clean dish towel and put in a warm, draft-free place 1½ hours, or until the dough has doubled in bulk.

Grease 2 9-by-5-inch loaf pans with the softened butter. Remove cover from the dough, punch the dough down, and remove from the bowl. Divide dough in half, form each half into a loaf, and place one in each pan. Set the pans in a warm place, cover again, and allow the dough to rise until doubled again, about 1 hour. Bake in a preheated 350° oven 45 minutes.

Makes 2 loaves, or serves 8 to 12.

Joseph Goldyne. *Strawberries*. 1980. Color monotype

EGGS, PANCAKES, AND WAFFLES

French Crepes for Sunday Breakfast ❧ Mason Wells

Heavenly Eggs on Toast ❧ Mary Gould

Imprisoned Eggs for Timothy Leary ❧ Lynn Hershman

Oven Eggs ❧ Mary Gould

Reuben Quiche ❧ Peter Plagens

Hang in the Well ❧ Mark Adams

Spanish Omelets Robert ❧ John Haley

Potato Omelet ❧ Richard Diebenkorn

Alexandra's Alive Pancakes ❧ Gerald Gooch

Zucchini Omelet ❧ Helen Lundeberg

Nora Shinaver's Cornmeal Pancakes ❧ Robert Freimark

Aunt Martha's Swedish Pancakes ❧ David Mackenzie

Swedish Oven Pancake ❧ Wally Hedrick

Quiche Florentine ❧ Coille Hooven

Sunday-Morning Special ❧ Hans Burkhardt

Whole-Wheat Waffles ❧ Carl Dern

Richard Diebenkorn.
Girl and Three Coffee Cups. 1957.
Collection Yale University
Art Gallery, New Haven.
Gift of Richard Brown Baker

FRENCH CREPES FOR SUNDAY BREAKFAST
Contributed by Mason Wells

⅔ cup unbleached all-purpose
    flour
2 tablespoons sugar
½ teaspoon salt
3 eggs, lightly beaten
1¾ cups milk
8 tablespoons butter, melted

Optional flavorings:
    1 teaspoon rum or brandy
    ½ teaspoon almond extract
    ½ teaspoon vanilla extract
    Grated rind of ½ lemon
      (no white part)

Optional coatings or fillings:
    1 cup confectioners' sugar,
      sifted
    1 cup maple syrup and 2
      tablespoons butter, heated
      together
    1½ cups marmalade, jelly,
      or jam

Sift the flour, sugar, and salt into a bowl. Add the eggs and beat vigorously with a wooden spoon. Gently stir in the milk, 2 tablespoons of the melted butter, and any of the optional flavorings, except the lemon rind. Alternatively, put all these ingredients, except the lemon rind, into the container of a food processor and, using the standard steel blade, process until smooth, or use an electric blender. Pour the mixture through a very fine sieve into a bowl. If using the lemon rind, add after the mixture has been sieved. Let the mixture rest in the refrigerator overnight or at least 4 hours. Remove from refrigerator and stir well. For convenience in making the crepes, pour the batter into a pitcher or have a ladle ready at hand.

Put about 1 teaspoon of the remaining butter in a crepe pan, or a 7-inch frying pan with sloping sides, over fairly high heat. Roll the pan around so that it is completely filmed with the butter. When the pan is very hot, add just enough batter to coat the bottom of the pan, about 2 or 3 tablespoons. Immediately roll the pan around over the heat so that the batter completely covers the bottom of the pan. Cook the crepe about 30 seconds, or until the edges begin to brown. Loosen the edges with an icing spatula or a round-ended knife and turn the crepe over. Cook on this side about 30 seconds longer and then turn out onto a plate. Repeat this process until all the batter is used, stacking the crepes one on top of another. They may be kept hot by placing the plate over barely simmering water and covering with foil or a bowl.

The crepes may be served sprinkled with confectioners' sugar and folded into triangles, or flat with maple syrup and butter, or spread with marmalade, jelly, or jam and rolled up.

Makes 18 to 20 crepes, or serves 4 to 6.

HEAVENLY EGGS ON TOAST
Contributed by Mary Gould

12 eggs
4 tablespoons butter
4 tablespoons cornstarch
2 cups cold milk
1 tablespoon curry powder, or
    more to taste
1 cup chutney
Salt
Freshly ground pepper
8 slices bread, crusts removed,
    toasted and buttered

Prick the more rounded ends of the eggs with a pin or needle. Put in a saucepan with cold water to cover, bring to a boil covered over high heat, reduce the heat, and simmer 10 minutes. Crack the shells of the eggs under running cold water and then peel. Keep the eggs warm in a bowl over very hot water.

Melt the butter in the top pan of a double boiler set over simmering water. Beat the cornstarch with one cup of the milk in a bowl and stir into the butter until the mixture thickens. Add the remaining milk, the curry powder, 2 tablespoons of the chutney (chopped if in large pieces), and salt and pepper to taste. Stir thoroughly and heat 5 minutes.

Cut the eggs in half lengthwise. Using a slotted spoon, lower each egg half, yolk up, into the sauce until well coated. Serve three halves on each slice of toast. Top with the remaining sauce and garnish with the remaining chutney. *Serves 8.*

Sketch by the artist

IMPRISONED EGGS FOR TIMOTHY LEARY
Contributed by Lynn Hershman

2 eggs
3 tablespoons sweet butter
1 teaspoon dry mustard
4 strips bacon
2 tablespoons heavy cream
Salt
Freshly ground pepper
12 ripe strawberries, washed,
    hulled, and lightly sugared
1 slice toast, cut in half
    diagonally and buttered

Meeting Timothy Leary at the Berkeley Psychic Institute led to the development of this dish. Leary was guest speaker and conducted a seminar on S.M.I.L.E. (Space Migration, Intelligence, Life Extension). I was working at San Quentin at this time and was particularly struck by his leering eyes, which seemed to pierce right through the skin of his audience. Timothy has an animal cunning that defies incarceration.

Samuel Butler once said that a chicken was only an egg's way of making another egg. Eggs are the reverse of themselves: their gentle interior liquid is their skeleton. A hard yet porous shell protects the nucleus yolk that swings in place like a hammock suspended by invisible threads of albumen. Eggs are worlds, stubbornly closed. With a bit of nudging they can be cracked, penetrated, siphoned so that the flowing wet internal cosmos becomes emancipated as it passes the inner and outer sides of the same fabric.

Test the eggs for freshness. Put them in a bowl of cold water. If they sink, they are fresh.

Melt the butter in a heavy skillet. Make certain the flame is moderate. Gas fire has a system of its own. "One can only compare the gait of fire to that of an animal; it must first leave one place before occupying another; it moves like an amoeba and a giraffe at the same time, its neck lurching, its foot dragging" (Francis Ponge: *The Voice of Things [Fire]*).

When the skillet is evenly heated, rub the dry mustard over the bacon and add to the pan. Allow the bacon to sizzle.

Liberate the eggs by cracking them into a small bowl. It is important that all the elements of this dish be collectively realized, like a Utopian community. That one assume the garb of the bacon, sizzling through time, reiterating a primordial chaos during its transformation, is essential. Watching the bacon fry is undergoing an initiation of death and resurrection. When the bacon begins to crisp, turn it over. When other side is crisp, remove bacon and drain on paper towels.

Lynn Hershman's *Eye Plate*
for Imprisoned Eggs
for Timothy Leary

Pour off all but 2 tablespoons of the fat in the skillet. Carefully pour the eggs into the skillet. Baste with some of the butter and fat. Top each egg with a spoonful of the heavy cream. Continue to cook until the cream heats thoroughly. Add salt and pepper to taste. Do not drain the eggs. When they are firm, lift them, like feathers, with a pancake turner and gently place them on an eye plate. Place the eggs on the center of the plate so that the eyes are covered by a new set of eyes. Arrange the bacon vertically, like bars, over the eggs. Circle the dish with the strawberries. Freeing individuality is the only way to organize a group. Arrange the toast to look like ears and serve with a SMILE.   *Serves 1.*

OVEN EGGS
Contributed by Mary Gould

6 tablespoons butter

3 scallions, trimmed and finely sliced, including the green tops

1 medium tomato, peeled, seeded, and chopped

¼ pound mushrooms, trimmed, cleaned, and finely chopped

1 tablespoon Tamari sauce, or more to taste

1 teaspoon garlic salt

6 eggs

⅓ cup grated Parmesan cheese

Salt

Freshly ground pepper

Melt 2 tablespoons of the butter in a saucepan over medium heat. Add the scallions and sauté 2 minutes. Add the tomato and mushrooms and simmer about 10 minutes, stirring frequently, until much of the liquid has evaporated and the mixture is well blended. Stir in the Tamari sauce and garlic salt. Cover the pan and reduce the heat to very low, just to keep the mixture hot.

Put the remaining butter in a baking dish large enough to accommodate the eggs and put it in a preheated 350° oven until the butter is melted and golden. Break the eggs into the dish, spacing them slightly apart from one another. Spoon the sauce around each egg and sprinkle with the cheese. Season additionally with salt and pepper to taste. Bake 10 minutes, or longer if desired. Transfer the eggs to serving plates and surround the eggs with the sauce. *Serves 3 to 6.*

REUBEN QUICHE
Contributed by Peter Plagens

1 tablespoon caraway seeds

1 unbaked 9-inch pie shell (page 194)

½ pound corned beef, shredded

1 tablespoon Dijon-type mustard

¾ cup sauerkraut packed in brine, drained and squeezed nearly dry

1 cup coarsely grated Gruyère cheese

3 eggs, lightly beaten

1 cup light cream

1 tablespoon grated onion

¼ teaspoon dry mustard

½ teaspoon salt

Sprinkle the caraway seeds over the pie crust and press them in lightly. Prick the bottom of the crust in several places with a fork. Bake in a preheated 425° oven 7 minutes. Remove from the oven and cool completely.

Spread the beef in the bottom of the shell and coat it lightly with the Dijon-type mustard. Spread the sauerkraut evenly over the beef and sprinkle with the cheese. Mix the remaining ingredients with a fork and pour into the shell. Bake in a preheated 350° oven 40 minutes. Let rest at least 5 minutes before serving.
Serves 4 to 6.

HANG IN THE WELL
Contributed by Mark Adams

2 quarts milk
4 eggs, lightly beaten
1 loaf homemade white bread
Salt
2 red onions, sliced
½ pound dried beef (jerky),
   sliced

This is a hot-weather lunch or supper dish from the farms of the Mohawk Valley in upstate New York and was often served to itinerant hop pickers at harvest time around the turn of the century. Since there was no refrigeration, it was hung down the well to cool.

Scald the milk in a large saucepan. Remove from the fire and slowly pour in the eggs, whisking gently but constantly. Chill in the refrigerator until very cold.

To serve, spoon into 2 very large soup bowls until they are three-quarters full. To eat, break chunks of firm white bread into the milk and season to taste with salt. It is essential to serve slices of raw sweet onion and dried beef to eat along with the eggs and milk. *Serves 2.*

Mark Adams

SPANISH OMELETS ROBERT

Contributed by John Haley

4 tablespoons olive oil
2 medium onions, coarsely
　chopped
1 clove garlic, minced
2 medium green peppers,
　cored, seeded, and coarsely
　chopped
8 medium ripe tomatoes,
　peeled, seeded, and coarsely
　chopped
2 teaspoons chili powder
½ teaspoon dried oregano
½ teaspoon dried basil
Salt
Freshly ground pepper
8 eggs
1 cup half-and-half
8 tablespoons butter
½ cup coarsely grated
　Parmesan cheese
½ cup coarsely grated
　Monterey Jack cheese

Put the olive oil in a saucepan over medium heat. Add the onions, garlic, and green peppers and stir about 5 minutes, or until the onion is soft and translucent but not brown. Add the tomatoes, chili powder, and herbs, and season lightly with salt and pepper. Cook, stirring frequently, until the mixture is well blended and most of the liquid has evaporated. Remove from the heat and set aside.

Break the eggs into a bowl, add the half-and-half, and season to taste with salt and pepper. Beat lightly with a fork. Do not overbeat. Divide the mixture into 4 equal portions in small bowls. Make 4 omelets as described in the preceding recipe, using 2 tablespoons of the butter for each and omitting the filling.

Reheat the tomato sauce briefly and spoon over each omelet. Sprinkle the top of each with a mixture of the cheeses and serve at once.

Serves 4.

POTATO OMELET

Contributed by Richard Diebenkorn

1 medium potato
2 thick slices bacon, coarsely
　chopped
1 small red onion, coarsely
　chopped
3 tablespoons butter
1 tablespoon minced parsley
4 eggs
Salt
Freshly ground pepper
½ cup sour cream
Salsa Ranchera (optional)

Boil the potato in lightly salted water to cover about 15 minutes, or until tender. When cool enough to handle, peel it and cut in small thin slices. Set aside.

Saute the bacon in a small frying pan over medium heat until crisp. Lift out the pieces with a slotted spoon, drain on paper towels, and set aside.

Saute the onion in 1 tablespoon of the butter in a saucepan over medium heat about 5 minutes, or until soft. Add the potato and bacon, stir over the heat another 5 minutes, remove from the heat, and sprinkle with the parsley. Set aside.

Break the eggs into a bowl, season to taste with salt and pepper, and beat lightly with a fork. Do not overbeat.

Heat the remaining butter in a 9-inch omelet pan over medium heat. Swirl the butter around in the pan so that it melts evenly. When it is very hot and golden but not brown, pour in the eggs. Stir the eggs 3 seconds with a fork and then leave them undisturbed until the center begins to bubble and the edges look cooked. Begin pulling the outer edges toward the center with a fork, allowing uncooked egg to run onto the exposed part of the pan. Reduce the heat slightly. Gradually the eggs will appear to be almost fully set. Shake the pan in a circular motion to be sure the omelet is not sticking to the pan. Spoon the potato-bacon filling over the top and, using a long narrow spatula or a fork, flip one-third of the omelet over the center. Slide the uncovered part of the omelet partly onto a plate and then invert the pan completely to form a neat rectangular package. You may spoon the sour cream over the omelet and top with a little of the optional Salsa Ranchera, or serve them on the side.
Serves 2.

ALEXANDRA'S ALIVE PANCAKES
Contributed by Gerald Gooch

4 cups unbleached all-purpose
   flour
1 teaspoon salt
6 teaspoons double-acting
   baking powder
3 tablespoons arrowroot
3½ cups milk
1 tablespoon vanilla extract
2 tablespoons honey
Grated rind of 1 orange
   (no white part)
8 tablespoons butter or bacon
   drippings
Maple syrup
Blackberry jam

Sift the flour, salt, baking powder, and arrowroot into a bowl. Mix the milk, vanilla, honey, and orange rind, pour over the flour mixture, and beat until the batter is smooth.

Fry large pancakes the usual way in the butter or bacon drippings on a hot griddle. Turn the pancakes when bubbles appear on the surface and the undersides are golden brown.

Serve as a Sunday breakfast with plenty of pure maple syrup and blackberry jam.
Serves 8.

ZUCCHINI OMELET

Contributed by Helen Lundeberg

2 medium zucchini
2 tablespoons olive oil
1 tablespoon butter
2 medium onions, thinly
   sliced
Salt
Freshly ground pepper
4 eggs
1 tablespoon grated Parmesan
   cheese
½ teaspoon garlic salt
¼-cup crumbled cooked
   bacon or sausage (optional)
¼ cup coarsely grated
   Monterey Jack cheese
   (optional)

Cook the zucchini whole for 8 minutes in lightly salted boiling water to cover. Drain; reserve the cooking liquid. Cut off the ends of the zucchini and cut the zucchini in ¼-inch slices.

Heat the olive oil and butter in an omelet pan or a 9-inch skillet over medium heat. Add the onions and stir about 5 minutes, until soft and translucent but not brown. Spread the onions evenly in the pan and reduce the heat. Spread the zucchini slices on top without disturbing the layer of onions. Season lightly with salt and pepper.

Break the eggs into a bowl, add ¼ cup of the zucchini cooking liquid, and season with the Parmesan cheese, garlic salt, and a little pepper. Beat lightly with a fork. Do not overbeat.

Sprinkle the optional bacon or sausage over the zucchini. Pour the eggs on top. Tip the pan to distribute the eggs evenly without stirring. Sprinkle the top with the Monterey Jack cheese, if desired. Reduce the heat to very low, cover the pan tightly, and cook until the eggs are just set, about 6 minutes.

Cut the omelet in 4 wedges and invert them onto warm serving plates. The onions on top should be delicately browned. *Serves 4.*

NORA SHINAVER'S CORNMEAL PANCAKES

Contributed by Robert Freimark

1 cup yellow cornmeal
1 cup Bisquick
1 teaspoon salt
2 cups milk, or more if
   necessary
1 teaspoon vanilla extract
2 tablespoons maple syrup
Bacon or sausage drippings
2 eggs, lightly beaten

My mother served cornmeal pancakes once a week in cold midwestern winters. They were delicious with melted butter flowing through the stack, drenched in pure maple syrup (we made our own), with sausage or bacon on the side. Other times of the year we marinated blueberries or sliced strawberries in the syrup before serving, or we covered the pancakes with sour cream, heaped raspberries or sliced apricots on top, and sprinkled with powdered sugar.

Old flat cast-iron griddles—the kind that sit over two

Beth Van Hoesen. *Fresno Basket.* 1974.
Color drypoint and aquatint

burners or a wood fire—are best for pancakes. Next in preference are the old heavy electric models from the forties. I think modern skillets and griddles are too dinky for the job.

Sift the cornmeal, Bisquick, and salt into a bowl. Add the milk, vanilla, syrup, and 4 tablespoons of the drippings. Beat thoroughly with a wooden spoon until the batter is smooth. Add the eggs and blend smoothly into the batter. If the batter seems too thick, add a little more milk.

Put a griddle over fairly high heat. When it is hot, test it with a few drops of water. When the drops sizzle and dance, the griddle is ready. Fry the pancakes the usual way, using plenty of drippings. Bring the pancakes, covered with a napkin and steaming, to the table.
Serves 2 to 4.

AUNT MARTHA'S SWEDISH PANCAKES
Contributed by David Mackenzie

3 eggs
1 cup milk
½ cup unbleached all-purpose
    flour
3 tablespoons vegetable oil,
    melted butter, or bacon
    drippings
1 teaspoon sugar
½ teaspoon salt
Oil
Maple syrup
Butter

Break the eggs into a bowl and beat lightly with a fork. Add the milk, flour, oil, sugar, and salt. Beat thoroughly with a whisk until the batter is smooth and the consistency of heavy cream.

Lightly oil an 8-inch iron skillet and put it over fairly high heat. When it is very hot, ladle ½ cup of the batter into the skillet. Immediately tilt the skillet so that the bottom is completely covered with the batter and pour the excess batter back into the bowl. Turn the pancake after 1 minute, when the underside is brown, and cook about 1 minute longer. Continue in this manner until all the batter is used.

Serve the pancakes, flat or rolled up, with maple syrup and butter. *Serves 2.*

SWEDISH OVEN PANCAKE
Contributed by Wally Hedrick

1 cup milk
⅔ cup unbleached all-purpose
   flour
2 tablespoons sugar
2 eggs
½ teaspoon salt
Grated rind of ½ lemon
   (no white part)
1 teaspoon cardamom seeds,
   freshly ground
4 tablespoons butter

Put all the ingredients except the butter into the container of a food processor and, using the standard steel blade, process into a smooth batter. Alternatively, beat by hand in a bowl with a wooden spoon or a whisk.

Put the butter in a 9-inch cake pan and place in a preheated 400° oven until the butter is melted. Remove pan from the oven and brush the bottom and sides evenly with the butter. Pour the batter into the pan and bake in the oven about 35 minutes, or until the pancake is deeply browned and puffy. Serve immediately with any desired topping. *Serves 4.*

QUICHE FLORENTINE
Contributed by Coille Hooven

1 10-ounce package frozen
   chopped spinach, cooked
   according to package directions,
   drained, and squeezed dry
1 cup heavy cream
3 eggs, lightly beaten
1 teaspoon salt
⅛ teaspoon cayenne pepper
1 deep 9-inch pie shell, prebaked
   10 minutes (page 194)
½ cup shredded Gruyère cheese
½ cup coarsely chopped walnuts

Mix the spinach, cream, and eggs in a bowl and season with the salt and cayenne. Pour the mixture into the pie shell and sprinkle with the grated cheese, pushing it down lightly into the spinach mixture. Sprinkle the walnuts on top. Bake in a preheated 350° oven 45 minutes, or until puffed and lightly browned. Serve hot, or allow to rest in a warm place 30 minutes and serve warm. *Serves 4 to 6.*

SUNDAY-MORNING SPECIAL
Contributed by Hans Burkhardt

2 eggs, separated
½ teaspoon salt
1 tablespoon butter
½ cup jam, jelly, or
   marmalade

Using a whisk or an electric mixer, beat the egg whites with the salt in a bowl until stiff but not dry. Beat the yolks in another bowl with a whisk until they are thick, add 2 tablespoons of cold water, and beat until smooth. Gently fold the whites into the yolks with a rubber spatula just until they are well incorporated. Do not overmix.

Melt the butter in an omelet pan or an 8-inch skillet over medium heat. Swirl the butter around to evenly

coat the bottom and sides of the pan. Spread the egg mixture in the pan and cook without stirring about 3 minutes. Reduce the heat and cover the pan with a tent of aluminum foil, leaving room for the omelet to rise under the foil. Cook about 5 minutes longer, or until the omelet is set. It should have risen about 3 inches. Slide it onto a hot plate and serve immediately with the jam, jelly, or marmalade spread on top. This is also good topped with creamed chicken, stewed vegetables, or a Spanish sauce of tomatoes, onions, and green peppers.
Serves 2.

WHOLE-WHEAT WAFFLES
Contributed by Carl Dern

1¾ cups whole-wheat flour
2 teaspoons double-acting
   baking powder
½ teaspoon salt
1 tablespoon sugar
1¾ cups buttermilk
3 eggs, separated
4 tablespoons butter, melted
¼ cup wheat germ
Maple syrup
Butter

Sift the dry ingredients into a bowl; sift again. Mix the buttermilk, egg yolks, and melted butter in another bowl. Make a well in the center of the dry ingredients, pour in the liquid mixture and the wheat germ, and stir just until well blended. Beat the egg whites in a bowl with a whisk or an electric mixer until stiff but not dry. Gently fold into the mixture with a rubber spatula just until they are well incorporated. Do not overmix.

Make waffles in a hot waffle iron. This is enough batter for about 6 waffles, depending on the size of the iron. Serve with pure maple syrup and butter.
Serves 3 to 6.

A breakfast still-life at the photographer's

DESSERTS

Joseph Goldyne. *Flan*. 1979. Color monotype. Collection the artist

Amardine Cream ✤ *Frederick Eversley*

Danish Apple Pudding-Cake ✤ *Roland Petersen*

Banana Ice Cream ✤ *Tyler James Hoare*

Carob Dream Bars ✤ *Betty and Clayton Bailey*

California Pie ✤ *Robert Freimark*

Martin Dangott's Cheesecake ✤ *Bill Kane*

Crostata di Frutta (Florentine Fruit Tart) ✤ *Rooney O'Neill*

Twenty-Five-Minute Cheesecake ✤ *Joan Brown*

Favorite Chocolate Cake ✤ *Hans Burkhardt*

Chinese Junk Pie ✑ Tyler James Hoare

David's Chocolate Cookies ✑ David Mackenzie

Bittersweet Chocolate Kisses ✑ Veronica and Rene di Rosa

Toulouse-Lautrec Chocolate Mayonnaise ✑ Betty and Clayton Bailey

Dampfnudeln ✑ Nell Sinton

Chocolate Silk Pie ✑ Pamela Kroner

Chocolate Mousse ✑ Richard and Margaret Mayer

Honey Cake ✑ Julius Wasserstein

Fig Pudding ✑ In honor of Manuel Neri

Grandma's Keks ✑ Richard Diebenkorn

Lemon Bars ✑ Chris Camacho

Key Lime Pie ✑ Priscilla Birge

Baked Lime Pudding ✑ Frederick Eversley

Loquat Pie ✑ Ruth Asawa

Mudflat Pie ✑ Tyler James Hoare

Mangoes for Reflective Moments ✑ Penelope Fried

Fresh Orange Dessert ✑ William Brice

Peach Upside-down Cake ✑ Pamela Kroner

Dragon-Skin Pears ✑ Amy Magill

Pears a la Braque's Guitar ✑ Irma Cavat

Pecan Squares ✑ Guy Diehl

Pie Crust ✑ Art Grant

Persimmon Pudding ✑ Nancy Genn

Raspberry Tarts ✑ Pamela Kroner

Rum-and-Chocolate Pie ✑ Robert Hartman

Sesame Thins ✑ Richard and Margaret Mayer

Mildred's Sweet-Potato Pies ✑ Ray Saunders

Frozen Soufflé Grand Marnier ✑ Paul Wonner

AMARDINE CREAM
Contributed by Frederick Eversley

1 pound dried, compressed
   apricot sheets*
Sugar to taste
½ cup slivered almonds
1 cup heavy cream, whipped
½ cup finely chopped
   pistachios

Cut apricot sheets into 3-inch sections. Soak in a saucepan with 3½ cups of water 3 hours. Put the pan over medium heat and bring to a boil. Stir briefly, reduce the heat to very low, cover the pan, and simmer 1 hour, stirring occasionally. The sheets should be nearly dissolved. Add sugar to taste, a teaspoon at a time. Raise the heat slightly and stir with a wooden spoon until the mixture thickens and is creamy. Be careful not to let it scorch.

Add the almonds, stir briefly, and pour the mixture into a serving bowl. Cool and then chill in the refrigerator 3 hours. Just before serving, mound the whipped cream over the top and sprinkle with the pistachios.
Serves 4.

Contributor's note: This is a classic Egyptian pudding served during Ramadan.

*Apricot sheets are available in fancy grocery stores. Dried whole apricots may be substituted and cooked in the same manner, but they should be puréed in a food processor or pressed through a sieve after being cooked.

DANISH APPLE PUDDING-CAKE
Contributed by Roland Petersen

¾ cup butter
3 cups dry bread crumbs,
   black or whole-wheat bread
   preferred, or substitute
   graham-cracker crumbs
2 cups heavy cream
¼ cup sugar
1 teaspoon vanilla extract
3½ cups applesauce, preferably
   homemade
½ cup raspberry jam

Melt the butter in a large skillet over medium heat until golden. Add the bread crumbs and stir constantly about 4 minutes, or until lightly toasted. Remove from the heat and set aside.

Beat the cream in a bowl with an electric mixer or a whisk until it begins to thicken. Gradually add the sugar and then the vanilla, continuing to beat until the cream is very stiff.

Spread ⅓ of the crumbs in the bottom of a glass serving bowl, spread a layer of ⅓ of the applesauce over the crumbs, and top with a layer of ⅓ of the whipped cream. Repeat with 2 more layers of each. Chill in the refrigerator 3 hours or longer.

Just before serving, decorate the top with small dabs of the jam.
Serves 6.

BANANA ICE CREAM
Contributed by Tyler James Hoare

3 egg yolks
3½ cups light cream
1½ cups milk
1¼ cups sugar
2 tablespoons vanilla extract
½ teaspoon salt
5 large ripe bananas
1½ teaspoons lemon juice

Beat the egg yolks in a large mixing bowl with an electric mixer or a whisk until thick and lemon-colored. Beat in the cream, milk, sugar, vanilla, and salt. Beat about 5 minutes, making sure that the sugar has dissolved. Mash the bananas in another bowl with the lemon juice and beat them thoroughly into the cream mixture. Pour the mixture into a freezing can fitted with a dasher and seal tightly with the lid.

If using an electric freezer, follow the manufacturer's directions. If using a hand-cranked freezer, lower the can into the freezer and pack rock salt and ice around it. Crank about 20 minutes, or until the crank becomes very hard to turn. Drain the excess water from the freezer. Wipe the lid dry and remove it, being careful not to allow any water to spill into the can, and extract the dasher. The ice cream may be served at once, but it improves by ripening at least 2 hours: pack the ice cream down in the can, replace the lid, and replenish the ice and rock salt as seems necessary.

Makes about 2 quarts, or serves 6 to 8.

Mark Adams. *Baking Bananas.* 1980. Watercolor. Collection the artist

CAROB DREAM BARS
Contributed by Betty and Clayton Bailey

Crumb base:
  1 cup sifted unbleached
    all-purpose flour
  2 tablespoons brown sugar
  ½ cup cold butter
  2 tablespoons butter,
    softened

Topping:
  ¼ cup sifted unbleached
    all-purpose flour
  1½ cups brown sugar,
    tightly packed
  ½ teaspoon double-acting
    baking powder
  ½ teaspoon salt
  2 eggs, lightly beaten
  1 teaspoon vanilla
  ¾ cup shredded coconut
  1 cup carob chips

Prepare the crumb base. Mix the flour and brown sugar in a bowl. Cut in the cold butter with a pastry blender or 2 knives until the mixture is crumbly. Spread the softened butter over the bottom and sides of a 9-by-13-inch baking pan. Press the crumb mixture evenly in the bottom. Bake in a preheated 350° oven 15 minutes.

While the crumb base is baking, prepare the topping. Sift the flour, brown sugar, baking powder, and salt into a bowl. Add the remaining ingredients and stir until well mixed.

After baking for 15 minutes, remove the pan from the oven and spread the topping evenly over the crumbs. Return the pan to the oven and bake 20 minutes longer. Cut into bars and serve warm or at room temperature. *Makes 18 bars.*

CALIFORNIA PIE
Contributed by Robert Freimark

½ pound dried prunes
½ pound dried apricots
Sugar
1 cup coarsely chopped
  walnuts
4 tablespoons butter, melted
1 unbaked 9-inch pie shell
  (page 194)
1 cup heavy cream
1 teaspoon vanilla extract

Soak the prunes and apricots separately in water only if package directions specify soaking. Put them in 2 separate saucepans, cover with water, and simmer covered over medium heat about 10 minutes, or until very tender. The prunes may take somewhat longer. Drain both fruits, reserving the cooking liquids. When the fruits are cool, pit the prunes and cut them and the apricots in pieces. Combine in a bowl. Add sugar to taste (up to ½ cup). Add the walnuts and butter and mix lightly. Stir in a few tablespoons of the cooking liquids to make the mixture moist but not runny.

Pour the mixture into the pie shell and bake on the middle rack of a preheated 350° oven about 30 to 40 minutes, or until the crust is golden. Let cool to room temperature on a rack; do not chill.

While the pie is cooling, beat the cream in a bowl with

an electric mixer or a whisk until it begins to thicken. Gradually add about 2 tablespoons of sugar and then the vanilla, continuing to beat until the cream is stiff. Chill in the refrigerator.

Mound the whipped cream over the pie and serve at once.   *Serves 6.*

Note: If desired, the pie may be covered with a top crust or a lattice of pie-crust dough, in which case serve whipped cream separately, if desired.

MARTIN DANGOTT'S CHEESECAKE
Contributed by Bill Kane

1 cup heavy cream
1½ pounds cream cheese, at
    room temperature
2 scant cups sour cream
2 egg yolks
1 teaspoon vanilla extract
1 teaspoon lemon juice, or
    more to taste
½ cup sugar, or more to taste
2 tablespoons butter, softened
Boiling water

Variations:
    Semisweet chocolate bits
    4 drops mint extract
    4 ounces peanut-butter
        chips
    3 tablespoons powdered
        instant espresso coffee

Whip the heavy cream in a bowl with an electric mixer or a whisk until quite stiff. Set aside.

Beat the cream cheese in a large bowl with an electric mixer or a whisk until light and slightly fluffy. Continue beating while adding the sour cream, egg yolks, vanilla, and lemon juice. Add sugar to taste. Add the whipped cream, using the mixer on its lowest speed.

Spread an 8-cup soufflé dish with the butter. Pour in the mixture. Set the dish in a larger pan containing 2 inches of boiling water. Bake in a preheated 325° oven about 45 minutes, or until the cake shrinks slightly from the sides of the dish. Remove the dish from the water bath, cool, and chill in the refrigerator 6 hours before serving.

Variations:

CHOCOLATE CHEESECAKE: Omit the lemon juice and add 4 ounces of semisweet chocolate bits, melted and slightly cooled, before adding the sugar.

CHOCOLATE MINT CHEESECAKE: Use above method for Chocolate Cheesecake. Add 4 drops of mint extract after adding the chocolate.

PEANUT-BUTTER CHEESECAKE: Omit the lemon juice and add 4 ounces of peanut-butter chips, melted and slightly cooled, before adding the sugar.

MOCHA CHEESECAKE: Omit the lemon juice and add 2 ounces of semisweet chocolate bits, melted and slightly cooled, and 3 tablespoons powdered instant espresso coffee before adding the sugar.   *Serves 6 to 8.*

CROSTATA DI FRUTTA
(FLORENTINE FRUIT TART)
Contributed by Rooney O'Neill

Pastry:

1¾ cups sifted unbleached
  all-purpose flour
½ cup sugar
½ teaspoon grated lemon
  rind (no white part)
1 teaspoon salt
7 tablespoons cold butter
3 egg yolks

Pastry cream:

3 egg yolks
½ cup sugar
¼ cup flour
1½ cups milk, scalded
1 teaspoon vanilla extract

Filling:

6 dry almond macaroons,
  dry ladyfingers, or vanilla
  cookies, crumbled
2 tablespoons fruit-flavored
  liqueur (optional)
1½ cups sliced fruit, such as
  peaches, strawberries, or
  oranges
1 cup jelly, the same flavor
  or color as the fruit,
  melted

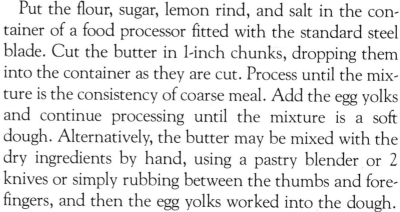

Put the flour, sugar, lemon rind, and salt in the container of a food processor fitted with the standard steel blade. Cut the butter in 1-inch chunks, dropping them into the container as they are cut. Process until the mixture is the consistency of coarse meal. Add the egg yolks and continue processing until the mixture is a soft dough. Alternatively, the butter may be mixed with the dry ingredients by hand, using a pastry blender or 2 knives or simply rubbing between the thumbs and forefingers, and then the egg yolks worked into the dough.

Wrap the dough in wax paper and chill in the refrigerator 3 hours. Flatten the dough on a sheet of wax paper with a rolling pin, pounding the dough vigorously if necessary. Cover it with another sheet of wax paper and roll it out into an 11-inch circle. Peel off the top sheet of wax paper, invert the dough over a 9-inch pie tin or glass pie dish, and quickly peel off the other sheet of wax paper. Try to work quickly, as the dough will become sticky at room temperature. Fit it into the tin or dish, cut off the excess, and flute the edge of the pastry. Chill for 1 hour.

Prick the bottom of the tart shell in several places with a fork and bake on the middle rack of a preheated 425° oven 10 minutes. Reduce the heat to 350° and bake about 15 minutes longer, or until the crust is lightly golden. Check occasionally as it bakes; if the bottom crust puffs up, prick lightly again with a fork to allow the air underneath to escape. Remove from the oven and cool.

Prepare the pastry cream. Beat the egg yolks and sugar with a wooden spoon in a saucepan until thick and lemon-colored. Stir in the flour and mix only until well blended. Set the pan over medium heat and gradually stir in the milk. Lower the heat and cook about 7 minutes, stirring constantly, until the mixture is thick and smooth. Remove from the heat, stir in the vanilla, and cool to room temperature.

Spread the cooled pastry cream in the bottom of the tart shell and strew the crumbled macaroons, ladyfin-

Priscilla Birge. *It Looks Good Enough to Eat.* 1968. Montage. Collection the artist

Left: Mark Adams. *Peaches.*
1978. Watercolor.
Collection the artist

Right: Mark Adams. *Peaches in a Bowl.*
1978. Watercolor.
Collection John Berggruen
Gallery, San Francisco

gers, or cookies over the top. Press them lightly into the cream. If desired, sprinkle them with a liqueur of the same flavor as the fruit you have chosen: Grand Marnier with oranges, etc. Arrange the fruit in a decorative pattern over the top and glaze with the jelly.

Chill the tart in the refrigerator 2 hours before serving. *Serves 6.*

TWENTY-FIVE-MINUTE CHEESECAKE
Contributed by Joan Brown

Crust:
   1½ cups graham-cracker
      crumbs (about 20
      crackers)
   2 tablespoons sugar
   6 tablespoons butter, melted

Filling:
   1½ pounds cream cheese, at
      room temperature
   4 eggs
   1 tablespoon dark rum
   1 cup sugar

Topping:
   2 scant cups sour cream
   1 tablespoon sugar
   1 tablespoon dark rum

Mix the graham-cracker crumbs in a bowl with the sugar, drizzle the butter over them, and mix thoroughly. Firmly but gently press the crumb mixture into the bottom of a 9-inch spring-form cake pan. Chill in the refrigerator at least 2 hours, or in the freezer 1 hour, to prevent the crust from disintegrating during baking.

Beat the cream cheese in a bowl with an electric mixer or a whisk until smooth and slightly fluffy. Continue beating while adding the eggs, the rum, and then, gradually, the sugar. Beat until the mixture is very smooth and creamy. Pour over the chilled crust and bake in a preheated 375° oven 20 minutes.

While the cake is baking, beat the sour cream, sugar, and rum in a bowl with an electric mixer or a whisk about 1 minute. After the cake has baked 20 minutes, spread the sour-cream mixture evenly over the top. Bake 5 minutes longer. Remove the cake from the oven, cool, and chill in the refrigerator at least 6 hours. Do not remove the sides of the pan until just before serving. *Serves 6 to 8.*

FAVORITE CHOCOLATE CAKE
Contributed by Hans Burkhardt

Cake:
  8 tablespoons butter,
    softened
  1 cup sugar
  2 ounces unsweetened
    chocolate, melted and
    slightly cooled
  3 eggs
  1½ cups sifted cake flour,
    and more as necessary
  1 teaspoon cream of tartar
  ½ teaspoon baking soda
  ½ teaspoon salt
  ½ cup milk
  1 teaspoon vanilla extract
2 tablespoons butter, softened

Icing and filling:
  6 ounces unsweetened
    chocolate
  8 tablespoons butter
  4 cups sifted confectioners'
    sugar
  1 cup milk, heated
  2 teaspoons vanilla extract
  2 cups heavy cream

Beat the butter in a bowl with an electric mixer until creamy. Gradually add the sugar and beat until fluffy. Add the melted chocolate, beating it in well. Beat in the eggs one at a time. Continue beating until the mixture is light and smooth. Sift the flour, cream of tartar, baking soda, and salt into a bowl. Mix the milk and vanilla in a small bowl. Alternately add the dry ingredients and the milk-vanilla mixture to the butter mixture, using the electric mixer on a low speed. Beat only until the batter is smooth. Alternatively, the batter may be mixed entirely by hand with a whisk or a wooden spoon.

Spread 2 8-inch cake pans with the softened butter and dust with flour, knocking out the excess. Pour the batter into the pans and bake in a preheated 350° oven about 30 minutes. When done, the cakes will have shrunk slightly from the sides of the pans and will be springy to the touch. Turn out onto 2 cake racks and cool.

While the cakes are cooling, prepare the icing. Melt the chocolate with the butter very slowly in the top pan of a double boiler over very hot but not simmering water. Gradually stir in the confectioners' sugar, then the hot milk, and last the vanilla. Remove from the heat and cool to room temperature.

Whip the heavy cream in a bowl with an electric mixer or a whisk until it begins to stiffen. Beat in 6 tablespoons, 1 at a time, of the cooled icing. Continue beating until well blended.

Cut each cake in half horizontally, making 4 layers. Fill the layers with the cream mixture and cover the whole cake with the remaining icing. If the icing has become too stiff, reheat briefly over hot water and beat until it has a spreading consistency.

Lightly cover the cake with foil or plastic wrap and chill in the refrigerator at least 24 hours. Two hours before serving, remove from the refrigerator, uncover, and let stand at room temperature.
Serves 6 to 8.

CHINESE JUNK PIE
Contributed by Tyler James Hoare

30 fortune cookies
4 tablespoons butter, melted
1 tablespoon unflavored
  gelatin
1 tablespoon orange-flavored
  gelatin-dessert powder
½ cup milk, scalded
1 tablespoon lemon juice
2 tablespoons grated orange
  rind (no white part)
⅓ cup sugar
2 egg yolks
8 ounces cream cheese
1 cup finely crushed ice
1 cup sour cream
1 cup mandarin-orange
  sections

Break the fortune cookies. Remove the fortunes and reserve. Crush the cookies on a board with a rolling pin until they are crumbs. Put the crumbs in a bowl, drizzle the melted butter over them, and mix well. Firmly but gently press the crumbs into the bottom and sides of a 9-inch pie tin or glass pie dish. Chill in the refrigerator at least 2 hours or in the freezer 1 hour.

Stir both gelatins into the hot milk in a bowl and pour into the container of a blender or a food processor fitted with the standard steel blade. Add the lemon juice and orange rind and blend or process about 40 seconds. Add the sugar, egg yolks, and cream cheese. Process 10 seconds. Add the ice and the sour cream, and process 15 seconds more.

Pour into the chilled pie crust and refrigerate at least 2 hours before serving. Decorate the top of the pie with the mandarin-orange sections and the fortunes.
Serves 6 to 8.

DAVID'S CHOCOLATE COOKIES
Contributed by David Mackenzie

1 ounce unsweetened
  chocolate
3 ounces semisweet chocolate
1 tablespoon butter
1 teaspoon vanilla extract
1 egg, lightly beaten
⅓ cup dark brown sugar,
  tightly packed
2 tablespoons flour
¼ teaspoon double-acting
  baking powder
1 cup coarsely chopped pecans
1 cup semisweet chocolate bits
Butter
18 pecan halves, or more if
  necessary

Melt the 4 ounces of chocolate very slowly with the butter in the top pan of a double boiler over very hot but not simmering water. Remove from the heat and cool slightly. Stir in the vanilla, 1 tablespoon of water, the egg, and the brown sugar. Sprinkle the flour and baking powder over the top and beat thoroughly until the mixture is smooth. Lightly stir in the chopped pecans and the chocolate bits. Chill in the refrigerator 1 hour.

Use 2 nonstick buttered baking sheets, or line 2 metal baking sheets with foil, and butter foil. Drop the batter by teaspoonfuls onto the sheets, spacing the cookies at least 2 inches apart. Press a pecan half in the center of each. Bake in a preheated 350° oven 12 minutes. While the cookies are still warm, remove from the baking sheet with a spatula.
Makes about 18 cookies.

BITTERSWEET CHOCOLATE KISSES
Contributed by Veronica and Rene di Rosa

6 ounces semisweet chocolate, cut in small pieces

3 ounces unsweetened chocolate, cut in small pieces

¼ cup freshly brewed strong coffee

⅛ teaspoon salt (optional)

½ cup (¼ pound) cold unsalted butter, cut in 1-inch pieces

¼ cup cognac or brandy

2 to 3 tablespoons sifted confectioners' sugar

½ cup unsweetened cocoa

Melt both chocolates very, very slowly in the coffee with optional salt in the top pan of a double boiler over 1 inch of very hot but not simmering water. Remove from heat, but keep in a warm place. After 5 minutes or so stir until the chocolate is completely melted and velvet smooth. Immediately remove the top pan and cool about 10 minutes, stirring occasionally. When the bottom of the pan is just warm to the touch, beat in the butter one piece at a time. Stir in the cognac by droplets and then beat in 2 tablespoons of the sugar. Taste and add more sugar if desired.

Cover 2 baking sheets with wax paper. Scrape the chocolate mixture into a large pastry bag fitted with a number-4 star tip. The bag must not be more than ⅔ full. Pipe ¾-inch rosettes of chocolate onto the paper-lined sheets. Try to work quickly and steadily, as the heat of your hands can melt the chocolate. The kisses may be placed close together, as they do not spread.

Veronica and Rene di Rosa

176

KISSES

When all are formed, sift cocoa over them generously and chill in the refrigerator 2 hours. When cold, they may be gently packed in an airtight container with wax paper between layers and then stored in the refrigerator. *Makes about 80 kisses.*

Contributor's note: Eat slowly and melt your heart out. They store perfectly in a cool place until you give in to temptation.

Editors' note: These are exceptional if the finest quality of chocolate, cognac, and cocoa is used. An orange-flavored liqueur, such as Grand Marnier or Cointreau, may be substituted for the cognac. Instead of forming kisses with a pastry bag, they may also be made into small balls and then rolled in the cocoa, in which case they are called truffles.

TOULOUSE-LAUTREC
CHOCOLATE MAYONNAISE
Contributed by Betty and Clayton Bailey

8 ounces unsweetened chocolate
½ cup plus 2 tablespoons sugar
1 tablespoon vanilla extract
4 eggs, separated
½ pound butter, softened
Pinch salt
Pinch cream of tartar

Melt the chocolate very slowly with ¼ cup water in the top pan of a double boiler over very hot but not simmering water. Stir occasionally. Remove from the heat, cool slightly, and scrape into a bowl. Using a whisk or a spoon, beat in ½ cup of sugar, then the egg yolks, the vanilla, and last the butter.

Beat the egg whites and salt in a bowl with an electric mixer or a whisk until foamy. Add the cream of tartar and beat 30 seconds more. Add the remaining 2 tablespoons of sugar gradually, continuing to beat until the whites are stiff and glossy but not dry. With a rubber spatula, gently fold ⅓ of the whites at a time into the chocolate mixture until none of the whites show. Pour or spoon into 6 individual serving bowls and chill 6 hours in the refrigerator before serving.
Serves 6.

DAMPFNUDELN
Contributed by Nell Sinton

Sponge:
- 1 package (¼ ounce) dry yeast
- 1 tablespoon sugar
- ⅓ cup lukewarm (115°) water
- ½ cup unbleached all-purpose flour

Dough:
- 1 cup sifted unbleached all-purpose flour, and more as necessary
- ½ teaspoon salt
- 1 egg yolk
- 1 teaspoon sherry (optional)
- ¼ teaspoon vanilla extract (optional)
- ⅓ cup milk
- 2 tablespoons butter, softened

2½ cups milk
½ cup butter
1 tablespoon sugar

Caramel topping:
- 1¼ cups sugar
- ½ cup boiling water

Vanilla sauce:
- ½ cup sugar
- 1 tablespoon cornstarch
- 1 cup milk
- 3 tablespoons butter
- 2 teaspoons vanilla extract

Sponge:
Put the yeast, sugar, and water in a large mixing bowl and stir briefly. Let sit about 10 minutes, or until bubbly. Stir in the flour with a wooden spoon to form a thick batter. Traditionally, this sponge, or starter, is supposed to sit "on the back of the stove" until it has doubled in bulk. Set it in any warm, draft-free place about 15 to 30 minutes, or until porous and spongy.

Dough:
Sift the flour with the salt into the bowl over the sponge after it has risen. Whisk the egg yolk in another bowl and stir in the optional sherry and vanilla and the milk. Pour over the flour and stir and beat vigorously with a wooden spoon to make a very soft dough. Add a little more flour only if the dough seems unmanageable; it will be sticky, however. Grease your hands with a little of the softened butter and knead the dough about 10 minutes, or until it becomes very elastic. Spread a large mixing bowl with the softened butter, put the dough in it, cover loosely with a clean dish towel, and set in a warm, draft-free place about 25 to 45 minutes, or until doubled in bulk. Punch down and let the dough rise again until doubled in bulk.

While the dough is rising again, put 2½ cups of milk, ½ cup of butter, and 1 tablespoon of sugar in a large, heavy, preferably enameled-iron pot or Dutch oven over low heat and stir just until the butter is melted. Do not simmer. Remove from the heat and cool to lukewarm.

Punch the dough down again and turn it out onto a floured board. Pat it out with floured hands into a circle about 9 inches in diameter. Using a floured 1¼-inch biscuit cutter, cut the dough into 12 to 16 rounds. Lay the rounds in the bottom of the pot of warm milk, turning gently to coat them well. Cover the pot loosely and set in a warm place until the dumplings have about doubled in bulk. If you have an oven-proof glass cover—or a large glass pie dish—use it as a lid; it will let you observe the progress of the rising and subsequent baking.

Put the pot, tightly covered, in a preheated 400° oven and bake 30 minutes. Check to see whether the dumplings have absorbed the liquid and are golden brown. Continue baking if necessary. Remove the pot from the oven and set on the back of the stove or in any convenient warm place.

Caramel topping:
Stir the sugar and ¼ cup of boiling water in a small, heavy saucepan over medium heat until the sugar has dissolved. Shake the pan gently over the heat until the syrup is a deep, ruddy gold. Do not allow it to become too dark or it will have a bitter taste. Remove from the heat and immediately pour in the remaining ¼ cup of boiling water. Take great care, as the syrup will bubble up furiously when the water hits it. After the bubbling has subsided, return the pan to the heat and simmer until the hardened caramel has dissolved. Pour a little of the syrup over each dumpling, making sure all are covered. Replace cover on pot.

Vanilla sauce:
Stir the sugar, cornstarch, and milk in a saucepan over medium heat until the sugar is dissolved and the mixture has thickened and is translucent. Remove from the heat and stir in the butter and then the vanilla. This sauce may be allowed to cool and then be reheated briefly over a low flame.

At serving time, transfer the dumplings to a warm platter and pass the sauce separately.
Serves 6 to 8.

Note: In place of the vanilla sauce, your favorite recipe for custard sauce, or crème anglaise, may be substituted.

Nell Sinton

CHOCOLATE SILK PIE
Contributed by Pamela Kroner

4 ounces unsweetened
    chocolate
½ cup butter, softened
1½ cups sifted confectioners'
    sugar
4 teaspoons vanilla extract
¼ teaspoon salt
3 eggs
1 prebaked 9-inch pie shell
    (page 194)
1½ cups heavy cream
¼ cup sugar

Melt the chocolate very slowly in the top pan of a double boiler over very hot but not simmering water. Remove from the heat and cool slightly.

Beat the butter in a bowl with an electric mixer or a whisk until creamy. Gradually add the confectioners' sugar, continuing to beat until the mixture is fluffy. Add the chocolate, 2 teaspoons of the vanilla, and the salt. Beat until well blended. Add the eggs one at a time, beating for 5 minutes after each is added. Pour the mixture into the pie shell and chill in the refrigerator 6 hours.

Beat the cream in a bowl with an electric mixer or a whisk until it begins to thicken. Gradually add the sugar and then the remaining 2 teaspoons of vanilla, beating constantly until the cream is stiff. Store in the refrigerator until serving time. Just before serving, spread the whipped cream over the pie.
Serves 6.

Sketch by the artist

CHOCOLATE MOUSSE
Contributed by Richard and Margaret Mayer

8 ounces semisweet chocolate
5 tablespoons Grand Marnier,
    dark rum, brandy, or water
6 eggs, separated
Pinch salt
Pinch cream of tartar
1½ cups heavy cream
3 tablespoons sugar
1 teaspoon vanilla extract

Melt the chocolate with the preferred liquid very slowly in the top pan of a double boiler over very hot but not simmering water. Stir occasionally. Remove from the heat and cool slightly. Beat in the egg yolks with a whisk and scrape the mixture into a bowl.

Beat the egg whites and salt in a bowl with an electric mixer or a whisk until foamy. Add the cream of tartar and beat until stiff but not dry. Gently fold into the chocolate mixture. Pour the mousse into a serving bowl and chill in the refrigerator 6 hours.

Beat the cream in a bowl with an electric mixer or a whisk until it begins to thicken. Gradually add the sugar and then the vanilla, continuing to beat until the cream is stiff. Mound the cream over the mousse or serve separately in a bowl.
Serves 6.

Wayne Thiebaud. *Cake on a Stand.* 1963–64. Courtesy Allan Stone Gallery, New York

Wayne Thiebaud. *Pie Rows.* 1961. Collection the artist

HONEY CAKE
Contributed by Julius Wasserstein

4 cups sifted unbleached
  all-purpose flour
2 teaspoons double-acting
  baking powder
2 teaspoons baking soda
6 eggs
½ cup brown sugar, tightly
  packed
2 cups honey
Grated rind of 2 lemons
  (no white part)
Juice of 2 lemons
¾ cup vegetable oil
1 cup cold coffee
½ teaspoon ground coffee
½ pound pecans or walnuts,
  finely ground
3 tablespoons butter, softened

Sift the flour, baking powder, and baking soda into a bowl. Set aside.

Beat the eggs lightly with a whisk in a large mixing bowl. Stir in the brown sugar until well mixed. Add the honey, lemon rind and juice, oil, cold coffee, and ground coffee. Mix thoroughly. Stir in all the nuts except ¼ cup. Add the flour mixture all at once. Stir vigorously with a wooden spoon or mix with your hands until the flour is well incorporated with the other ingredients.

Spread a 9-by-13-inch baking pan with half the butter. Line the pan with wax paper, and spread the paper with the remaining butter. Pour the batter into the pan and sprinkle the top with the reserved nuts. Bake in a preheated 350° oven 1 hour.
Serves 6 to 8.

Note: This cake improves if wrapped in foil or plastic and left to stand 2 or 3 days or even a week.

Julius Wasserstein

FIG PUDDING
Contributed in honor of Manuel Neri

1 pound dried figs, coarsely
chopped
2 cups milk
1½ cups sifted unbleached
all-purpose flour
1¼ cups fresh bread crumbs
1 cup sugar
2½ teaspoons double-acting
baking powder
1 teaspoon freshly grated
nutmeg
1 teaspoon cinnamon
¾ teaspoon salt
3 eggs, lightly beaten
¾ pound suet, finely ground
in a meat grinder or grated
2 teaspoons grated lemon rind
1 tablespoon butter, softened

Hard sauce:
1 cup unsalted butter,
softened to room
temperature
1½ cups light or dark
brown sugar, tightly
packed
6 tablespoons dark rum
1 tablespoon grated orange
rind (no white part)
1 tablespoon grated lemon
rind (no white part)
¼ teaspoon freshly grated
nutmeg
¼ cup cognac or brandy,
heated

Put the figs and milk in a saucepan over medium heat, bring to a boil, cover the pan, lower the heat, and simmer 25 minutes. Remove from the heat and set aside.

Mix all the dry ingredients thoroughly in a large bowl. Using an electric mixer, a whisk, or a wooden spoon, beat in the eggs, suet, lemon rind, and the fig mixture.

Grease a 1½-quart pudding mold and its lid with the softened butter. Pour the batter into the mold and cover tightly. If desired, the pudding may now be refrigerated 24 hours before steaming.

Set the mold on a trivet in a large pot, add boiling water to come halfway up the sides of the mold, cover the pot, and steam 2 hours. As the pudding steams, add more boiling water as necessary to maintain the original level and check that the water is actually boiling, not simmering, or the pudding will be heavy.

While the pudding is steaming, prepare the hard sauce. Beat the butter with an electric mixer or a whisk until pale and fluffy. Press the brown sugar through a fine sieve to eliminate lumps and beat gradually into the butter. Beat in the orange rind, lemon rind, and nutmeg. Chill in the refrigerator until about 20 minutes before serving time. Whisk the sauce briefly to restore fluffiness and transfer to a serving bowl.

After steaming the pudding, remove it from the pot and let rest 20 minutes before serving; if you wish it to wait slightly longer, turn off the heat and let it rest on its trivet in the pot (which should be uncovered). Unmold it onto a hot serving plate, pour the cognac over it, and ignite. Serve the hard sauce on the side.
Serves 6.

Editors' note: The pudding may be steamed in a 6-cup earthenware or stainless-steel bowl. In England these are called pudding basins. The bowl should be covered with buttered wax paper and then heavy aluminum foil, which are tied securely with string around the rim. True suet, incidentally, is not just any beef fat, but the fat surrounding the kidneys. It is waxy and white.

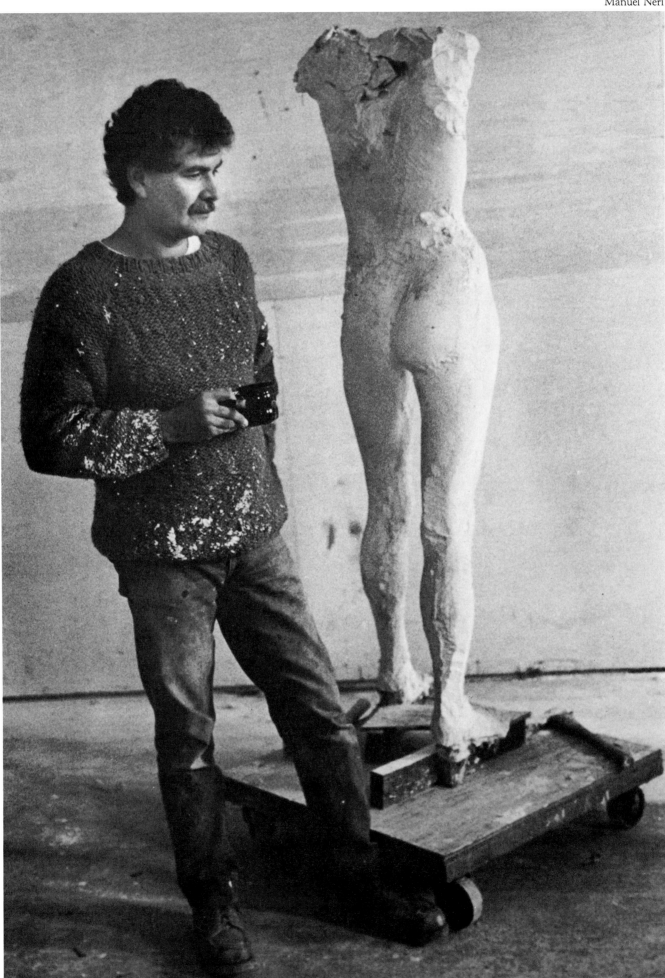

GRANDMA'S KEKS
Contributed by Richard Diebenkorn
With many thanks to C. L. V.

1½ cups sifted unbleached
  all-purpose flour
1 teaspoon baking soda
1 tablespoon ground ginger
½ teaspoon cinnamon
½ teaspoon ground nutmeg
2 eggs
½ cup brown sugar
½ cup sour cream
½ cup molasses
½ cup butter, melted
½ cup finely chopped
  crystallized ginger
Confectioners' sugar

Sift the flour, baking soda, ginger, cinnamon, and nutmeg into a bowl. Add all the remaining ingredients except the confectioners' sugar and beat vigorously with a spoon until the batter is well mixed and smooth.

Insert fluted paper or aluminum cups in a 12-cup muffin pan. Spoon the batter into the cups, filling them about halfway. Bake in a preheated 325° oven about 15 minutes, or until the cakes are firm to the touch. Remove from the pan and cool on a rack. Sprinkle with confectioners' sugar before serving.
Makes 12 keks or cupcakes.

Note: If fluted cups are unavailable, grease muffin tins with softened butter, dust well with flour, knocking out excess, and proceed as above.

LEMON BARS
Contributed by Chris Camacho

1 cup plus 2 tablespoons
  butter, softened
½ cup sifted confectioners'
  sugar
¾ cup sifted bleached
  all-purpose flour
3 eggs
1 cup sugar
½ cup lemon juice

Spread a 9-by-9-inch baking pan generously with 2 tablespoons of the butter. Set it aside.

Beat the remaining butter in a bowl with a whisk or an electric mixer until creamy. Gradually add the confectioners' sugar, beating until the mixture is fluffy. Add the flour and stir with a spoon until the mixture is well blended and smooth. Spread this pastry evenly in the bottom of the baking pan.

Beat the eggs lightly in a bowl and gradually beat in the sugar and lemon juice. Spread evenly over the pastry. Bake in a preheated 350° oven 25 minutes. Remove from the oven, cool slightly, and cut into bars.
Makes 12 bars.

KEY LIME PIE
Contributed by Priscilla Birge

Crust:
   1½ cups zwieback crumbs
   ¼ cup confectioners' sugar
   6 tablespoons butter, melted

Filling:
   4 egg yolks
   1 14-ounce can sweetened
      condensed milk
   1 teaspoon grated lime rind
      (no white part)
   ½ cup lime juice
1 pre-baked 9-inch pie shell
   (page 194)

Topping:
   4 egg whites
   ¼ teaspoon salt
   ⅛ teaspoon cream of tartar
   6 tablespoons sugar

Put the crumbs in a bowl with the confectioners' sugar and drizzle the butter over them. Stir until well mixed. Press firmly but gently into the bottom and sides of a 9-inch pie dish or pie tin. Chill in the refrigerator at least 2 hours or in the freezer 1 hour.

When the pie shell is well chilled, prepare the filling. Whisk the egg yolks in a bowl until thick and lemon-colored. Add the condensed milk, lime rind, and lime juice. Stir until well blended and immediately pour into the pie shell. Chill in refrigerator for at least 3 hours.

Beat the egg whites with the salt in a bowl with an electric mixer or a whisk until frothy. Add the cream of tartar and beat until glossy. Gradually add the sugar, beating until the whites are very stiff. Spread this meringue over the pie filling, making sure the edges are well covered. Bake in a preheated 300° oven 15 minutes, or until the peaks of the meringue are golden.
Serves 6 to 8.

BAKED LIME PUDDING
Contributed by Frederick Eversley

⅓ cup superfine sugar
3 tablespoons unbleached
   all-purpose flour
½ teaspoon cinnamon
¼ teaspoon salt
2 eggs, separated, plus 1 yolk
3 tablespoons rum
1 teaspoon grated lime rind
   (no white part)
¼ cup lime juice
1¼ cups milk
2 tablespoons butter, softened
Boiling water

Sift the sugar, flour, cinnamon, and salt into a bowl. Set aside. Whisk the 3 egg yolks in a bowl until thick and lemon-colored. Add the rum, lime rind, lime juice, and milk. Stir until smooth. Combine with the dry ingredients, stirring with a whisk until the mixture is well blended.

Beat the 2 egg whites in a bowl with an electric mixer or a whisk until barely stiff. With a rubber spatula, fold very gently into the other mixture until none of the whites show.

Spread the butter on the bottom and sides of a 9-inch glass pie dish and pour the pudding mixture into it. Set the dish in a larger pan containing boiling water that will come up to half the height of the dish. Bake in a preheated 350° oven 30 minutes. Remove the pudding from the oven, cool, and chill in the refrigerator 6 hours.
Serves 6.

LOQUAT PIE
Contributed by Ruth Asawa

2 quarts fresh loquats, stems
and flower tips removed,
skinned and pitted
Juice of 1 lemon
1 cup sugar
2 tablespoons flour
1 unbaked 9-inch pie shell
(page 194)
2 tablespoons butter

Put the loquats in a bowl and sprinkle with the lemon juice, sugar, and flour. Stir lightly with a wooden spoon, without breaking the fruit, until it is well mixed with the sugar and flour. Pour the fruit with all the juice into the pie shell, spreading it evenly. Dot the top with the butter.

Bake in a preheated 425° oven 10 minutes. Reduce the heat to 350° and bake about 30 minutes longer. The loquats should be very tender and the juices thickened. Remove from the oven, cool, and chill in the refrigerator 3 hours.
Serves 6.

MUDFLAT PIE
Contributed by Tyler James Hoare

12 Oreo cookies
4 tablespoons butter, melted
1 quart chocolate-chip/mint
ice cream
1½ cups Hershey's chocolate
syrup
2 cups heavy cream
4 tablespoons sugar
1 teaspoon vanilla extract
2 ounces semisweet chocolate,
chilled
12 maraschino cherries

Crush the cookies on a board with a rolling pin until they are crumbs. Put the crumbs in a bowl, drizzle the butter over them, and mix thoroughly. Firmly but gently press the crumbs into the bottom and sides of a 9-inch pie dish or pie tin. Freeze at least 1 hour.

Allow the ice cream to soften at room temperature until it reaches a spreading consistency. Gently spread it evenly over the chilled crust, taking care not to dislodge the crumb crust, and pour the chocolate syrup over it. Freeze at least 2 hours.

Just before serving, beat the cream in a bowl with an electric mixer or a whisk until it begins to thicken. Gradually add the sugar, beating constantly, and then beat in the vanilla. Spread the cream over the frozen pie. Using a vegetable peeler, scrape curls of the chocolate over the top. Garnish with the cherries.
Serves 6.

Note: Plain chocolate-chip ice cream may be substituted for the chocolate-chip/mint.

Sandy Shannonhouse. *Gateau.* (n.d.) Porcelain.
Courtesy Quay Gallery, San Francisco

Penelope Fried sharing a reflective moment with a friend

MANGOES FOR REFLECTIVE MOMENTS
Contributed by Penelope Fried

4 large very ripe mangoes,
  peeled and sliced
2 tablespoons lime juice
¼ cup rose-petal syrup
  (see *Editors' note*)
¾ cup heavy cream, whipped,
  or 1 cup *crème fraîche*
¼ cup fresh rose petals
Edible silver leaf (optional—
  see *Editors' note*)

Gently mix the mango slices with the lime juice in a bowl and then arrange them on a beautiful serving plate. Gently fold 1 tablespoon of the rose-petal syrup into the whipped cream or the *crème fraîche* and drizzle the remainder over the mangoes. Spoon the cream over the mangoes. Decorate with the rose petals and, if desired, bits of the edible silver leaf.
Serves 4.

Editors' note: Rose-petal syrup is imported from Bulgaria and is available in shops specializing in Near Eastern delicacies. Rose-petal jam may be substituted, but it should be strained and thinned slightly with rose water before being folded into the cream and drizzled over the mangoes. Edible silver leaf may be found in shops specializing in Indian delicacies. (Under *no* circumstances may it be substituted with regular silver leaf.)

FRESH ORANGE DESSERT
Contributed by William Brice

6 navel or blood oranges
1 6-ounce can frozen orange
   juice, thawed
2 tablespoons apricot
   preserves, strained
¼ cup thinly sliced blanched
   almonds, lightly toasted
¼ cup fresh mint leaves,
   lightly packed

Using a very sharp knife, pare all the rind from the oranges, leaving none of the white membrane. Cut the oranges crosswise into slices and then cut the slices in half. Remove any seeds. Put the slices in a serving bowl.

Heat the orange juice with the apricot preserves in a small saucepan. Bring just to a boil, stir thoroughly, remove from the heat, and cool. Pour the orange-apricot mixture over the oranges, toss lightly, and chill in the refrigerator at least 2 hours.

Just before serving, toss lightly again and sprinkle with the almonds and mint.
Serves 4.

PEACH UPSIDE-DOWN CAKE
Contributed by Pamela Kroner

4 tablespoons butter
1¾ cups sugar
4 large fresh peaches, peeled,
   pitted, and sliced
1 cup sifted unbleached
   all-purpose flour
1 teaspoon double-acting
   baking powder
¼ teaspoon salt
2 eggs
½ teaspoon almond extract
1 teaspoon vanilla extract
½ cup milk, scalded with
   1 tablespoon butter
1 cup heavy cream, whipped,
   seasoned to taste with sugar
   and vanilla extract

Melt the butter in a 9-by-9-inch cake pan over very low heat. Do not allow it to brown. Remove from the heat and sprinkle 1 cup of the sugar evenly in the bottom of the pan. Arrange the peach slices in an attractive pattern over the sugar. Set aside.

Sift the flour, baking powder, and salt into a bowl. Set aside.

Whisk the eggs in another bowl until very light. Gradually beat in the remaining ¾ cup of sugar. Add the almond, vanilla, and scalded milk and stir until well blended. With a rubber spatula, fold in the reserved flour mixture, about ¼ cup at a time, until the batter is smooth. Alternatively, the eggs, and then the added sugar, may be beaten with an electric mixer on high speed and the other ingredients added with the mixer on low speed.

Pour the batter over the peaches and bake in a preheated 350° oven 45 minutes, or until the cake is springy to the touch. Cool 5 minutes in the pan. Run a knife around the edges of the pan to loosen the cake and invert it onto a platter. Serve the cake warm or at room temperature. Pass the whipped cream in a bowl.
Serves 6.

DRAGON-SKIN PEARS
Contributed by Amy Magill

Approximately 3 cups assorted fresh, canned, or candied Oriental fruits, such as papaya, pineapple, mandarin oranges, lichees, dragon's eyes (longans), kumquats, candied ginger, and sugarcane, cut in ½-inch chunks or cubes

2 cups freshly squeezed orange juice

1 cup sugar

2 tablespoons Grand Marnier or other fruit liqueur (optional)

¼ teaspoon five-spice powder* (optional)

4 barely ripe pears, with attractive skin markings

2 cups colored rock-sugar crystals

½ cup brandy, heated

Spear the fruit chunks or cubes on the top 2 inches of 24 3-inch toothpicks, alternating colors and flavors and making them look as attractive as possible. Set aside.

Stir the orange juice and sugar in a saucepan over medium heat until the sugar has dissolved, boil 2 minutes, and reduce the heat to very low. Stir in the optional liqueur and five-spice powder and any syrups from canned fruits you have used.

Cut the pears in half and core them. Slide them into the simmering syrup, raise the heat slightly, and poach 3 to 10 minutes. The time will depend on the ripeness of the pears. They should be poached till tender but not mushy. Transfer the pears, skin up, to a warm platter, stick 3 of the fruit-topped toothpicks in each half, and sprinkle with the rock sugar. Present the pears at once to your guests. Ignite the heated brandy and pour over the pears. The effect should be of a cluster of flaming jewels. *Serves 4 to 8.*

*Five-spice powder contains anise, star anise, fennel, cloves, and cinnamon. It is available in Chinese markets.

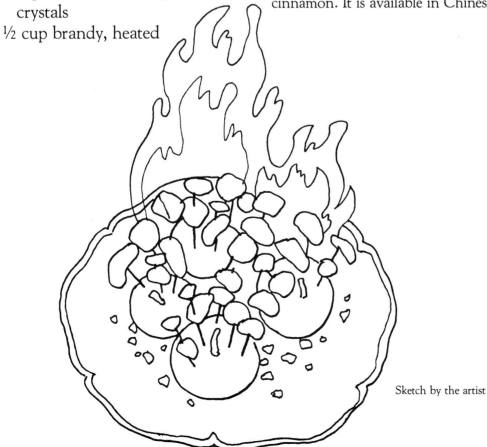

Sketch by the artist

PEARS À LA BRAQUE'S GUITAR
Contributed by Irma Cavat

1 orange

7 tablespoons sugar or honey

2-inch piece vanilla bean, split, or 2 teaspoons vanilla extract

6 firm (but not underripe) pears

2 tablespoons cornstarch

3 or 4 tablespoons rum, brandy, or cognac

2 3-inch sticks cinnamon

3 tablespoons chopped pecans, walnuts, or almonds (optional)

Peel the orange in lengthwise strips with a rotary peeler (do not include any white part). Cut each strip into very thin lengthwise strips (these will eventually serve as the strings of the pear guitars). Poach strips in a small saucepan of boiling water 5 minutes, drain, and pat dry with paper towels. Squeeze the juice from the orange and strain.

Place sugar or honey in a low-sided enameled-iron or stainless-steel pan or deep skillet large enough to hold the pears in a single layer. Add the orange juice, 1½ cups water, and the vanilla bean (if using vanilla extract, add it as directed below). Bring to a boil, stirring until the sugar has dissolved, and simmer uncovered 5 minutes.

Peel the pears and cut in half lengthwise. Remove cores neatly (a small melon-ball cutter is ideal for this purpose) and with a paring knife carefully cut away the tough, stringy strip that runs from the core up to the stem end and down to the blossom end.

Place the pear halves and the orange peel in the simmering syrup and poach gently 10 or 15 minutes, or until the pears can be easily pierced with a fork. Do not overcook: the pears should be tender but not mushy. Carefully remove with a slotted spoon to a large plate or a platter and let cool. Simmer the syrup 5 minutes longer to reduce somewhat. Some of the orange peel will have stuck to the pears and some will have remained in the syrup: don't let that worry you.

While pears are poaching, split the cinnamon sticks lengthwise into 12 strips with a large, heavy knife.

Dissolve the cornstarch in two tablespoons of cold water and stir into the syrup. Stir constantly until the syrup is clear. Remove from stove. Stir in the rum. (Add the vanilla extract, if used.)

When the pears are cool enough to handle, carefully insert a strip of cinnamon stick in the stem end of each pear half to represent the neck of the guitar. Arrange the pear halves, flat side up, on a deep platter. Pick off and reserve any of the orange peel that may have adhered to the pears.

Pour the syrup over the pear halves, straining out the orange peel and vanilla bean (discard vanilla bean). Arrange 3 or 4 orange strips lengthwise down the center of each pear half to resemble the strings of a guitar. If desired, sprinkle chopped nuts around the pears. Serve barely warm, at room temperature, or well chilled. *Serves* 6.

Note: If one wants to gild the lily, serve the pears with a bowl of *crème fraîche* or sour cream. Incidentally, these pears are not supposed to look like realistic guitars; remember, neither did Braque's.

Mark Adams. *Bosc Pears.*
1980. Watercolor.
Collection the artist

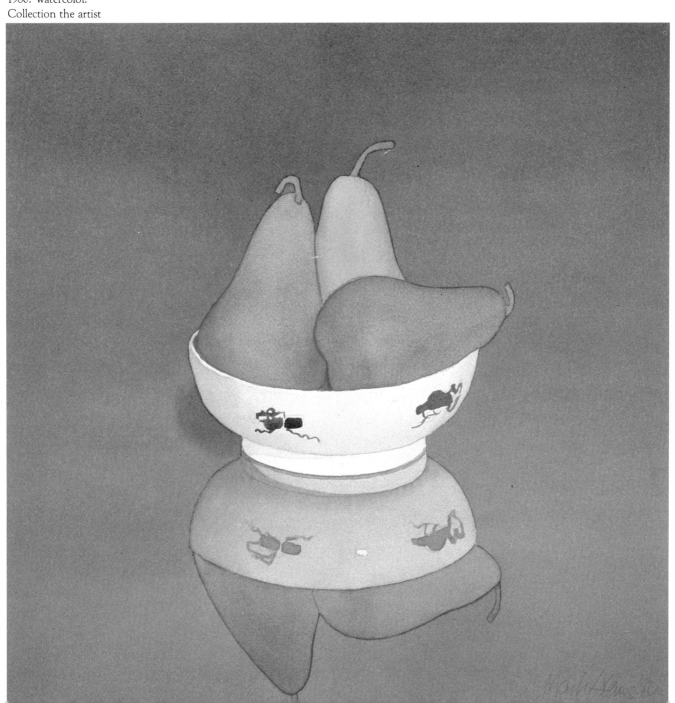

PECAN SQUARES
Contributed by Guy Diehl

½ pound shelled pecans

2 eggs

1 cup brown sugar, tightly
  packed

8 ounces pitted dates, cut in
  small pieces

1 cup shredded coconut

2 tablespoons butter, softened

Put the nuts in the container of a food processor and, using the standard steel blade, finely grind. Transfer to a bowl and set aside.

Reattach the container and the blade to the processor. Put the eggs, brown sugar, and dates in the container and thoroughly blend. Alternatively, use a blender instead of a processor. Add the date mixture with ¾ cup of the coconut to the nuts and mix thoroughly. Grease a 9-by-9-inch baking pan with the butter. Spread the batter evenly in it, sprinkle with the remaining coconut, and bake in a preheated 350° oven 15 minutes. Remove from the oven, cool slightly, and cut into squares. Serve warm or at room temperature.

Makes 16 squares.

PIE CRUST
Contributed by Art Grant

2 cups sifted unbleached
  all-purpose flour, and more
  as needed

2 teaspoons salt

1 tablespoon sugar

1 cup cold butter

7 tablespoons ice water

3 tablespoons currant or apple
  jelly, melted (optional)

Put the flour, salt, and sugar in the container of a food processor fitted with the standard steel blade. Cut the butter into 1-inch chunks; then begin processing, dropping them into the container as they are cut. Process until the mixture is the consistency of coarse meal. Alternatively, the butter may be mixed with the dry ingredients by hand, using a pastry blender or 2 knives, or simply by rubbing between the thumbs and forefingers.

Transfer the mixture to a large bowl. Stirring rapidly with a 2-pronged fork, add the ice water. Mix lightly with your hands, pressing the dough down in the bowl and turning it over several times until it forms a cohesive mass. Do not knead or overmix. Wrap the dough in wax paper and chill in the refrigerator at least 2 hours, or store as long as 3 days. This rest, which relaxes the gluten, is essential for a good, flaky pastry.

Using half the dough at a time, roll out with a rolling pin on a well-floured board into an 11-inch circle. Fit the circle into a 9-inch pie tin or glass pie dish. Try not to stretch the dough as it is fitted into the dish. Trim off the excess and flute the edge of the pastry or not, as desired.

To prebake an unfilled pie shell, fit a piece of foil over the pastry and press it lightly against the sides and bottom. Spread about 2 cups of dried beans evenly over the foil. Bake on the middle rack of a preheated 425° oven 10 minutes. Remove the foil and beans from the shell, reserving the beans for repeated use. Optionally, the shell may now be brushed with the jelly, which helps keep the crust from becoming soggy when it later receives a moist filling. Prick the bottom of the shell in several places with a fork. Reduce the oven to 350° and bake about 15 minutes longer, or until the crust is lightly golden. Check occasionally during this last baking; if the bottom of the crust puffs up, prick very lightly with a fork to allow the air underneath to escape.
Makes 2 pie shells.

Art Grant

PERSIMMON PUDDING

Contributed by Nancy Genn

2 to 4 ripe persimmons,
  peeled and seeded
1 cup sifted unbleached
  all-purpose flour
1 cup sugar
2 teaspoons baking soda
¼ teaspoon cinnamon
¼ teaspoon salt
1 egg
½ cup milk
¼ teaspoon vanilla extract
6 tablespoons butter, melted
Boiling water

Put the persimmons in the container of a food processor and, using the standard steel blade, purée. Alternatively, force them through a food mill. You will need 2 scant cups of purée for the pudding.

Sift all the dry ingredients into a mixing bowl. Set aside.

Beat the egg in another bowl until it is light and frothy and then stir in the milk, the persimmon purée, the vanilla, and 4 tablespoons of the butter. Add this mixture to the dry ingredients and stir with a wooden spoon until well blended.

Brush an 8-cup pudding mold with the remaining butter and pour the mixture into it. The mold should not be more than ⅔ full. Cover the mold tightly with its lid. Place the mold on a trivet in a large pot containing 1 to 2 inches of boiling water. Cover the pot tightly and steam the pudding 3 hours over low to medium heat, replenishing the boiling water when necessary. Alternatively, though not as satisfactorily, steam the pudding in the top pan of a double boiler over simmering water. (For an alternative method of covering a pudding mold, see Fig Pudding, p. 184.)

Just before serving, unmold the pudding onto a warm dish. Serve hot or warm.   *Serves 4 to 6.*

Note: Whipped cream, sweetened to taste and flavored with vanilla, may accompany the pudding, if desired.

RASPBERRY TARTS
Contributed by Pamela Kroner

1 recipe pie-crust dough
(page 194)

Filling:
    8 ounces cream cheese,
        at room temperature
    4 tablespoons ricotta
    ½ cup sugar
    1 teaspoon vanilla extract
    1 teaspoon brandy, or
        kirsch
    1½ cups fresh raspberries

Glaze:
    1 cup thinly sliced fresh
        strawberries
    4 tablespoons sugar
    1 tablespoon cornstarch,
        mixed with 2 tablespoons
        water

Divide the dough into 6 equal portions. Roll each out on a well-floured board into a 6-inch circle; or, to make very neat tart shells, roll each into a slightly larger circle and then cut in perfect rounds with a can that is 6 inches in diameter. Turn a muffin pan upside down and fit each circle over an inverted cup, spacing them 1 cup apart from each other to avoid their sticking together. Alternatively, use individual ½-cup round molds inverted on a baking sheet. Bake the shells in a preheated 350° oven about 25 minutes, or until golden brown. Using the side of a knife, raise each shell slightly from the baking cup to make sure it is not sticking. Let the shells cool completely, still inverted on the cups. Very gently lift each shell off its cup and transfer to a platter.

Beat the 2 cheeses in a bowl with a whisk or an electric mixer until fluffy. Gradually beat in the sugar and then the vanilla and the brandy. Spoon this mixture into the bottom of each tart shell and arrange the raspberries, stem side down, neatly on top.

Sketches by the artist

Put the sliced strawberries and the sugar in a saucepan over medium heat and, stirring constantly, bring to a boil. Add the cornstarch and water, reduce the heat, and stir until the liquid is clear and thickened. Remove from the heat, cool slightly, and spoon over the raspberries in each tart. Chill in the refrigerator about 2 hours before serving.   *Makes 6 tarts.*

Note: If desired, substitute melted strawberry, raspberry, or currant jelly for the sliced strawberry glaze.

SESAME THINS
Contributed by Richard and Margaret Mayer

1¾ cups sifted unbleached
    all-purpose flour
½ teaspoon baking soda
½ teaspoon salt
1 cup butter, softened
1 cup sugar
1 egg
1 teaspoon vanilla extract
½ cup sesame seeds, or more
    if necessary
3 tablespoons butter, melted

Sift the flour, baking soda, and salt into a bowl. Set aside.

Beat the softened butter with an electric mixer or a whisk until creamy. Gradually add the sugar, beating continually until fluffy, and then beat in the egg and vanilla. Stir in half the flour mixture with a wooden spoon and then fold in the remainder with a rubber spatula to form a soft dough. Wrap in wax paper and chill in the refrigerator at least 8 hours.

Sprinkle the sesame seeds over a pastry board. Drop the chilled dough, a generous teaspoon at a time, onto the board, and roll with the palm of the hand into a small ball, coating ball thoroughly with sesame seeds.

Brush 2 cookie sheets with the melted butter and put the balls of dough on them about 2 inches apart. Bake in a preheated 350° oven 10 minutes, or until golden brown. Remove the thins from the cookie sheets with a spatula while they are still hot.
Makes about 48 thins.

RUM-AND-CHOCOLATE PIE
Contributed by Robert Hartman

1½ cups milk
½ cup evaporated milk
4 eggs, separated
¾ cup sugar
1 tablespoon cornstarch
1 teaspoon vanilla extract
6 ounces semisweet chocolate
    bits
¼ cup dark rum
1 9-inch prebaked pie shell
    (page 194)
1 tablespoon unflavored
    gelatin, dissolved in ¼ cup
    water

Combine the milks in a saucepan and scald over medium heat. Whisk the egg yolks in a bowl until thick and lemon-colored. Gradually stir in the milks. Sift ½ cup of the sugar with the cornstarch into the same bowl and stir or whisk until the mixture is smooth. Pour into the top pan of a double boiler over simmering water. Stir with a wooden spoon until the mixture is thick enough to coat the spoon. Remove from the heat and stir in the vanilla.

Pour 1 cup of the mixture into a bowl and immediately add the chocolate bits. Stir until the chocolate has melted and add the rum. Pour this custard into the pie shell, spreading it evenly over the bottom. Chill in the refrigerator 1 hour.

Pour the remaining custard into a bowl and stir in the gelatin and water. Chill in the refrigerator about 45 minutes, stirring occasionally. The custard should thicken slightly but not stiffen. Remove from the refrigerator and stir vigorously with a whisk to smooth out any lumps.

Beat the egg whites in a bowl with an electric mixer or a whisk until they begin to stiffen. Gradually add the remaining ¼ cup of sugar, continuing to beat until the egg whites are stiff and glossy. Fold them gently into the custard with a rubber spatula until none of the whites show. Spread this custard over the chocolate one in the pie shell and continue chilling the pie 3 hours, or until both custards are firmly set.
Serves 6.

MILDRED'S SWEET-POTATO PIES
Contributed by Ray Saunders

6 cups cooked sweet potatoes
8 eggs
1¾ cups heavy cream
1½ cups light or dark brown
   sugar, tightly packed
1 teaspoon ground nutmeg
1 tablespoon vanilla extract
1 cup butter, melted
2 teaspoons salt
3 unbaked 9-inch pie shells
   (page 194)
2 cups heavy cream, whipped,
   sweetened to taste with
   sugar, and flavored with
   1 teaspoon vanilla extract
   (optional)

Beat the sweet potatoes with an electric mixer in a large bowl until they are very smooth and have no lumps. Beat in the eggs, one at a time, and then the cream, sugar, nutmeg, vanilla, butter, and salt. Divide the mixture into the pie shells and bake on the lowest rack of a preheated 350° oven 1 hour. Serve slightly warm or at room temperature with optional whipped cream.
Serves 18 to 20.

Note: For 1 pie, use the following proportions:
2 cups cooked sweet potatoes
3 eggs
½ cup plus 2 tablespoons
   heavy cream
½ cup light or dark brown
   sugar, tightly packed
¼ teaspoon ground nutmeg
1 teaspoon vanilla extract
⅓ cup butter, melted
Scant ¾ teaspoon salt
1 unbaked 9-inch pie shell
   (page 194)
⅔ cup heavy cream and
   ¼ teaspoon vanilla extract
   (optional)

FROZEN SOUFFLÉ GRAND MARNIER
Contributed by Paul Wonner

1 quart vanilla ice cream
½ cup fresh orange juice,
   chilled
½ cup Grand Marnier, chilled
6 almond macaroons, coarsely
   chopped and chilled
¼ cup slivered almonds,
   lightly toasted and chilled
1½ cups heavy cream
½ cup sugar
1 teaspoon vanilla extract
2 cups thinly sliced fresh
   strawberries

Allow the ice cream to soften slightly at room temperature and stir into it ¼ cup each of the orange juice and Grand Marnier. Stir in the macaroons and almonds. The ice cream must not be allowed to become liquid. If necessary, store it briefly in the freezer between additions of ingredients.

Beat the heavy cream in a bowl with an electric mixer or a whisk until it begins to thicken. Gradually add ¼ cup of the sugar, beating constantly, and then the vanilla. Beat until the cream is stiff. Using a rubber spatula, fold the whipped cream into the ice cream. Pour or scrape the mixture into a chilled 8-cup mold, packing it down lightly, and freeze at least 6 hours.

Put the strawberries and the remaining ¼-cup each of sugar and orange juice in a saucepan over medium heat. Stir lightly, without mashing the fruit, and bring just to a boil. Remove from the heat and stir in the remaining ¼ cup of Grand Marnier. Cool to room temperature.

At serving time, unmold the ice cream onto a cold platter, using a hot towel around the mold to loosen it. If the surface of the ice cream melts during the process, return the ice cream, unmolded, briefly to the freezer. Pass the sauce in a bowl.
Serves 8.

Irma Cavat. *Apple Picture (Los Angeles)*. 1981. Courtesy Kennedy Galleries, New York.

LIST OF ARTISTS

ANSEL EASTON ADAMS
Photographer
Born: San Francisco, 1902
Studied: Yale University
Exhibits: San Francisco Museum of Modern Art; Museum of Modern Art, New York; Metropolitan Museum of Art, New York
Resides: Carmel, California

MARK ADAMS
Tapestry artist; painter
Born: Fort Plain, New York, 1925
Studied: Syracuse University; with Hans Hoffmann and Jean Lurçat in France
Exhibits: International Biennial of Tapestry, Lausanne, Switzerland; San Francisco Museum of Modern Art; California Palace of the Legion of Honor, San Francisco; John Berggruen Gallery, San Francisco
Resides: San Francisco

ROBERT ARNESON
Sculptor
Born: Benicia, California, 1930
Studied: Mills College; California College of Arts and Crafts, Oakland
Exhibits: San Francisco Museum of Modern Art; Museum of Contemporary Art, Chicago; Museum of Modern Art, New York; Whitney Museum of American Art, New York
Resides: Benicia, California

CHARLES ARNOLDI
Sculptor
Born: Dayton, Ohio, 1946
Studied: Chouinard Art Institute, Los Angeles
Exhibits: San Francisco Museum of Modern Art; Santa Barbara Museum of Art; Museum of Modern Art, N.Y.; Albright-Knox Art Gallery, Buffalo
Resides: Venice, California

RUTH ASAWA
Sculptor; painter
Born: Norwalk, California, 1926
Studied: Milwaukee State Teachers College; with Joseph Albers at Black Mountain College

Exhibits: Whitney Museum of American Art, New York; San Francisco Museum of Modern Art; De Young Museum, San Francisco
Resides: San Francisco

CLAYTON BAILEY
Sculptor; museum director; curator, Kaolithic Curiosities Wonders of the World Museum, Port Costa, California
Born: Antigo, Wisconsin, 1939
Studied: University of Wisconsin
Exhibits: De Young Museum, San Francisco; Milwaukee Art Center; Museum of Contemporary Crafts, New York
Resides: Port Costa, California

LARRY BELL
Sculptor
Born: Chicago, 1939
Studied: Chouinard Art Institute, Los Angeles
Exhibits: Los Angeles County Museum of Art; San Francisco Museum of Modern Art; Oakland Museum; Museum of Modern Art, New York; Jewish Museum, New York; 8th Bienal de São Paulo, Brazil; Stedelijk Museum, Amsterdam
Resides: Taos, New Mexico, and Los Angeles, California

KARL S. BENJAMIN
Painter
Born: Chicago, 1925
Studied: Northwestern University, Evanston, Illinois; Claremont Men's College, Claremont, California
Exhibits: Los Angeles County Museum of Art; San Francisco Museum of Modern Art; Walker Art Center, Minneapolis; Whitney Museum of American Art, New York; Museum of Modern Art, New York; Corcoran Gallery of Art, Washington, D.C.; Smithsonian Institution, Washington, D.C.
Resides: Claremont, California

FLETCHER BENTON
Sculptor
Born: Jackson, Ohio, 1931
Studied: Miami University, Oxford, Ohio
Exhibits: Whitney Museum of American Art, New York; Albright-Knox Art Gallery, Buffalo, N.Y.; San Francisco Museum of Modern Art
Resides: San Francisco

VICTOR BERGERON
Painter; sculptor; owner, Trader Vic's Restaurant
Born: San Francisco, 1902
Opened first restaurant in 1934; has written numerous cookbooks; completed first sculpture in 1968
Resides: San Francisco

PRISCILLA BIRGE
Painter
Born: New York City, 1934
Studied: Brown University; San Francisco Art Institute; University of California, Berkeley
Exhibits: San Francisco Museum of Modern Art; Oakland Museum
Resides: Berkeley

Robert Arneson among friends

Joan Brown, a self-portrait

CHOTSIE BLANK
(Charlotte Skall Blank)
Photographer; member, Modern Art Council, San Francisco Museum of Modern Art
Born: Cleveland
Studied: Bradford Junior College, Bradford, Massachusetts; University of Chicago; San Francisco Art Institute
Resides: San Francisco

KAREN BRESCHI
Sculptor
Born: Oakland, 1941
Studied: California College of Arts and Crafts, Oakland; Sacramento State University; San Francisco Art Institute
Exhibits: Oakland Museum; San Francisco Museum of Modern Art; Whitney Museum of American Art, New York; Smithsonian Institution, Washington, D.C.
Resides: San Francisco

WILLIAM BRICE
Painter; printmaker
Born: New York, 1921
Studied: Chouinard Art Institute, Los Angeles
Exhibits: Dallas Museum of Fine Arts; University of California, San Diego; San Francisco Museum of Modern Art; Los Angeles Institute of Contemporary Art
Resides: Los Angeles

JOAN BROWN
Painter
Born: San Francisco, 1938
Studied: San Francisco Art Institute
Exhibits: Whitney Museum of American Art, New York; San Francisco Museum of Modern Art; California Palace of the Legion of Honor, San Francisco
Resides: San Francisco

HANS BURKHARDT
Painter; printmaker
Born: Basel, Switzerland, 1904
Studied: Cooper Union, New York; Grand Central School of Art, New York; Arshile Gorky's studio, New York
Exhibits: Metropolitan Museum of Art, New York; Art Institute of Chicago; San Francisco Museum of Modern Art
Resides: Los Angeles

CHRIS CAMACHO
Painter; sculptor
Born: Fall River, Massachusetts, 1946
Studied: Rhode Island Junior College; San Francisco Art Institute
Exhibits: 63 Bluxome Street Gallery, San Francisco; Whitney Museum of American Art, New York
Resides: Los Angeles

IRMA CAVAT
Painter
Born: Brooklyn, New York
Studied: with José de Creeft and Alexander Archipenko in New York and Woodstock, New York; Hoffmann School of Fine Arts, Provincetown, Massachusetts
Exhibits: Santa Barbara Museum of Art; Feingarten Galleries, San Francisco; Main Street Gallery, Chicago; Kennedy Galleries, New York
Resides: Santa Barbara

JUDY CHICAGO
Painter
Born: Chicago, 1939
Studied: University of California, Los Angeles
Exhibits: Los Angeles County Museum of Art; San Francisco Museum of Modern Art; Seattle Art Museum; Whitney Museum of American Art, New York; Philadelphia Museum of Art
Resides: Benicia, California

MARIAN CLAYDEN
Fiber artist
Born: England, 1937
Studied: Kesteven College, England; Nottingham School of Art, England

Exhibits: California Crafts Museum, Palo Alto; San Francisco Museum of Modern Art; Museum of Contemporary Crafts of the American Crafts Council, New York; Smithsonian Institution, Washington, D.C.
Resides: Los Gatos, California

VAN DEREN COKE
Photographer; writer; director, Department of Photography, San Francisco Museum of Modern Art
Born: Lexington, Kentucky, 1921
Studied: University of Kentucky, Lexington; Indiana University; Harvard University
Exhibits: Oakland Museum; Focus Gallery, San Francisco; Art Museum, University of New Mexico, Albuquerque; Witkin Gallery, New York; Galerie A. Nagel, West Berlin
Resides: San Francisco

BARNABY CONRAD
Artist; author
Born: San Francisco, 1922
Studied: University of North Carolina; Yale University; University of Mexico
Exhibits: Maxwell Gallery, San Francisco
Resides: Santa Barbara, California

TONY COSTANZO
Ceramist
Born: Schenectady, New York, 1948
Studied: San Francisco Art Institute; Mills College, Oakland
Exhibits: San Francisco Art Institute; Quay Gallery, San Francisco; Oakland Museum
Resides: Oakland

TAFFY DAHL
Ceramist
Born: San Francisco
Studied: University of California; Southampton College of Art
Exhibits: San Francisco Museum of Modern Art; Oakland Museum; Philadelphia Museum of Art
Resides: San Anselmo, California

JERROLD DAVIS
Painter
Born: Chico, California, 1926
Studied: University of California, Berkeley
Exhibits: Newport Harbor Art Museum, Newport Beach, California; Los Angeles County Museum of Art; California Palace of the Legion of Honor, San Francisco
Resides: Berkeley

TONY DELAP
Sculptor
Born: Oakland, 1927
Studied: California College of Arts and Crafts, Oakland; Claremont Men's College, Claremont, California
Exhibits: Los Angeles County Museum of Art; LaJolla Museum of Art; Whitney Museum of American Art, New York; Museum of Modern Art, New York; Jewish Museum, New York
Resides: Corona del Mar, California

CARL DERN
Sculptor
Born: Salt Lake City, 1936
Studied: San Francisco Art Institute; University of California, Berkeley
Exhibits: San Francisco Art Institute; Stanford University Art Museum; University Art Museum, Berkeley
Resides: Fairfax, California

STEPHEN DE STAEBLER
Sculptor
Born: St. Louis, Missouri, 1933
Studied: San Francisco Art Institute; Princeton University; University of California, Berkeley
Exhibits: San Francisco Museum of Modern Art; Oakland Museum
Resides: Berkeley

ELEANOR DICKINSON
Painter; graphic and video artist
Born: Knoxville, Tennessee, 1931
Studied: University of Tennessee; San Francisco Art Institute
Exhibits: Corcoran Gallery of Art, Washington, D.C.; Smithsonian Institution traveling exhibitions; San Francisco Museum of Modern Art
Resides: San Francisco

A window at Eleanor Dickinson's

RICHARD DIEBENKORN
Painter
Born: Portland, Oregon, 1922
Studied: Stanford University; University of California, Berkeley; California School of Fine Arts; University of New Mexico
Exhibits: Whitney Museum of American Art, New York; M. H. De Young Museum, San Francisco; San Francisco Museum of Modern Art; Biennale, Venice
Resides: Santa Monica, California

GUY DIEHL
Painter
Born: Pittsburgh, 1949
Studied: California State University, Hayward; San Francisco State University
Exhibits: Hank Baum Gallery, San Francisco; Walnut Creek Art Gallery, Walnut Creek, California; Oakland Museum
Resides: Concord, California

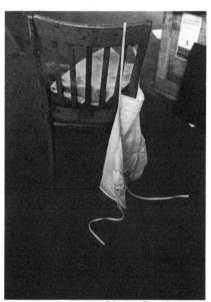

Nancy Genn's apron

LADDIE JOHN DILL
Painter; sculptor
Born: Long Beach, California, 1943
Studied: Chouinard Art Institute, Los Angeles
Exhibits: Walker Art Center, Minneapolis; San Francisco Museum of Modern Art; Smithsonian Institution, Washington, D.C.; Albright-Knox Art Gallery, Buffalo, N.Y.
Resides: Venice, California

VERONICA DI ROSA
Illustrator; painter; writer
Born: British Columbia, Canada, 1934
Studied: Vancouver School of Art; Art Center, Los Angeles
Wrote and illustrated *Chocolate Decadence, Sinful Strawberries, Virtuous Vanilla,* and *Good News Brown Bread.* Illustrated *Flavors of Mexico* and *Sweets for Saints and Sinners*
Resides: Napa, California

WILLIAM DOLE
Painter
Born: Angola, Indiana, 1917
Studied: Olivet College, Olivet, Michigan; University of California, Berkeley
Exhibits: De Young Museum, San Francisco; Hirshhorn Museum and Sculpture Garden, Smithsonian Institution, Washington, D.C.; Phillips Collection, Washington, D.C.; Allentown Art Museum, Pennsylvania; Indianapolis Art Museum
Resides: Santa Barbara, California

FREDERICK EVERSLEY
Sculptor
Born: Brooklyn, New York, 1941
Studied: Carnegie Institute, Pittsburgh; in Allende, Mexico
Exhibits: Whitney Museum of American Art, New York; National Academy of Science, Washington, D.C.; Smithsonian Institution, Washington, D.C.; Museum of Contemporary Art, Chicago
Resides: Venice, California

CLAIRE FALKENSTEIN
Sculptor
Born: Coos Bay, Oregon
Studied: University of California, Berkeley
Exhibits: Institute of Contemporary Art, Boston; Louvre, Paris; Carnegie Institute, Pittsburgh; Whitney Museum of American Art, New York; Los Angeles County Museum of Art
Resides: Venice, California

AL FARROW
Sculptor
Born: New York, 1943
Studied: City College of New York; College of Marin
Exhibits: San Francisco Museum of Modern Art; Munich
Resides: San Rafael

BELLA FELDMAN
Sculptor
Born: New York
Studied: Queens College, New York; Cali-

A corner of Al Farrow's studio

NANCY GENN
Painter
Born: San Francisco, 1929
Studied: San Francisco Art Institute; University of California, Berkeley
Exhibits: San Francisco Museum of Modern Art; Aldrich Museum, Ridgefield, Connecticut; Museum of Modern Art, New York; National Museum of American Art, Smithsonian Institution, Washington, D.C.; Smithsonian Institution traveling exhibitions
Resides: Berkeley

DAVID GILHOOLY
Ceramist
Born: Auburn, California, 1943
Studied: University of California, Davis
Exhibits: Institute of Contemporary Art, Boston; Whitney Museum of American Art, New York; Museum of Contemporary Art, Chicago; San Francisco Muse-

fornia College of Arts and Crafts, Oakland; California State University, San Jose
Exhibits: California Palace of the Legion of Honor, San Francisco; San Francisco Museum of Modern Art; San Francisco Art Institute
Resides: Berkeley

BARBARA FOSTER
Printmaker
Born: Glendale, California, 1947
Studied: University of California, Santa Barbara; San Francisco State University
Exhibits: Oakland Museum
Resides: San Francisco

ROBERT FREIMARK
Painter; tapestry artist
Born: Doster, Michigan, 1922
Studied: Cranbrook Academy of Art, Bloomfield Hills, Michigan
Exhibits: De Saisset Art Gallery and Museum, University of Santa Clara, California; Minneapolis Institute of Arts; Detroit Institute of Arts; Museum of Modern Art, New York
Resides: San Jose, California

PENELOPE FRIED
Painter
Born: Reading, England
Studied: San Francisco Art Institute
Exhibits: San Francisco Museum of Modern Art
Resides: San Francisco

Judith Golden

um of Modern Art; National Museum of American Art, Smithsonian Institution, Washington, D.C.; Montreal Museum of Art

Resides: Davis, California

JUDITH GOLDEN
Photographer
Born: Chicago, 1934
Studied: School of the Art Institute of Chicago; University of California, Davis
Exhibits: San Francisco Museum of Modern Art; Friends of Photography, Carmel, California; De Saisset Art Gallery and Museum, University of Santa Clara, California; Herbert F. Johnson Museum of Art, Cornell University, Ithaca, New York; Fogg Art Museum, Harvard University
Resides: Tucson, Arizona, and San Francisco

JOSEPH GOLDYNE
Painter
Born: Chicago, 1942
Studied: University of California, Berkeley; Harvard University
Exhibits: San Francisco Museum of Modern Art; John Berggruen Gallery, San Francisco; Quay Gallery, San Francisco
Resides: San Francisco

GERALD GOOCH
Ceramist; painter; professor, San Francisco Art Institute
Born: Mannington, West Virginia, 1933
Studied: California College of Arts and Crafts, Oakland
Exhibits: San Francisco Museum of Modern Art; San Francisco Art Institute
Resides: San Francisco

A corner of Marian Clayden's studio

MARY GOULD
Sculptor
Born: Seattle, 1923
Studied: San Francisco Art Institute; University of California, Davis
Exhibits: Oakland Museum; San Jose Museum of Art; University Art Museum, University of California, Berkeley
Resides: Berkeley

ART GRANT
Sculptor; performing artist
Born: San Francisco, 1927
Studied: San Francisco State College; San Francisco Art Institute
Exhibits: San Francisco Art Institute; Oakland Museum
Resides: Mill Valley, California

JOHN HALEY
Painter; sculptor
Born: Minneapolis, 1905
Studied: With Hans Hoffmann and Cameron Booth
Exhibits: Art Institute of Chicago; Metropolitan Museum of Art, New York; Museum of Modern Art, New York; San Francisco Museum of Modern Art
Resides: Richmond, California

FRANK HAMILTON
Ceramist; painter
Born: Tennessee, 1923
Studied: Colorado College, Colorado Springs; Stanford University
Exhibits: Quay Gallery, San Francisco
Resides: San Francisco

JO HANSON
Sculptor
Born: Carbondale, Illinois
Studied: University of Illinois; San Francisco State University
Exhibits: Corcoran Gallery of Art, Washington, D.C.; San Francisco Museum of Modern Art; Pennsylvania Academy of the Fine Arts, Philadelphia
Resides: San Francisco

John Haley

ROBERT HARTMAN
Painter
Born: Sharon, Pennsylvania, 1926
Studied: University of Arizona; Colorado Springs Fine Arts Center; Brooklyn Museum of Art School
Exhibits: Santa Barbara Museum of Art; Whitney Museum of American Art, New York
Resides: Oakland, California

TYRONE HEAD
Painter
Born: Bakersfield, California, 1940
Studied: San Jose State College
Exhibits: Stanford University Museum and Art Gallery and other California galleries
Resides: Mountain View, California

WALLY HEDRICK
Sculptor; painter
Born: Pasadena, 1928
Studied: Otis Art Institute, Los Angeles; California School of Fine Arts; California College of Arts and Crafts, Oakland; San Francisco State College
Exhibits: Museum of Modern Art, New York; San Francisco Museum of Modern Art; Dallas Museum of Fine Arts
Resides: San Geronimo, California

MARY HEEBNER
Born: Los Angeles, 1951
Studied: University of California, Santa Barbara
Exhibits: Los Angeles County Museum of Art; University of California, Santa Barbara; The Allrich Gallery, San Francisco
Resides: Santa Barbara, California

LYNN HERSHMAN
Painter; sculptor
Born: Cleveland, 1941
Studied: Case Western Reserve University; Ohio State University, Columbus; Cleveland Institute of Art; San Francisco State University; California College of Arts and Crafts, Oakland; University of California, Los Angeles; Otis Art Institute, Los Angeles
Exhibits: Butler Institute of American Art, Youngstown, Ohio; San Francisco Museum of Modern Art; Contemporary Arts Museum, Houston; National Gallery, Australia; Centre National d'Art et de Culture Georges Pompidou, Paris
Resides: San Francisco

TYLER JAMES HOARE
Sculptor; printmaker
Born: Joplin, Missouri, 1940
Studied: University of Colorado; Sculpture Center, New York; University of Kansas; California College of Arts and Crafts, Oakland
Exhibits: Pratt Graphics Center, Brooklyn, New York; Library of Congress, Washington, D.C.; California Palace of the Legion of Honor, San Francisco
Resides: Berkeley

RAY HOLBERT
Graphic artist
Born: Berkeley, 1945
Studied: University of California, Berkeley
Exhibits: San Francisco Museum of Modern Art; Helen Euphrat Gallery, Cuppertino, California; Studio Museum (Harlem), New York; Museum of Howard University, Washington, D.C.
Resides: Berkeley

Frank Hamilton

COILLE HOOVEN
Ceramist
Born: New York, 1939
Studied: University of Illinois, Urbana
Exhibits: Quay Gallery, San Francisco; De Young Museum, San Francisco
Resides: Berkeley

HENRY T. HOPKINS
Director, San Francisco Museum of Modern Art
Born: Idaho Falls, Idaho, 1928
Studied: School of the Art Institute of Chicago; University of California, Los Angeles
Resides: San Francisco

JULIA HUETTE
Painter
Born: St. Louis, Missouri, 1948
Studied: University of Michigan, Ann Arbor; University of California, Berkeley
Exhibits: Quay Gallery, San Francisco; Oakland Museum; Van Straaten Gallery, Chicago; Baltimore Museum of Art
Resides: Oakland

ROBERT IRWIN
Sculptor
Born: Long Beach, California, 1928
Studied: Jepson Art Institute, Los Angeles; Chouinard Art Institute, Los Angeles
Exhibits: Los Angeles County Museum of Art; Chicago Museum of Contemporary Art; Walker Art Center, Minneapolis; Museum of Modern Art, New York; Whitney Museum of American Art, New York; Fogg Art Museum, Harvard University
Resides: Los Angeles

YNEZ JOHNSTON
Painter; printmaker
Born: Berkeley, 1920
Studied: University of California, Berkeley
Exhibits: San Francisco Museum of Modern Art; California Institute of Technology, Pasadena; Florence, Italy
Resides: Los Angeles

BILL KANE
Photo-neon artist
Born: Holden, Massachusetts, 1951
Studied: University of Massachusetts, Amherst; San Francisco State University
Exhibits: Foster Goldstrom Fine Arts Gallery, San Francisco; Washington Project

Some Coille Hooven ceramics

for the Arts, Washington, D.C.; Kyoto Museum of Modern Art; Tokyo Museum of Modern Art
Resides: San Francisco

TOBY JUDITH KLAYMAN
Painter
Born: Providence, Rhode Island, 1935
Studied: Brandeis University, Waltham, Massachusetts
Exhibits: Fort Mason Art Center, San Francisco
Resides: San Francisco

PAMELA KRONER
Painter
Born: San Francisco, 1948
Studied: San Francisco Art Institute
Exhibits: San Francisco Museum of Modern Art; Oakland Museum; Ritz Gallery, Point Reyes, California
Resides: Inverness, California

CHRISTOPHER LANE
Painter
Born: New York, 1937
Studied: Goddard College, Vermont; Atelier de la Grand Chaumière, Paris
Exhibits: Whitney Museum of American Art, New York; San Francisco Museum of Modern Art; Beaux Arts Gallery, London; Dana Reich Gallery, San Francicso
Resides: San Francisco

SYLVIA LARK
Painter; printmaker
Born: New York, 1947

Studied: State University of New York; University of Wisconsin; Mills College, Oakland
Exhibits: Ivory/Kempton Gallery, San Francisco; University Gallery, University of Southern California, Los Angeles; Memorial Union Art Gallery, University of California, Davis; N.A.M.E. Gallery, Chicago; Allan Stone Gallery, New York
Resides: Sacramento

HELEN LUNDEBERG
Painter
Born: Chicago, 1908
Studied: With Lorser Feitelson
Exhibits: Museum of Modern Art, New York; Whitney Museum of American Art, New York; Amon Carter Museum, Fort Worth; Des Moines Art Center; San Francisco Museum of Modern Art
Resides: Los Angeles

DAVID MACKENZIE
Painter
Born: Los Angeles, 1942
Studied: Orange Coast College, Costa Mesa, California; San Francisco Art Institute
Exhibits: De Young Museum, San Francisco; University Art Museum, Berkeley; Whitney Museum of American Art, New York
Resides: San Francisco

AMY MAGILL
Painter; muralist; ceramist
Born: Houston, Texas, 1941
Studied: Self-taught
Exhibits: San Francisco Museum of Modern
Art
Resides: San Francisco

K. LEE MANUEL
Fiber artist
Born: Southern California
Studied: San Francisco Art Institute
Exhibits: University of California; San
Francisco Museum of Modern Art
Resides: Santa Cruz, California

RALPH MARADIAGA
Gallery director; designer
Born: San Francisco, 1934
Studied: City College, San Francisco; San
Francisco State University; Stanford Uni-
versity
Exhibits: San Francisco Museum of Modern
Art; Museum of Modern Art, New York
Resides: San Francisco

RICHARD MAYER
Painter; sculptor
Born: Chicago, 1935
Studied: San Francisco Art Institute
Exhibits: San Francisco Museum of Art;
California Palace of the Legion of Honor,
San Francisco; Oakland Museum
Resides: San Francisco

ALBERTA MAYO
Graphic artist
Born: Oakland, 1949
Studied: Franconia College, New Hamp-
shire; Fat City School of Finds Art, Holly-
wood
Exhibits: Zwickers Gallery, Halifax, Nova
Scotia; Augusta's Cafe-Restaurant, Berke-
ley
Resides: Riverside, California

DONNA MOSSHOLDER
(-HERRESHOFF)
Painter; printmaker
Born: Pasadena, 1946
Studied: California College of Art, Oakland
Exhibits: San Francisco Art Institute; Oak-
land Museum; Newport Harbor Museum,
Newport, California
Resides: Berkeley

LEE MULLICAN
Painter
Born: Chickasha, Oklahoma, 1919
Studied: Abilene Christian College; Uni-
versity of Oklahoma; Kansas City Art In-
stitute; San Francisco Art Institute
Exhibits: San Francisco Museum of Modern
Art; Oklahoma Art Center, Oklahoma
City; Whitney Museum of American Art,
New York; Chile
Resides: Santa Monica, California

ARTHUR NELSON
Ceramist
Born: Denver, 1942
Studied: University of Colorado; California
College of Arts and Crafts, Oakland
Exhibits: Anna Gardner Gallery, Stinson
Beach, California
Resides: Oakland

MANUEL NERI
Sculptor
Born: Sanger, California, 1930
Studied: University of California, Berkeley;
California College of Arts and Crafts,
Oakland; San Francisco Art Institute
Exhibits: University Art Museum, Berke-
ley; Oakland Museum; San Francisco
Museum of Modern Art; Museum of Fine
Arts, London; New York galleries
Resides: Benicia, California

GEORGE NEUBERT
Sculptor; Associate Director of Art, San
Francisco Museum of Modern Art
Born: Minneapolis, 1942

Studied: Hardin-Simmons University, Abi-
lene, Texas; San Francisco Art Institute;
Mills College, Oakland
Resides: Oakland

NATHAN OLIVEIRA
Painter
Born: Oakland, 1928
Studied: Mills College, Oakland; California
College of Arts and Crafts, Oakland
Exhibits: San Francisco Museum of Modern
Art; Corcoran Gallery of Art, Washing-
ton, D.C.; Art Institute of Chicago; Whit-
ney Museum of American Art, New York;
Museum of Modern Art, New York; Solo-
mon R. Guggenheim Museum, New York
Resides: Stanford, California

ROONEY O'NEILL
Painter
Born: Sacramento, 1945
Studied: University of Santa Clara, Califor-
nia; University of California, Berkeley;
California State University, Sacramento
Exhibits: California galleries
Resides: Emeryville, California

JOHN PEETZ
Director, Oakland Museum
Born: McMinnville, Oregon, 1929
Studied: Armstrong College, Berkeley
Resides: Oakland

ROLAND PETERSEN
Painter; printmaker
Born: Denmark, 1926
Studied: University of California, Berkeley;

Fred Reichman

Irma Cavat. *Pomegranates I*. 1980. Courtesy Kennedy Galleries, New York

San Francisco Art Institute; California College of Arts and Crafts, Oakland; Atelier, Paris; Islington Studio, London
Exhibits: De Young Museum, San Francisco; La Jolla Museum of Art; Santa Barbara Museum of Art; Carnegie Institute, Pittsburgh; Art Institute of Chicago; Virginia Museum of Fine Arts, Richmond; National Gallery of Art, Washington, D.C.
Resides: Davis, California

PETER PLAGENS
Painter
Born: Dayton, Ohio, 1941
Studied: University of Southern California, Los Angeles; Syracuse University
Exhibits: Los Angeles County Museum of Art; Whitney Museum of American Art, New York
Resides: Los Angeles and New York

CHARLES PRENTISS
Sculptor
Born: Los Angeles, 1942
Studied: El Camino College, Los Angeles
Exhibits: Portland Art Museum, Oregon; Newport Harbor Art Museum, Newport Beach, California; University of Illinois; Long Beach Museum of Art, California; Denver Art Museum; University of California, Los Angeles; Phoenix Art Museum
Resides: Northridge, California

JOSEPH RAFFAEL
Painter; printmaker
Born: Brooklyn, New York, 1933
Studied: Cooper Union, New York; Yale University
Exhibits: Whitney Museum of American Art, New York; Richmond Art Museum, Richmond, Virginia; Chicago Art Institute; Corcoran Gallery of Art, Washington, D.C.; San Francisco Museum of Modern Art; Des Moines Art Center; Joslyn Art Museum, Omaha; Denver Art Museum; Germany; Japan
Resides: San Geronimo, California

SONYA RAPOPORT
Computer artist; painter
Born: Boston, 1923
Studied: New York University; University of California, Berkeley
Exhibits: San Francisco Museum of Modern Art; De Young Museum, San Francisco; Oakland Museum
Resides: Berkeley

FRED REICHMAN
Painter
Born: Bellingham, Washington, 1925
Studied: University of California, Berkeley; San Francisco Art Institute
Exhibits: California Palace of the Legion of Honor; Santa Barbara Museum of Art; San Francisco Museum of Modern Art; Whitney Museum of American Art, New York; Japan
Resides: San Francisco

JOANNE RRUFF
Mixed-media sculptor
Born: Detroit, 1949
Studied: Wayne State University, Detroit
Exhibits: Quay Gallery, San Francisco; San Francisco Museum of Modern Art; Smithsonian Institution traveling exhibition
Resides: San Francisco

RAYMOND SAUNDERS
Painter
Born: Pittsburgh, 1934
Studied: Pennsylvania Academy of Fine Arts, Philadelphia; University of Pennsylvania; Carnegie Institute, Pittsburgh; California College of Arts and Crafts, Oakland
Exhibits: Museum of Modern Art, New York; Contemporary Arts Museum, Houston; San Francisco Museum of Modern Art; Providence Museum of Art; Amsterdam; Paris
Resides: Oakland

ANN SEYMOUR
Writer; art critic, *Art Week*; member, Modern Art Council, San Francisco Museum of Modern Art
Born: San Francisco
Studied: Stanford University
Resides: San Francisco

SANDY SHANNONHOUSE
Sculptor; ceramist
Born: Petaluma, California, 1947
Studied: University of California, Davis
Exhibits: Oakland Museum; San Francisco
   Museum of Modern Art; Quay Gallery,
   San Francisco; Seattle Art Museum; Car-
   borundum Museum, Niagara Falls, New
   York; Museum of Contemporary Crafts,
   New York; Queens Museum, New York
Resides: Benicia, California

NELL SINTON
Painter
Born: San Francisco
Studied: San Francisco Art Institute
Exhibits: San Francisco Museum of Mod-
   ern Art; American Academy of Arts and
   Letters, New York; Smithsonian Institu-
   tion, Washington, D.C.
Resides: San Francisco

PATRICIA TAVENNER
Collage artist; photographer
Born: Doster, Michigan, 1941
Studied: Michigan State University; Cali-
   fornia College of Arts and Crafts, Oak-
   land
Exhibits: Los Angeles County Museum of
   Art; Museum of Contemporary Crafts,
   New York; Paris
Resides: Oakland

GAGE TAYLOR
Painter
Born: Fort Worth, 1942
Studied: University of Texas; Michigan
   State University
Exhibits: Whitney Museum of American
   Art, New York; San Francisco Museum of
   Modern Art; Museum of Contemporary
   Art, Chicago; National Museum of
   American Art, Smithsonian Institution,
   Washington, D.C.; Musée d'Art Mod-
   erne, Paris
Resides: Woodacre, California

WAYNE THIEBAUD
Painter
Born: Mesa, Arizona, 1920
Studied: Sacramento State College
Exhibits: San Francisco Museum of Modern
   Art; Pasadena Art Museum; De Young
   Museum, San Francisco; Whitney Mu-
   seum of American Art, New York; Bay-
   ton Art Institute; São Paulo, Brazil; West
   Germany
Resides: San Francisco and Sacramento

ANN THORNYCROFT
Painter
Born: Petersfield, England, 1944
Studied: San Francisco Art Institute; Chou-
   inard Art Institute, Los Angeles
Exhibits: Rosamund Felson Gallery, Los
   Angeles; Ivory-Kimpton Gallery, San
   Francisco
Resides: Venice, California

GARNER TULLIS
Painter; printmaker
Born: Cincinnati, 1939
Studied: Pennsylvania Academy of Fine
   Arts, Philadelphia; University of Pennsyl-
   vania; John Berggruen Gallery, San Fran-
   cisco
Exhibits: San Francisco Museum of Modern
   Art and other California museums
Resides: San Francisco

Sandy Shannonhouse

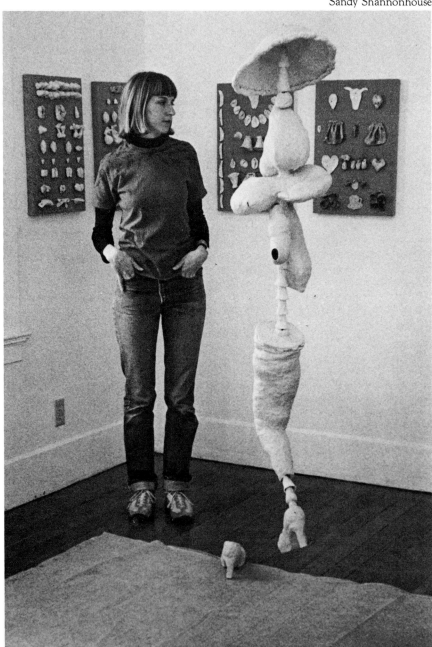

Irma Cavat. *Fromagerie*. 1980. Courtesy Kennedy Galleries, New York.

BETH VAN HOESEN (Mrs. Mark Adams)
Printmaker; painter
Born: Boise, Idaho, 1926
Studied: Stanford University; San Francisco Art Institute; San Francisco State University; École d'Art Americaines de Fontainebleau; Académie de la Grande Chaumière, Paris; Académie Julien, Paris
Exhibits: Oakland Museum; Fine Arts Museum, San Francisco; Brooklyn Museum; Pennsylvania Academy of Fine Arts, Philadelphia
Resides: San Francisco

JULIUS WASSERSTEIN
Painter
Born: Providence, Rhode Island, 1924
Studied: San Francisco Art Institute; San Francisco State University
Exhibits: San Francisco Museum of Modern Art; Paule Anglim Gallery, San Francisco; California Palace of the Legion of Honor, San Francisco
Resides: San Francisco

MASON WELLS
Painter
Born: Southbridge, Massachusetts
Studied: Harvard University; Yale University; San Francisco Art Institute
Exhibits: Quay Gallery, San Francisco
Resides: San Francisco

COLE WESTON
Photographer
Born: Carmel, California, 1919
Studied: With father, Edward Weston, and Ansel Adams
Exhibits: San Francisco Museum of Modern Art; University Art Museum, University of California, Berkeley; Carmel Weston Gallery, Carmel, California
Resides: Carmel, California

WILLIAM WILEY
Painter
Born: Bedford, Indiana, 1937
Studied: San Francisco Art Institute
Exhibits: Joslyn Art Museum, Omaha; San Francisco Museum of Modern Art; Art Institute of Chicago; Corcoran Gallery of Art, Washington, D.C.; Albright-Knox Art Gallery, Buffalo, N.Y.; Museum of Modern Art, New York; Whitney Museum of American Art, New York; J.P.L. Fine Arts, London; Netherlands; Switzerland
Resides: San Francisco

PAUL WONNER
Painter
Born: Tucson, 1929
Studied: California College of Art, Oakland; University of California, Berkeley
Exhibits: Carnegie Institute, Pittsburgh; Museum of Modern Art, New York; Whitney Museum of American Art, New York; Art Institute of Chicago; San Francisco Museum of Modern Art
Resides: San Francisco

JACK ZAJAC
Sculptor; painter
Born: Youngstown, Ohio, 1929
Studied: Scripps College, Claremont, California; American Academy, Rome
Exhibits: Smithsonian Institution, Washington, D.C.; Virginia Museum of Fine Arts, Richmond; Whitney Museum of American Art, New York; California museums; Italy
Resides: Santa Cruz

INDEX